Great Lakes
SHIPWRECKS

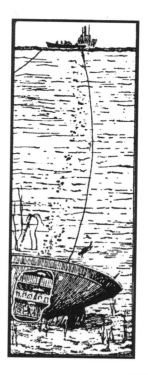

New Discoveries and Updates

Other Works by Cris Kohl and Joan Forsberg

BOOKS:

Dive Southwestern Ontario! (1985; expanded edition 1988)
Shipwreck Tales: The St. Clair River (to 1900) (1987)
Dive Ontario! The Complete Guide to Shipwrecks and
    Scuba Diving in Ontario (1990; expanded edition 1995)
Dive Ontario Two! More Ontario Shipwreck Stories (1994)
Treacherous Waters: Kingston's Shipwrecks (1997)
The 100 Best Great Lakes Shipwrecks, Volume I (1998; updated ed. 2005)
The 100 Best Great Lakes Shipwrecks, Volume II (1998; updated ed. 2005)
TITANIC, *The Great Lakes Connections* (2000)
The Great Lakes Diving Guide (2001; expanded edition 2008)
Diver's Guide to the Kitchen (2003)
Shipwreck Tales of the Great Lakes (2004)
Shipwrecks at Death's Door (2008)
Our World--Underwater, The First 40 Years (Editors; 2010)
The Christmas Tree Ship (2012)
The Wreck of the **GRIFFON** (2014)

DOCUMENTARIES:

Shipwreck Tales of the Great Lakes (2009)
Great Lakes Shipwrecks of the World Wars (2009)
Tales of Great Lakes Shipwreck Pairs (2009)
The Shipwrecked Whalebacks (2009)
Deep Shipwrecks of the Great Lakes (2009)
Shipwrecks at Death's Door (2010)
Exploring Canada's Great Lakes Shipwrecks (2010)
Thirteen Shipwrecks: The Great Lakes' Worst Maritime Disasters (2011)
Shipwrecks off Whitefish Point (2011)
Shipwreck Tales of Chicago (2012)
TITANIC, *The Great Lakes Connections* (2012)
The War of 1812 on the Great Lakes (2012)
Point Pelee Shipwrecks (2013)
The Great Storm of 1913 (2013)
The Wreck of the **GRIFFON** (2015)
Shipwreck Tales of Georgian Bay (2015)

MAPS:

The 100 Most Famous Great Lakes Shipwrecks (2013)
The War of 1812 on the Great Lakes (2013)
Door County Lighthouses and Shipwrecks (2014)
Lake Superior Lighthouses and Shipwrecks (2014)
Lake Huron Lighthouses and Shipwrecks (2014)

GREAT LAKES SHIPWRECKS

NEW DISCOVERIES AND UPDATES

To John —
Enjoy the many
shipwreck stories!

Cris Kohl
Joan Forsberg

CRIS KOHL
AND
JOAN FORSBERG

Great Lakes Shipwrecks -- New Discoveries and Updates
by Cris Kohl and Joan Forsberg

Published by
Seawolf Communications, Inc.
West Chicago, Illinois   USA

Photo credits are shown in terms of the author's source for the photograph rather than a specific photographer who might have taken it, except where the photographer is known and specifically named. Photographs are © of any photographers or institutions as indicated, excluding authors Cris Kohl and Joan Forsberg. Artwork is © of the artists as indicated. Text, maps, artwork, and photos by authors Cris Kohl and/or Joan Forsberg are © Seawolf Communications, Inc.

Cover Designs: Cris Kohl and Joan Forsberg

Printed in Canada

FIRST EDITION
5 4 3 2 1

FRONT COVER IMAGE: The ship's wheel on the wreck of the tug, *Sport,* in Lake Huron, commands attention from diver Joan Forsberg. (Photo by Cris Kohl)
BACK COVER IMAGES (TOP TO BOTTOM, LEFT TO RIGHT): The very visible wreck of the *Lynda Hindman* in Lake Huron off Bayfield, ON, sets imaginations on fire (Photo by Cris Kohl); a detailed drawing of the Lake Huron wreck of the *Keystone State* (Courtesy of the artist, Robert McGreevy); an early 1900's colorized postcard of the *Henry B. Smith* before it was lost in Lake Superior (Kohl-Forsberg Archives); the *City of Cleveland* in Lake Huron (Photo by Vlada Dekina); the steam engine gauges on Lake Superior's *A. A. Parker* (photo by Jitka Hanakova); the schooner *Rouse Simmons*, the famous "Christmas Tree Ship," in Lake Michigan (Photo by Cal Kothrade); Cris Kohl and Joan Forsberg at Whitefish Point (Photo by Darryl Ertel).

TABLE OF CONTENTS

GREAT LAKES SIDEBARS

INTRODUCTION

In 2001, we compiled much of the material that had appeared in our earlier books, plus information from the extensive notes in our collection (which, since then, has outgrown the term "collection" and become an "archive") about Great Lakes maritime history, particularly shipwrecks, into a 416-page book. This book listed every shipwreck in the Great Lakes known to have been located, giving both its history, each shipwreck's present condition, and usually specific location coordinates, and was called, *The Great Lakes Diving Guide,* which indicated an audience limited to scuba divers. Regardless of its title, this book proved to be very popular with divers and non-divers alike, especially among maritime-history-minded people, because it really was the "encyclopedia of Great Lakes shipwrecks."

We enlarged the book in late 2007, adding all of the new shipwreck discoveries since 2001, plus ones that had been unknown to us at the time of the first edition, with that second edition being a truly encyclopedic 608 pages long. This second edition indicated that we are in the midst of a "golden age of Great Lakes shipwreck discovery," having come a long way from the days when divers at one end of a lake had no idea what divers at the other end were exploring, and when people somehow found shipwrecks using primitive, narrow-range depth-sounders compared to today's affordable and wide-range sidescan sonar systems.

In 2015, we determined that it was once again time to update our best-selling shipwrecks book. However, its length of 608 pages could not be increased, and, since no information could be removed, the decision was made to produce a "companion volume" to *The Great Lakes Diving Guide*, giving it the title, *Great Lakes Shipwrecks, New Discoveries and Updates*.

This new book does not replace *The Great Lakes Diving Guide* -- it complements it. It provides information about newly located or revealed shipwrecks, plus updates, such as expanded history details and newer-format GPS coordinates, on older ones, thus making it the perfect COMPANION to the massive amount of information already in *The Great Lakes Diving Guide*.

In this new book, we again provide a venue for talented Great Lakes photographers and artists to display some of their work. The advertising in this book serves two purposes: to provide a clearinghouse of scuba services available for those wishing to actually explore Great Lakes shipwrecks, and to provide a means of keeping this book's retail price affordable.

Join us for the adventure of discovery in the Great Lakes!

Cris Kohl and Joan Forsberg
February, 2016

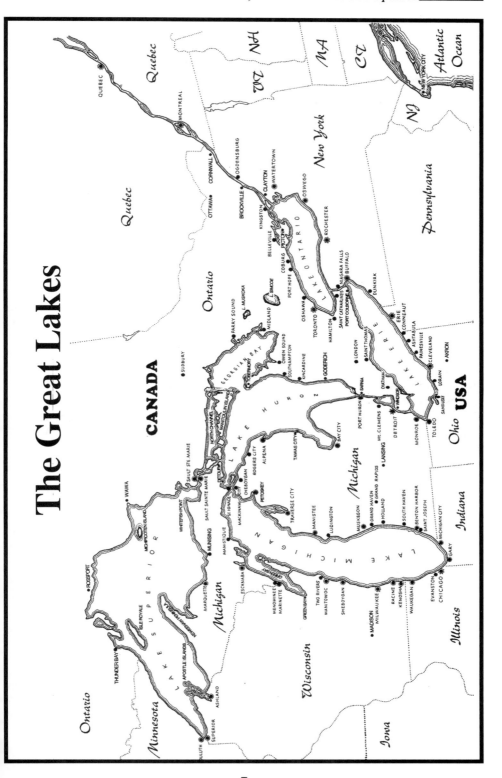

ACKNOWLEDGEMENTS

We sincerely thank all the individuals, organizations, and institutions who have contributed so much to this book, and without whom a project of this kind would not have been possible.

The following individuals and organizations provided invaluable information, expertise, and insight: Jeff Gray and Wayne Lusardi of the NOAA National Marine Sanctuary; Kevin Magee, Dr. David Van Zandt, Tom Kowalczk, Cindy LaRosa, and Jim Pasker of Cleveland Underwater Explorers; Michael and Georgann Wachter; Roy Pickering of Save Ontario Shipwrecks; Ken Merryman and Jerry Eliason of the Great Lakes Shipwreck Preservation Society; Wally Peterson of Ontario's Thunder Country Diving; Jim Jarecki, Bob Rushman, and Dr. John Bell and the Underwater Archaeological Society of Chicago; Jim Baye of Neptune Dive Club; Art Vermette; Richard Tappenden, Jr.; Clive Cussler for sharing his wisdom about shipwreck hunting, and NUMA (National Underwater Marine Agency); Valerie Van Heest and Michigan Shipwreck Research Association (MSRA); Steve Radovan; David Trotter of Undersea Research Associates; the Great Lakes members of the Women Divers Hall of Fame: Gina Bier, Lynn Funkhouser, Dr. Sue Morra, Robin MacFadden Parish, Becky Kagan Schott, Pat Stayer, Tamara Thomsen, Valerie van Heest and Georgann Wachter; Al Hart; Harold V. Cooley; Darryl Ertel; Jim and Pat Stayer; Tim Juhl; Joe Porter of *Wreck Diving Magazine*; the George Thomas Archer Marine Arts Collection; and Dr. Lara Hernandez Corkrey.

It is always a pleasure to make use of the following remarkable research facilities and helpful staff: Robert Graham of the Center for Archival Collections at Bowling Green State University, Bowling Green, Ohio; Runge Collection, Milwaukee Public Library; Door County Historical Museum, Sturgeon Bay, WI; Library and Archives of Canada, Ottawa, Ontario; Glenn Longacre of the National Archives, Great Lakes Branch, Chicago, Illinois; Ontario Archives, Toronto, Ontario; Northern Illinois University, DeKalb, Illinois; and the University of Windsor, Windsor, Ontario.

We are proud to provide a showcase for the stunning images provided to us by the talented Artists and Photographers listed on page 9 with the pages where their work can be found, and we thank each and every one of them: Robert Doornbos, Cal Kothrade, Robert McGreevy, Peter Rindlisbacher, Roland "Chip" Stevens, Marcel Blanchette, Vlada Dekina, Chris Doyal, Jerry Eliason, Jitka Hanakova, the late Joyce Hayward, Joe Hoyt, John Janzen, Warren Lo, Bill Martinez, Ken Merryman, Andy Morrison, Scott Reimer, Becky Kagan Schott, David Trotter, Bob Underhill, and Valerie Van Heest.

Finally, and most importantly, we are very grateful to the advertisers listed on page 221 whose support has enabled this book to be affordable, and for being our partners in the goal of making the Great Lakes the great dive destination they deserve to be.

ARTISTS

Sincere thanks go to these remarkable artists and organizations, listed alphabetically, who very generously allowed their work to be used in this book:

Marcel Blanchette (Ontario) 81

Robert Doornbos (Michigan).....143, 144, 146, 147, 148, 167

Cal Kothrade (Wisconsin)....141, 176, 179

Kevin Magee & Cindy LaRosa, Cleveland Underwater Explorers (Ohio) CLUE 51, 52, 53

Robert McGreevy (Michigan)...... 95, 99, 100, 101, 102, 103, 106, 112, 122, 124, 125, 134, 137, 157

NOAA Thunder Bay Sanctuary and Preserve (Michigan) 107, 128, 129, 131, 135

Peter Rindlisbacher (Ontario) 32

Roland "Chip" Stevens (New York) 27, 28, 29, 30, 31, 32

Underwater Archaeological Society of Chicago (Illinois) 151

UNDERWATER PHOTOGRAPHERS

While quite a few of the images in this book were taken by the authors, Cris Kohl and Joan Forsberg, many were taken by others, including an impressive new generation of Great Lakes underwater photographers. We thank the following talented people, listed alphabetically, who contributed images for use in this book. We are pleased to have been able to provide a showcase for their exceptional work:

Vlada Dekina (Ontario)...........14, 15, 17, 18, 19, 20, 21, 26, 63, 65, 66, 123, 126

Chris Doyal (Michigan) 140, 159

Jerry Eliason, Ken Merryman, et al., (Minnesota) 194, 196, 197, 204

Jitka Hanakova (Wisconsin) 125, 126, 130, 133, 134, 135, 136, 154, 155, 158, 199, 202

Joyce Hayward (Ohio) 122

Joe Hoyt (Michigan) 132, 135

John Janzen (Minnesota) 109, 110, 152, 153, 157, 158, 179

Cal Kothrade (Wisconsin)........141, 167, 168, 170, 171, 172, 173, 175, 177, 179, 181, 183, 203

Warren Lo (Ontario)................20, 34, 37, 38, 40, 42, 43, 115, 117

Bill Martinez (Michigan) 146

Andy Morrison (Michigan)......61, 74, 118, 124, 125, 157

Scott Reimer (Illinois).............150, 151

Becky Kagan Schott (Pennsylvania) 110, 135, 155

David Trotter (Michigan) 99, 103

Bob Underhill (Michigan)........164

Valerie Van Heest (Michigan).. 146, 147, 148, 160

David Van Zandt, Cleveland Underwater Explorers (Ohio) CLUE 52, 53

1. St. Lawrence River

"NEW SHIPWRECKS" refers to those that are not in the book, *The Great Lakes Diving Guide,* second edition, 2008 (*GLDG2*), either because they had not yet been discovered, or because the authors had not yet learned about their locations.

NEW SHIPWRECKS

A. Ash Island barge
B. Small steam launch
C. *General Hancock*
D. North Colborne Island barge
E. *Gipsey*

F. *Elk*
G. *W. H. G.*
H. *Schoolcraft*
I. North Bay wreck

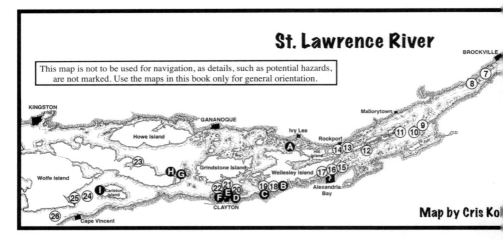

"UPDATED SHIPWRECKS" refers to ones that are in the book, *The Great Lakes Diving Guide* (shortened to *GLDG2* when referenced in this chapter). The UPDATED information about each of these shipwrecks could be new or corrected GPS coordinates, additional maritime history, and/or modern-day news about that particular wreck.

UPDATED SHIPWRECKS

1. 'Belly Dumper' wreck
2. *Eastcliffe Hall*
3. *Weehawk*
4. 'Loblaw's' wreck
5. *Rothesay*
6. *Muscallonge*
7. *Sam Cook?*
8. *Roosevelt*
9. *America*

10. *Keystorm*
11. *Pentland* and
    F. A. Georger
12. *Clara White*
13. *Kinghorn*
14. *Sophia*
15. *Catherine*
16. *Islander*
17. *Roy A. Jodrey*

18. *Oconto*
19. *A. E. Vickery*
20. *Dauntless*
21. *Squaw*
22. *Maggie L.*
23. Holliday Point wreck
24. *Lewiston* and barges
25. *Harvey J. Kendall*
26. *Arizona*

The sidewheel steamer, *Bohemian*, spent decades traveling on the upper St. Lawrence River. Built in Montreal in 1873, this ship burned there to a total loss on August 27, 1909.
(Kohl-Forsberg Archives)

Map by Cris Kohl

A. ASH ISLAND BARGE (NEW)

DEPTH: 80-130 feet   LEVEL: Advanced
COORDINATES: 44° 21' 23.000"N/075° 59' 48.419"W
(44.3582N/075.9969W)

LOCATION: This wreck lies 0.6 miles (1 kilometre) upstream of the Thousand Islands Bridge, on the Canadian side, in a small bay on the northeast tip of Ash Island.

This relatively intact, wooden shipwreck, sitting upright on the steep slope of Ash Island, is an unnamed, belly-dumper type of barge, measuring about 130 feet long and 42 feet wide. It was scuttled, along with its stone cargo, after the completion of the Thousand Islands (Ivy Lea) Bridge in 1938.

Often a buoy, placed there by volunteers from the maritime conservation organization called Save Ontario Shipwrecks (S. O. S.) marks the site. This buoy is thoughtfully attached to an anchor cage rather than to the shipwreck in order to avoid any damage to the wreck, but as such, this anchor cage can be dragged if too big or too heavy a boat is tied to it, or if the already strong, three-to-four-knot current increases due to rough weather.

B. SMALL STEAM LAUNCH (NEW)

DEPTH: 88 feet   LEVEL: Advanced
COORDINATES: 44° 17.213'N/076° 00.242'W

LOCATION: This shipwreck is located between two historic wrecks: the *Iroquois,* or *Iroquoise* (*GLDG2* p. 80-81) and the *Sir Robert Peel* (*GLDG2* p. 80). The *Iroquois* lies about 300 feet upstream of this small, unidentified steam launch.

Although this little wreck, only about 30 feet in length, is badly deteriorated, it appears to have been a steam launch from about the year 1900. The fact that its engine was removed suggests that this vessel was stripped and purposely abandoned and sunk at this location. Beware of depth (the wreck sits on a ledge next to a severe slope that drops to over 200 feet) and the very strong current.

C. GENERAL HANCOCK (NEW)

> **DEPTH: above water to 12 feet deep   LEVEL: Novice**
> **COORDINATES: 44° 16.940′N/076° 00.734′W**

LOCATION: This wreck can be found just off the south shore of Mandolin Island in the middle of a cluster of islands about half a mile north of Fisher's Landing, New York.

Built of steel in 1896 at Wilmington, Delaware, originally for the U.S. Army (official number 228755), and after spending more than a dozen years working as a ferry to Governor's Island in New York City, this 96-foot-long ship, with a beam of 23′5″ feet, a draft of 9′6″ feet, and a displacement of 131 gross tons, came to the Thousand Islands in 1924 as part of the Hutchinson brothers' two-vessel fleet servicing Alexandria Bay, New York, and Rockport, Ontario (the other ship was the *Theodore Roosevelt*; see p. 15). The opening

The ferry, **General Hancock.** (KOHL-FORSBERG ARCHIVES)

of the Thousand Islands Bridge between Canada and the USA in 1938 put the ferries out of business, and the *General Hancock* was abandoned at its current location in 1942.

Part of the twisted steel hull rises out of the water, making it easy to locate, and, while much of this ship's metal was removed for its scrap value, numerous items of interest remain in place, particularly both propellers, one at each end of this double-ender.

D. NORTH COLBORNE ISLAND BARGE (NEW)

> **DEPTH: 11-21 feet   LEVEL: Novice**
> **COORDINATES: 44° 15.490′N/076° 03.958′W**

LOCATION: Between green buoy #221 and the shore of North Colborne Island.

This small, rectangular, work barge is believed to have been abandoned here after work was completed in 1938 on the Thousand Islands Bridge. This boxy barge, which rests among aquatic weeds on mud and rock, attracts many fish. Beware of unusual currents.

E. GIPSEY (NEW)

> **DEPTH: In 11 feet   LEVEL: Novice**
> **COORDINATES: 44° 14.712′N/076° 04.346′W**

LOCATION: Off Board Island, just east of Clayton, New York.

This small, two-masted schooner, built in 1847 at Sackets Harbor, New York, as the *Isaac Walton*, was rebuilt in 1859 at Sodus, NY, and renamed *Gipsey*, both vessels having the same official number: 10162. Measuring 47 feet in length, 13 feet in beam, 5 feet in draft, and displacing 33 tons, the *Gipsey* was enrolled at Oswego, NY, from 1860 to 1866, and at French Creek, NY, in 1866-67, before changing ownership to Clayton, NY, in 1868. In the 1870's, the ship was owned by Captain A. Cook of Clayton, who apparently still owned her when the schooner stranded and sank at this site in 1901. She was abandoned in place after her hardware was removed.

Very little remains of this tiny shipwreck sticking up out of the mud and weeds.

F. ELK (NEW)

> **DEPTH: 10-14 feet   LEVEL: Novice**
> **COORDINATES: 44° 14.630′N/076° 04.856′W**

LOCATION: Off the east side of Clayton, NY, at the head of Washington Island.

The *Elk*, a small schooner that hauled grain, sank here in the 1850's, circumstances unknown. Only the bottom of the hull, with its keelson and some framing, remains in place.

G. W. H. G. (NEW)

> **DEPTH: 30 feet   LEVEL: Novice-Intermediate**
> **COORDINATES: 44° 14.40′ 102″N/076° 11.16′ 059″W**

LOCATION: At the foot of Wolfe Island, Ontario, near Quebec Head.

This wreck is that of a small, wooden speedboat lost in the early 1900's. Historically, this was an early example of a boat converted from steam power to gasoline power. Badly disintegrated today, these remains lie among rocks on a weedy bottom.

H. SCHOOLCRAFT (NEW)

> **DEPTH: To 20 feet   LEVEL: Novice**
> **COORDINATES: 44° 13.978′N/076° 12.115′W**

LOCATION: On the eastern tip of Wolfe Island, Ontario, halfway between Brakey Bay and Quebec Head.

The wooden steamer, Schoolcraft, burned at Wolfe Island, Ontario, in 1920. (KOHL-FORSBERG ARCHIVES)

This burned hull, previously thought to be that of the schooner, *Julia* (see page 83 of *GLDG2*), is actually what is left of the wooden-hulled steamer named the *Schoolcraft*. Launched at Trenton, Michigan, in 1884 and measuring 185'6″ in length and 34' in beam, this ship, returning to Kingston from Montreal, light after delivering its final load of coal of the season, on December 3, 1920 caught on fire 14 miles from its destination. All 14 people on board were rescued by the small steamer, *Missisiquoi* (see p.42). This shallow shipwreck site is protected from the wind.

I. NORTH BAY WRECK (NEW)

> **DEPTH: to 10 feet   LEVEL: Novice**
> **COORDINATES: 44° 10.201′N/076° 18.599′W**

LOCATION: This wreckage is located in privately-owned North Bay on Carleton Island, just northeast of Cape Vincent, New York.

This very old, wooden vessel (only the keel and frames remain) appears to have been a twin-masted sailing ship from the 18th century. Historic Carleton Island was a strategic naval and shipbuilding base for first British, then American, forces in the late 1700's.

Because this bay is privately owned, no boat may anchor or disturb the bottom without permission from the owner. Excavation and study in the 1960's found that this wreck could be the *Halifax*, built at Oswego in 1756, but that ship's fate is undetermined.

1. 'BELLY DUMPER' WRECK   (UPDATE -- *GLDG2* p. 56)

> **DEPTH:** 65 to 92 feet   **LEVEL:** Advanced
> **COORDINATES:** 45° 01′ 39.600″N/074° 50′ 41.399″W

2. *EASTCLIFFE HALL*   (UPDATE -- *GLDG2* p. 57-58)

> **DEPTH:** 40-65 feet   **LEVEL:** Advanced
> **COORDINATES:** 44° 55′ 28.800″N/075° 06′ 4.200″W

3. *WEEHAWK*   (UPDATE -- *GLDG2* p. 61)

> **DEPTH:** To 22 feet   **LEVEL:** Novice-Intermediate
> **COORDINATES:** 44° 46.615′N/075° 23.990′W

The spelling of this steel ferry's name has also been seen as *Wee Hawk*. This ship, built in 1926 at Camden, New Jersey, was a powerful (700 horsepower), capacious (500 passengers and 36 railroad cars) vessel measuring 145′6″ in length, 37′1″ in beam, with a draught of 12′7″ that worked for the St. Lawrence Seaway Development Corporation running between Cornwall Island, Ontario, and Rooseveltown, New York. Sold for scrap in 1960 for the sum of $3,150.00, the buyer never scrapped his purchase, so, to this day, it lies alongside the St. Lawrence River in the abandoned ship canal (Lock 28). In recent years, the lock gate has been opened to allow fresh water into the canal, greatly imcreasing the water visibility.

4. 'LOBLAW'S' WRECK   (UPDATE -- *GLDG2* p. 64)

> **DEPTH:** 52 feet   **LEVEL:** Intermediate
> **COORDINATES:** 44° 41.598′N/075° 30.812′W

This unidentified wreck lies about 1,500 feet off the U.S. shoreline.

5. *ROTHESAY*   (UPDATE -- *GLDG2* p. 63-64)

> **DEPTH:** 22-30 feet   **LEVEL:** Novice-Intermediate
> **COORDINATES:** 44° 41.585′N/075° 31.397′W

Left: *The bow of the 193-foot-long sidewheel steamer,* **Rothesay,** *which sank in a collision with a tug boat on Sept. 12, 1889, attracts a visiting scuba diver.*
(PHOTO BY VLADA DEKINA)

Right: *A diver photographs one of the* **Rothesay's** *toppled paddlewheels lying in 30 feet of water in the St. Lawrence River near Prescott, Ontario.*
(PHOTO BY VLADA DEKINA)

6. MUSCALLONGE (UPDATE -- *GLDG2* p. 66)

DEPTH: 99 feet **LEVEL: Advanced**
COORDINATES: 44° 36.245′N/075° 39.212′W

TUG EXPLODES BURNS TO WATER CREW ESCAPES

7,000 Gallons of Burning Oil Spread Flames 1,000 Feet

Brockville, Aug. 16 (CP). -- The Montreal tug Muscallonge burned to the water's edge early Saturday after the craft had been beached a mile and a half east of here on the St. Lawrence River. Origin of the fire is unknown. Captain S. Ahearn and the crew of ten escaped.
The Muscallonge was bound up river from Montreal with the smaller tug Ajax and the barge Bruce Hud-

Left: The loss of the Muscallonge *made dramatic headlines in the Toronto Globe on Aug. 17, 1936.* (KOHL-FORSBERG ARCHIVES)

Right: *A diver shines a light on the* Muscallonge. (PHOTO BY VLADA DEKINA)

7. NOT THE *SAM COOK* (UPDATE -- *GLDG2* p. 72)

DEPTH: To 60 feet **LEVEL: Advanced**
COORDINATES: 44° 33.110′N/075° 43.339′W

This shipwreck, lying in a strong current just a short distance upstream of Brockville, Ontario, at first nicknamed the "Battersby Island Wreck" and later believed to be the schooner, *Sam Cook*, is not the *Sam Cook*.

While the *Sam Cook* (143′6″ x 26′2″ x 11′) was wrecked near this location on July 6, 1882, the Chicago *Inter Ocean* newspaper reported 12 days later that, while "her stern is in sixty feet of water and her bow is fast on the rocks,...it is likely that she will be raised." Despite George Hall of Ogdensburg, NY, stripping this ship of her sails, anchors, and rigging in October 1882, in July 1883, Port Huron wrecker Capt. Merryman began work on recovering the vessel, which he succeeded in doing by October that year. The *Sam Cook*, rebuilt at Ogdensburg over that winter, upon completion on June 11, 1884, was renamed the *William Wheeler* (which foundered in a Lake Ontario storm on August 29, 1893.)

So, the mystery of the Battersby Island Wreck remains unsolved.

8. ROOSEVELT (UPDATE -- *GLDG2* p. 72)

Of the three abandoned ships, collectively known as the "Molly's Gut Wrecks," near the Brockville, Ontario, waterfront, lying in about 20 feet of water, one is believed to be the remains of the ferry boat *Roosevelt,* or *Theodore Roosevelt,* built in 1906 and burned to a total loss on October 7, 1936, at Edgewood Park, Alexandria Bay, NY. This was one of the two ferries operating here (the other was the *General Hancock* -- see page 12) that were no longer needed in 1938 when the Thousand Islands Bridge was built.

The ferry, Roosevelt. (KOHL-FORSBERG ARCHIVES)

9. AMERICA (UPDATE -- *GLDG2* p. 75-76)

> **DEPTH: 55-78 feet   LEVEL: Advanced**
> **COORDINATES: 44° 26.997'N/075° 48.670'W**

NOTE: This wreck lies just inside U.S. waters, and the correct date of loss is July 19, 1932, not June 20, 1932. This article is from the Toronto *Globe*, dated July 20, 1932.

Blast on Drill Boat Claims Seven Lives Near Alexandria Bay

Nine Men Injured by Dynamite Explosion Few Miles From Scene of Tragedy Caused by Lightning in 1930—St. Lawrence Valley Shaken for Miles—Motor Boats Hasten to Aid as Oil Tanker Proceeds on Way

(Associated Press Dispatch.)
ALEXANDRIA BAY, N.Y., July 19.—Seven men were believed killed and nine were injured late today at Chippewa Bay when a dynamite explosion on the drill boat America blew the boat to bits, and shook the St. Lawrence Valley for

Left: KOHL-FORSBERG ARCHIVES. *The* **America,** *including its sunken barge.* (PHOTOS BY VLADA DEKINA)

10. KEYSTORM (UPDATE -- *GLDG2* p. 76-77)

> **DEPTH: 35-120 feet   LEVEL: Advanced**
> **COORDINATES: 44° 25.770'N/075° 49.361'W**

A diver examines the **Keystorm's** *engine* (left) *and propeller* (right). (PHOTOS BY VLADA DEKINA)

11. PENTLAND AND F. A. GEORGER (UPDATE -- *GLDG2* p. 77-78)

> **DEPTH: To 14 feet   LEVEL: Novice**
> **COORDINATES: 44° 24.960'N/075° 50.925'W**
> **(44° 24' 53.399"N/075° 50' 57.599"W)**

Known locally as "The Twisted Sisters," these two, abandoned, wooden ships are the *Pentland* (the more southern one) and the *F. A. Georger* (the more northern one). The propeller, *Pentland* (192'8" x 35'5" x 14'3"), was built at Grand Haven, Michigan, in 1894, while the immense, three-masted schooner, *F. A. Georger* (200'6" x 35'4" x 15'), was constructed at Tonawanda, New York, in 1874. Save Ontario Shipwrecks has surveyed both.

(KOHL-FORSBERG ARCHIVES)

12. CLARA WHITE (UPDATE -- *GLDG2* p. 78)

> **DEPTH: To 15 feet   LEVEL: Novice**
> **COORDINATES: 44° 23.672'N/075° 53.240'W**

The small schooner, *Clara White*, built at Dog Lake, Storrington, Ontario in 1871, burned to a complete loss on July 29, 1889 (not July 11, 1889, as reported earlier). The Kingston (Ontario) *Daily British Whig* reported that "...The crew lost all their effects," and that is why so many clay pipes were located at this site!

13. KINGHORN (UPDATE -- *GLDG2* p. 78)

> **DEPTH: 80-93 feet   LEVEL: Advanced**
> **COORDINATES: 44° 22.606'N/075° 55.838'W**
> **(44° 22' 35.821"N/075° 55' 54.000"W)**

The official name of this shipwreck is *Kinghorn*, not *Kingshorn*, as previously reported, and the loss of this 303-gross-ton schooner-barge (131' x 24'8" x 9'1") just off Rockport, Ontario, occurred on May 3, 1897. This ship, an early example of composite (both wood and iron) construction, was built at Montreal in 1871.

The **Kinghorn's** *wheel* (left) *and stove inside the wreck* (right) *attract visiting divers.* (PHOTOS BY VLADA DEKINA)

14. SOPHIA (UPDATE -- *GLDG2* p. 79)

> **DEPTH: 65-75 feet   LEVEL: Advanced**
> **COORDINATES: 44° 22.650'N/075° 56.090'W**

LOCATION: This wrecked schooner, which lies at Rockport, Ontario, has a vague history. It could be the schooner-barge named the *Sophia* that was built at Sorel, Quebec, in 1854, and worked at hauling bulk cargoes (e.g. grain, coal) between Lake Ontario and Montreal. This may be one of the two vessels reported wrecked here in November, 1888.

15. CATHERINE (UPDATE -- *GLDG2* p. 79)

> **DEPTH: 65-75 feet   LEVEL: Advanced**
> **COORDINATES: 44° 20.925'N/075° 54.780'W**

This wreck, reported earlier as being a schooner, is actually the small steamer that tragically sank with the loss of several lives after colliding with the large excursion steamer, *St. Lawrence*, on July 17, 1890.

16. ISLANDER (UPDATE -- *GLDG2* p. 79)

> **DEPTH: 15-60 feet   LEVEL: Intermediate**
> **COORDINATES: 44° 20.300'N/075° 55.210'W**

17. Roy A. Jodrey (UPDATE -- *GLDG2* p. 80)

DEPTH: 140-250 feet   LEVEL: Technical
COORDINATES: 44° 19.858′N/075° 56.055′W

The 640-foot-long freighter, *Roy A. Jodrey*, sunk after striking a shoal in November 1974, is a deep shipwreck sitting in dangerous, fast-moving water, so it is to be explored ONLY by prepared divers with proper training and extreme experience. This is NOT the *Sweepstakes*!

The enormous, intact freighter, Roy A. Jodrey, is difficult to reach. Penetration diving on this shipwreck is doubly dangerous. (Photos by Vlada Dekina)

18. *OCONTO* (UPDATE -- *GLDG2* p. 81)

> **DEPTH: 145 to 180 feet   LEVEL: Technical**
> **COORDINATES: 44° 17.005′N/076° 00.972′W**

On July 10, 1886, the wooden steamer, *Oconto*, (143′ x 32′ 8″ x 10′1″), built at Manitowoc, Wisconsin, in 1872, struck a rock, was impaled, and eventually slid into deep water.

Left: *Steamer* Oconto. (KOHL-FORSBERG ARCHIVES) **Right:** Oconto's *anchor.* (PHOTO BY VLADA DEKINA)

19. *A. E. VICKERY* (UPDATE -- *GLDG2* p. 81-82)

> **DEPTH: 65 to 121 feet   LEVEL: Advanced**
> **COORDINATES: 44° 16.820′ 076″N/076° 01.183′W**

The 28-year-old *A. E. Vickery* sank on August 15, 1889, due to the carelessness of a hired pilot. The wreck lies on a slope on the U.S. side near the Rock Island Lighthouse.
Be aware of, and take precautions against, the strong currents at this site.

Clockwise from top left: *The 136-foot schooner,* A. E. Vickery, *closely resembled this ship, the 139-foot* **Elgin** *(1874 - 1910).* (KOHL-FORSBERG ARCHIVES). *Highlights include* **Vickery's** *windlass and chain* (PHOTO BY WARREN LO), *bow railings, and vast cargo holds.* (PHOTOS BY VLADA DEKINA)

20. DAUNTLESS (UPDATE -- *GLDG2* p. 82)

> **DEPTH: 50 feet   LEVEL: Intermediate**
> **COORDINATES: 44° 14.937′N/076° 04.311′W**

The sleek, 86-foot-long, excursion steamer, *Dauntless*, started running between Clayton and Alexandria Bay in the summer of 1921, delivering mail and as many as 100 tourists at a time to waiting trains. The fancy bow scrollwork identified this burned, engineless wreck, which was likely scuttled when the ship grew old and river traffic slowed down.

21. SQUAW (UPDATE -- *GLDG2* p. 82)

> **DEPTH: 50 feet   LEVEL: Intermediate**
> **COORDINATES: 44° 14.603′N/076° 05.606′W**

22. MAGGIE L. (UPDATE -- *GLDG2* p. 83)

> **DEPTH: 75 feet   LEVEL: Advanced**
> **COORDINATES: 44° 14.646′N/076° 05.680′W**

The *Maggie L.* was a small, wooden, two-masted schooner (67′ x 17′4″ x 5′2″), built at Picton, Ontario, in 1889, by the Redmond Ship Builders, and was used to haul bulk cargoes such as coal. On October 31, 1929, the *Maggie L.* was cut in two in a collision with the steel freighter, *Keystate*. No lives were lost, but the smaller vessel, one of the last of the old-time schooners still working on the lakes, was a total loss.

The 72-foot-long **Glen Cuyler** *(1859-1911),* **left,** *closely resembled the 67-foot-long schooner,* **Maggie L.,** *which was cut in two in a collision with the 250-foot-long, steel freighter,* **Keystate, right.** *The* **Keystate,** *built in 1927 in England, was scrapped in 1961.* (KOHL-FORSBERG ARCHIVES)

23. HOLLIDAY POINT WRECK (UPDATE -- *GLDG2* p. 83)

> **DEPTH: 36-46 feet   LEVEL: Novice-Intermediate**
> **COORDINATES: 44° 14.190′N/076° 16.630′W**

Only the bow and the centerboard box in midship remain intact on this unidentified sailing vessel lying alongside eastern Wolfe Island, Ontario.

24. LEWISTON AND THREE BARGES (UPDATE -- *GLDG2* p. 84)

> **DEPTH: To 20 feet   LEVEL: Novice-Intermediate**
> **COORDINATES: 44° 09.000020′N/076° 20.924′W**

The wooden propeller barge named the *Lewiston* (about 200 feet long), was possibly towing the three unidentified barges that lie just downstream. One of these barges could be the old steamer, stripped of its equipment, named the *Oatland* (ex-*William J. Averell*).

25. *HARVEY J. KENDALL* (UPDATE -- *GLDG2* p. 84)

> **DEPTH: 20-29 feet   LEVEL: Novice-Intermediate**
> **COORDINATES: 44° 08.555'N/076° 21.981'W**

26. *ARIZONA* (UPDATE -- *GLDG2* p. 84)

> **DEPTH: to 34 feet   LEVEL: Novice-Intermediate**
> **COORDINATES: 44° 07.36'N/076° 23.05'W**

NOTE: Regarding the "Eel City" dive site between Brockville and Mallorytown (see *GLDG2*, p. 75) -- These snakelike, slimy creatures, named American eels, have nearly disappeared. Breeding in the Atlantic Ocean's Sargasso Sea, taking 10 to 12 years to mature, and being a popular food in Europe and Japan are factors that have decimated the species, once so common in the St. Lawrence River, including in the Thousand Islands.

A Great Lakes Sidebar

A U-Boat Wreck in the Thousand Islands?

Wilbur Wahl, the owner of the French Creek Marina in Clayton, New York, has amassed an amazing collection of old anchors from the St. Lawrence River which he openly exhibits in his marina, including a controversial one from World War II. Displaying a bold swastika on one of its flukes, it allegedly came from a German U-boat that was sunk in the Thousand Islands in 1942!

Mr. Wahl states that, as a youth, he witnessed a 1942 bombing of the area in the Thousand Islands just upstream of Linda Island by Canadian aircraft from the

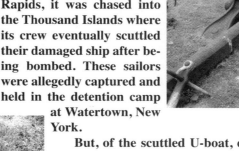

nearby Trenton Air Force Base on Lake Ontario. According to the long-circulated story, after a U-boat was seen running up the Lachine Rapids, it was chased into the Thousand Islands where its crew eventually scuttled their damaged ship after being bombed. These sailors were allegedly captured and held in the detention camp at Watertown, New York.

But, of the scuttled U-boat, only this anchor was found -- reportedly by a diver back in 1970. Is the rest of this U-boat still out there, waiting to be discovered?

Joan Forsberg listens to some of Wilbur Wahl's anchor tales -- including the story of the one that allegedly came from a Nazi submarine in the Thousand Islands in 1942! (PHOTOS BY CRIS KOHL)

2. Lake Ontario

"NEW SHIPWRECKS" refers to those that are not in the book, *The Great Lakes Diving Guide,* second edition, 2008 (*GLDG2*), either because they had not yet been discovered, or because the authors had not yet learned about their locations.

NEW SHIPWRECKS

A. 'Confederation Wreck No. 1'
B. Ships' Graveyard:
   Sarnor/Hattie Hutt
   'Queen Mary'
C. *Shannon*
D. *Roberval*
E. *Gordon*
F. *Atlas*
G. *Three Brothers*
H. *Ocean Wave*
I. *Bay State*

J. *Queen of the Lakes*
K. *Isaac G. Jenkins?*
L. *Samuel F. Hodge*
M. *C. Reeve*
N. *Nisbet Grammer*
O. *P. B. Locke*
P. *Ontario*
Q. *Salvage Queen*
R. 'Two Bits'/'Rumrunner'
S. Berringham crane & tug
T. *La Grande Hermine*

"UPDATED SHIPWRECKS" refers to ones that are in the book, *The Great Lakes Diving Guide* (shortened to *GLDG2* when referenced in this chapter). The UPDATED information about each of these shipwrecks could be new or corrected GPS coordinates, additional maritime history, and/or modern-day news about that particular wreck.

UPDATED SHIPWRECKS

1. *Wolfe Islander II*
2. *Prince Regent/Princess Charlotte*
3. *St. Lawrence*
4. *Munson*
5. *Cornwall*
6. 'Glendora'
7. *Comet*
8. *George T. Davie*

9. *George A. Marsh*
10. *City of Sheboygan*
11. *Katie Eccles*
12. *Olive Branch*
13. *Alexandria*
14. *Sligo*
15. The 'Tiller Wreck'
16. *Julia B. Merrill*
17. *Lyman M. Davis*

A. 'CONFEDERATION WRECK NO. 1' (NEW)

> **DEPTH: 10 feet**   **LEVEL: Novice-Intermediate**
> **COORDINATES: : 43.245970N/-79.740768W**

LOCATION: This unidentified, abandoned wreck lies approximately 300 feet off Confederation Park B in Kingston, Ontario.

The wreck, lying in 10 feet of water, appears to have been a wooden sidewheel steamer.

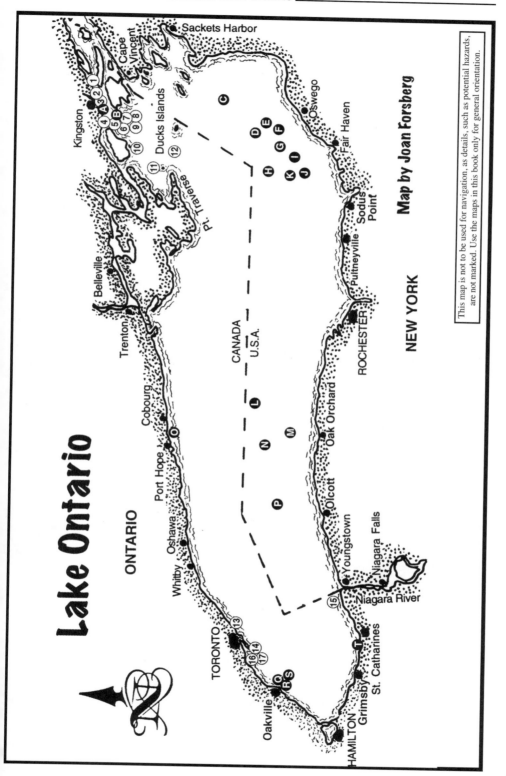

Lake Ontario

ONTARIO

Kingston

Cape Vincent

Sackets Harbor

Belleville

Trenton

Cobourg

Port Hope

Oshawa

Whitby

TORONTO

Oakville

HAMILTON

Grimsby

St. Catharines

Ducks Islands

Pt. Traverse

CANADA
U.S.A.

Oswego

Fair Haven

Sodus Point

Putneyville

ROCHESTER

Oak Orchard

Olcott

Youngstown

Niagara Falls

Niagara River

NEW YORK

Map by Joan Forsberg

B. SHIPS' GRAVEYARD: *SARNOR, HATTIE HUTT,* 'QUEEN MARY' (NEW)

LOCATION: These vessels lie in a ships' graveyard, one of three near Kingston, Ontario, off Nine Mile Point. Depth is about 90 feet. The *Sarnor* and the *Hattie Hutt* lie so close together that they are connected by a line and are usually done as a single dive.

The large, wooden steamer, *Sarnor,* launched at West Bay City, Michigan, in 1888 as the *Brittanic* and renamed in 1913, was already sitting idle when the ship caught on fire at Kingston on March 15, 1926. The hulk was towed out into the lake and scuttled on November 1, 1937, as part of a major harbor clean-up.

Built in 1873 at Saugatuck, Michigan, and launched as the *F. B. Stockbridge* before being renamed in 1881, the "gracious schooner" *Hattie Hutt,* used as a tow barge in her latter years, was abandoned at Kingston in the late 1920's and finally raised and scuttled in Lake Ontario on November 6, 1937.

The complete stories of the *Sarnor* and the *Hattie Hutt,* along with photos of them in their prime as well as being raised from Kingston harbor after having been abandoned, appear in the 1997 book, *Treacherous Waters: Kingston's Shipwrecks,* by Cris Kohl.

Above: *The wrecks of the 128-foot-long schooner,* **Hattie Hutt** *(left and right), and the 227-foot-long steamer,* **Sarnor** *(center), were both scuttled in deep, Lake Ontario waters in 1936 after spending years as abandoned eyesores in Kingston harbor.* (PHOTOS BY VLADA DEKINA)

The huge, unidentified, scuttled wreck, nicknamed the **'Queen Mary'** *due to its enormous size, features considerable scattered debris in the hull* (left) *and a large, four-bladed propeller* (right).
(PHOTOS BY VLADA DEKINA)

C. *SHANNON* (NEW)

LOCATION: This wreck lies in deep water about 20 miles north of Oswego, NY.

The *Shannon* was a small (77'5" x 18'7" x 5'7") scow-schooner, built by Robert Davis at Battersea (Kingston), Ontario, in 1867, the year that Canada became a country. This 120-ton, wooden vessel, owned in Gananoque, Ontario, sprang a leak and foundered on June 20, 1874, enroute from Oswego to Gananoque with a coal cargo. No lives were lost.

This small shipwreck, which was reported found on June 24, 2011, by Dan Scoville and Chris Koberstein, is amazingly intact; both masts (with some rigging!) remain standing, along with the upright bowsprit perpendicular to its flat-faced bow, and, on deck, the cabin is still in place (a rarity!) near the ship's wheel (another rarity!) The heavy coal cargo in the holds is visible, and helped identify this shipwreck.

D. *ROBERVAL* (NEW?)

LOCATION: The *Roberval* rests about 12 miles off Oswego, NY.

We included this shipwreck in the book, *GLDG2* (p. 127), in 2008 because Great Lakes historian Wes Oleszewski showed ROV video footage of a deep shipwreck, stated as being the *Roberval*, at Milwaukee's annual "Ghost Ships Festival" in 2002. But when the *Roberval* was located in October, 2013, by Jim Kennard, Roger Pawlowski, and Roland "Chip" Stevens, it received a much higher level of media attention.

CREW OF WRECKED FREIGHTER SAVED

Lake Ontario Gale Swamps Boat, Washing Hands From the Deck.

Captain, Woman Cook and Others Save Themselves On Improvised Raft.

Oswego, N. Y., Sept. 26.—Four members of the crew of the steamer Roberval, of Ottawa, which foundered yesterday in Lake Ontario nine miles from here, were picked up late today on an improvised raft, after having been buffeted by the sea for 24 hours without food. Two others reported missing were seen in a

Clockwise from upper left: *The small, steel bulk freighter, Roberval, in 1915. Many newspapers reported the* Roberval's *tragic loss, this one being the start of a long article in the* Detroit Free Press, *Sept. 27, 1916* (KOHL-FORSBERG ARCHIVES). *Discovery team member Roland "Chip" Stevens painted the wreck.* (COURTESY OF ROLAND STEVENS)

The diminutive (it was about half the length of a standard, 250-foot-long "canaler" common on the Great Lakes at the time) *Roberval* (128' x 24' x 8'), built in Toronto in 1907, was hauling lumber from Cape Vincent to Oswego on September 25, 1916, when overcome by a sudden storm. The lumber piled on deck created a high profile which the strong winds caught, and the ship rolled onto its starboard side. Capt. Peter Eligh saved the cook by pulling her by her hair onto a makeshift raft of lumber which also carried two other sailors, while three others reached shore in a damaged lifeboat. Two crew members, however, perished when the ship sank. The wreck's superstructure is heavily damaged.

E. *GORDON* (NEW)

LOCATION: This dredge lies approximately 10 miles off Oswego, NY.

A small flotilla of tug boats towing dredges set out towards Oswego from Cape Vincent on November 17, 1879, when a strong storm hit them, disrupting their cohesion. The relatively new, 51-foot-long tug, *Philip Becker*, struck the *Gordon*, damaging both vessels and causing them to leak badly. Just before the *Becker* sank, her three crew members jumped on board the *Gordon* -- which also sank, taking the lives of all 6 people then on board!

The rectangular, box-like wreck of the dredge *Gordon* was reportedly located in deep waters on July 5, 2012, by Dan Scoville and Chris Koberstein. The *Becker* remains lost.

F. ATLAS (NEW)

LOCATION: One of the oldest commercial ships in the Great Lakes lies off Oswego, NY, harbor, in nearly 300' of water. Her heavy, limestone cargo plummeted this one-year-old, two-masted, 27-ton, 52-foot-long schooner, the *Atlas*, to the lake bottom on May 4, 1839, in a storm. All 5 people on board perished. In an attempt to render assistance, the steamer, *Telegraph*, found only small items of flotsam.

This wreck was found in June 2013, by Jim Kennard, Roger Pawlowski and Roland "Chip" Stevens.

Left: *The wreck of the* **Atlas,** *with its toppled masts.* (COURTESY OF ARTIST ROLAND STEVENS)

G. THREE BROTHERS (NEW)

LOCATION: Deep, off Oswego, NY.

An early, two-masted, dagger-board (like a centerboard) schooner, the *Three Brothers*, built in 1827, disappeared with all hands in a storm on November 12, 1833.

This shipwreck was located in July 2014, by Jim Kennard, Roger Pawlowski and Roland "Chip" Stevens.

Right: *The* **Three Brothers,** *as the wreck sits today.* (COURTESY OF ARTIST ROLAND STEVENS).

H. OCEAN WAVE (NEW)

LOCATION: This wreck lies about 15 miles off Oswego, NY.

Carrying a heavy deckload of lumber for Oswego, the twin-masted, 98-ton schooner, *Ocean Wave* (81' x 20'1" x 7'6"), built at Picton, Ontario, in 1868, departed Trenton, Ontario, on Nov. 9, 1890, but the vessel foundered in a storm with all hands, including the two co-owners who planned to retire after this trip. The capsized ship was seen just prior to sinking, north of Oswego, with no one on board.

Jim Kennard, Roger Pawlowski and Roland "Chip" Stevens found the wreck in 2012.

Right: *News of the* **Ocean Wave** *appeared in the* **Detroit Free Press** *on Nov. 11, 1890.* (KOHL-FORSBERG ARCHIVES)

SUNK IN LAKE ONTARIO.

A Schooner, Supposed to be the Ocean Wave, Lost.

NO TIDINGS OF HER CREW WHO, IT IS FEARED, ARE DROWNED.

Story of the Engineer of the Wrecked Steam Barge Bruno.

The *Ocean Wave* Supposed to be Lost With All on Board.

OSWEGO, November 10.—*Special.*—The schooner Cornelia arrived here this afternoon and reported that she passed a vessel bottom side up about twelve miles up the Lake. The tug Ferris left for the vessel at 3:30. The captain of the Cornelia says the vessel is about twelve miles due north of this port. She was loaded with lumber, and that the vessel was the Ocean Wave, which was due here with lumber. There was no one on board her, and it is thought the crew has perished.

LATER.—The tug Ferris has just returned [0:30 ?, and ??????] her search for the vessel reported as having been seen bottom side up some miles out. Capt. Ferris reports...

I. BAY STATE (NEW)

LOCATION: This wreck lies in deep water off Fair Haven, NY.

Built in 1852 at Buffalo, NY, the wooden propeller, *Bay State* (137'3" x 25'7" x 11'4"), foundered with the loss of all (at least 23) people who were on board on November 4, 1862.

The *Bay State* was located in August 2015, by Jim Kennard and Roger Pawlowski.

Left: *The tragic wreck of the* **Bay State,** *an early propeller-driven ship on Lake Ontario.* (COURTESY OF ARTIST ROLAND STEVENS)

J. QUEEN OF THE LAKES (NEW)

LOCATION: This wreck, in 200'-300' of water, sits about 8 miles off Sodus Point, NY.

The schooner, *Queen of the Lakes* (128' x 23'3" x 10'3"), built at Portsmouth (Kingston), Ontario in 1853 in Canada West (later Ontario), foundered with its coal cargo on Nov. 28, 1906. The crew rowed to shore safely.

Jim Kennard, Dan Scoville, and Roland "Chip" Stevens found this shipwreck in August 2009, but did not publicly announce its discovery until July 2011.

The Canadian schooner, Queen of the Lakes, *worked for 53 years!* (KOHL-FORSBERG ARCHIVES)

K. ISAAC G. JENKINS (NEW)

LOCATION: This wreck is located approximately 15 miles northwest of Oswego, NY.

This upright schooner, found in more than 750 feet of water, is most likely the *Isaac G. Jenkins* (137' x 25'6" x 12'). Built in 1873 at Algonac, Michigan, it foundered two years later, on December 2, 1875, while bound from the Welland Canal to Oswego. All 10 hands were lost.

Left: *The wreck that is probably the* Isaac G. Jenkins, *painted from remote-operated (ROV) video.* (COURTESY OF ARTIST ROLAND STEVENS)

L. SAMUEL F. HODGE (NEW)

LOCATION: This shipwreck lies in mid-lake off Oak Orchard, NY.

The 586-gross-ton, wooden propeller, *Samuel F. Hodge* (149′4″ x 30′ x 12′8″), constructed in 1881 at Detroit, Michigan, was hauling 600 tons of wire when the ship caught on fire on July 5, 1896, and sank. One sailor, the fireman in the boiler room, lost his life. The remainder of the crew was rescued by the passing propeller, *St. Joseph*.

Detected by sidescan sonar in 2007 by Jim Kennard and Dan Scoville, this shipwreck, lying in several hundred feet of water, was not examined, investigated or identified until they returned to the site in 2009. They had been searching for a schooner considerably smaller than this shipwreck, so they put this one "on hold" (yes, they eventually located their small schooner -- see the story of the *Milan* in *GLDG2* on p. 126).

This larger shipwreck carried a steam engine and a propeller, indicating clearly that it was not a schooner. It was also evident that a fire had destroyed the superstructure and much of the decking. A later search reportedly located two masts on the lake bottom several miles away, probably at the spot where the fire burned them off at their bases. The steamer, *Hodge*, carried two, short masts. Hull measurements provided the final evidence needed to identify this shipwreck as the *Samuel F. Hodge*.

The 149-foot propeller, **Samuel F. Hodge.**
(KOHL-FORSBERG ARCHIVES)

M. C. REEVE (NEW)

LOCATION: This wreck lies in deep water (nearly 400') off Oak Orchard, NY.

The two-masted, gaff-rigged schooner, *C. Reeve* (119' x 25'8" x 10'), built in 1853 at Buffalo, NY, was known for two things: hauling a valuable cargo of black walnut across the Atlantic Ocean to Liverpool in 1858, and being in collisions with other ships, the final one of which, with the schooner *Exchange*, permanently sank the corn-cargoed *C. Reeve* on November 22, 1862, during a blinding blizzard. No lives were lost. Wreck hunters Jim Kennard and Dan Scoville located the *C. Reeve* in 2009.

LOCAL INTELLIGENCE.

COLLISION—VESSEL LOST.—The schooner *C. Reeve*, Captain Donahue, was run down on Lake Ontario, near Oak Orchard, about four miles from land, on Saturday night last, by the schooner *Exchange* from Cleveland. The night was dark and it was snowing at the time. The

Information about the final **C. Reeve** *collision appeared in the* **Detroit Free Press** *on Nov. 27, 1862.* (KOHL-FORSBERG ARCHIVES)

N. NISBET GRAMMER (NEW)

LOCATION: This steel-hulled shipwreck lies in 500+ feet of water 30 miles east of the Niagara River, off Thirty-Mile Point, NY.

The 1,725-gross-ton *Nisbet Grammer* (253' x 43'4" x 20'), built in England in 1923, is reputedly the largest shipwreck in Lake Ontario. On May 31, 1926, the *Grammer,* carrying grain from Port Colborne, Ontario, bound for Montreal, sank in a collision with the freighter, *Dalwarnic*, during severe fog, the crew escaping in a lifeboat. Dan Scoville, Jim Kennard, Craig Hampton and Roland Stevens located the wreck in August 2014.

The 253-foot freighter, **Nisbet Grammer** *(left,* KOHL-FORSBERG ARCHIVES*) sank after being struck in fog by the bow of the 253-foot freighter,* **Dalwarnic** *(right,* COURTESY OF ARTIST ROLAND STEVENS*)*

O. P. B. LOCKE (NEW)

DEPTH: 80 feet   LEVEL: Advanced
COORDINATES: 43.916182N/-78.298781W

LOCATION: This wreck lies approximately three miles (five kilometres) off Port Hope, Ontario.

The three-masted, 344-gross-ton, centerboard schooner, *P. B. Locke* (135'9" x 26' x 11'4"), built by the Bailey Brothers at Toledo, Ohio, in 1872, was converted to a schooner-barge the following year. After 40 years of service on the Great Lakes, the *Locke*, while in tow of the wooden steamer, *Juno,* met her demise. During a violent storm on November 1, 1912, the *P. B. Locke* was cut adrift from the *Juno*, which hightailed it back to Cobourg, Ontario, where she

Both the steamer, **Juno,** *and its tow, the schooner-barge,* **P. B. Locke,** *sank at the same time, but the* **Juno** *was recovered.* (KOHL-FORSBERG ARCHIVES)

MARINE

JUNO AND LOCKE SINK IN ONTARIO

Crew of Canadian Barge, Including Woman, Make Perilous Trip to Shore.

Special to The Free Press.
Port Hope, Ont., November 1.—The steambarge Juno, with the barge P. B. Locke in tow, sprang a leak when half way between Port Hope and Cobourg late Thursday night.
The Locke was cut adrift and the Juno put back to Cobourg, where she sank at the pier. The Locke's anchor failed to hold and the barge sank near Gull light, east of Port Hope.
The Locke's crew of three men and one woman took to the yawl and reached Port Hope alive on a perilous trip. The

promptly sank at the pier. The *Locke* dropped her anchor to ride out the storm, but the anchor failed to hold, and the ship's seams opened, sinking her near Gull Light, east of Port Hope. The three men on the *Locke* (Capt. Dan McVicar, mate Hilton Fuller, and sailor Jack Marrigan) and the woman cook (Minnie Holland) took to their small yawl boat and, after a perilous trip, reached Port Hope safely.

The three-masted schooner, **P. B. Locke,** *prior to being cut down to a tow-barge.*
(KOHL-FORSBERG ARCHIVES)

(The towing steamer, *Juno*, which also sank, was recovered, but eventually ended her days on the bottom of Lake Ontario. See *GLDG2*, p. 119, for the story of the *Juno*.)

The *P. B. Locke*, since its discovery by the Nautilus Scuba Club in August 2000, has become the most popular shipwreck dive in the northwestern part of Lake Ontario. The wreck sits upright and retains all of its artifacts, including the ship's wheel.

P. ONTARIO (NEW)

LOCATION: This very significant (one of the most historic in the lake!) shipwreck lies in about 400 feet of water off Olcott, NY.

The wreck of the British sailing vessel, the H.M.S. *Ontario*, used during the American Revolution and sunk in a violent storm on the U.S. side of Lake Ontario on Oct. 31, 1780, with the loss of everyone -- anywhere from 84 to 130 people, including women, children, and possibly about 30 U.S. prisoners of war -- was found on May 31, 2008, by wreck hunters Jim Kennard and Dan Scoville.

Several cannons lie on the deck of this 22-gun, 77-foot-long warship, resting partially on its side. Both masts remain upright, complete with crow's nests, rising 70 feet above the deck. The bow stem is decoratively carved, and two windows on the stern remain unbroken. The ROV video of this wreck is absolutely amazing!

Clockwise from right: *The H.M.S.* **Ontario** *under sail* (COURTESY OF THE ARTIST, PETER RINDLISBACHER); *the ship struggled in a violent storm* (COURTESY OF THE ARTIST, ROLAND STEVENS); *the wreck as it rests in very deep water today.* (COURTESY OF THE ARTIST, ROLAND STEVENS)

Q. SALVAGE QUEEN (NEW)

DEPTH: 60 to 71 feet   LEVEL: Advanced
COORDINATES: 43° 25.111′N/079° 39.969′W

LOCATION: This scuttled wreck lies just outside Hamilton, Ontario, harbor.

Dive shop owner Robb Shannon purchased this old ship in 2005, and, after renaming it *Jessie Ann* (after his grandmother), has been using it as a scuba diver training site.

Launched in 1899 as the *H.C.M. No. 15* (85′4″ x 27′6″ x 7′6″) by the Harbor Commissioners of Montreal for use as a floating grain elevator, this vessel was converted to a salvage tugboat in the 1920's when it was purchased by the Pyke Salvage Company and renamed *Salvage Queen* (not *SA Queen*, as incorrectly indicated on at least one web site due to a keyboarding error). The *Salvage Queen's* exciting history included recovering ships stranded on shoals (e.g. the *Gilchrist* and the *Armonda* in 1929, with assistance from the other Pyke boats, namely the tug *Salvage Prince* and the lighter *George T. Davie* -- see p. 39; the *Calgarian* in 1933; the *Kingston* in 1941), cleaning up the damage from the tragic St. Lawrence River explosion of the drill boat, *John B. King*, which killed 30 workers in 1930 (see *GLDG2*, p. 68-69), raising the tug *Dalhousie Rover* from the Welland Canal in 1946, and laying the telephone cable to Wolfe Island in 1960. Now divers can be trained on this wreck knowing more of its history!

Left: *The salvage tug, Salvage Queen.* (KOHL-FORSBERG ARCHIVES)

Right: *The deck of the Jessie Ann (ex-Salvage Queen).* (PHOTO BY WARREN LO)

R. 'TWO BITS' / 'RUMRUNNER' (NEW)

DEPTH: 75 feet   LEVEL: Advanced
COORDINATES: 43° 25.216′N/079° 39.725′W

LOCATION: Just over a mile out of Oakville harbor, Ontario, at Six Mile River.

The 'Two Bits' (left) *reportedly once worked as a dive charter boat at Penetanguishene, Ontario. Nothing is known about the nicknamed 'Rumrunner'* (right). (PHOTOS BY WARREN LO)

S. BERRINGHAM CRANE AND TUG (NEW)

DEPTH: 148 feet   LEVEL: Technical
COORDINATES: 43° 26.020′N/079° 36.986′W

LOCATION: In deep water about 2.5 miles (4 kilometers) off Oakville harbor, Ontario.

Reportedly some time in the 1980's, a large crane and a small work boat, both owned by the Berringham Construction company in Hamilton, ended up on the dark, lake bottom.

Right: *The Berringham crane lies flat in deep water.* (PHOTO BY WARREN LO)

T. LA GRANDE HERMINE (NEW)

LOCATION: This stranded "pirate ship" lies just west of St. Catharines, Ontario, in Jordan Harbour, its masts visible and eyecatching from the Queen Elizabeth Way (QEW).

This "wreck" actually has a long, real history! Built in 1914 at Lauzon, Quebec, for use as a ferry at Trois-Rivieres and named the *Le Progres* (127' x 34'), the ship was renamed *La Verendrye* in 1930, and later, *La Marjolaine*. After conversion to a floating restaurant, it was rebuilt in 1991 as a lifesize replica of the Jacques Cartier vessel, *La Grande Hermine* ("The Big Weasel"). Planned re-use as a restaurant lacked funding, and the ship lay idle at Jordan Harbour. In 2003, vandals set fire to the vessel, precluding any further use.

As the St. Lawrence River ferry, Le Progres, at Trois-Rivieres, Quebec. (KOHL-FORSBERG ARCHIVES)   *As La Grande Hermine, abandoned at Jordan Harbour, Ontario.* (PHOTO BY CRIS KOHL)

1. WOLFE ISLANDER II (UPDATE -- GLDG2 p. 88-89)

DEPTH: 40 to 85 feet   LEVEL: Intermediate-Advanced
COORDINATES: 44° 13.545'N/076° 25.044'W
44.225901N/-76.417381W

2A. PRINCE REGENT   (UPDATE -- GLDG2 p. 86-87)

DEPTH: 6 feet   LEVEL: Novice
COORDINATES: 44.235572N/-76.446530W

2B. PRINCESS CHARLOTTE   (UPDATE -- GLDG2 p. 86-87)

DEPTH: 15 feet   LEVEL: Novice-Intermediate
COORDINATES: 44.232466N/-76.451058W

LOCATION: In Deadman Bay, Kingston, ON.

The *Prince Regent* (56 guns) was previously mis-identified as the *Psyche*, and the *Princess Charlotte* (42 guns), as the *Prince Regent*. Both schooners were launched into Kingston's Navy Bay on April 14, 1814, near the end of the War of 1812, and both vessels were abandoned after the war in the shallows of Deadman Bay. Salvage of cannons used as ballast on the *Princess Charlotte* took place in 1938. The skeletal frames of both wrecks can be reached from shore.

Frames from the Prince Regent in Deadman Bay. (PHOTO BY CRIS KOHL)

3. ST. LAWRENCE (UPDATE -- GLDG2 p. 87)

DEPTH: 8 feet   LEVEL: Novice
COORDINATES: 44.220591N/-76.505026W

LOCATION: This historic wreckage lies in the small, manmade harbor of a private residence at the foot of Morton Street, just east of Kingston's infamous penitentiary.

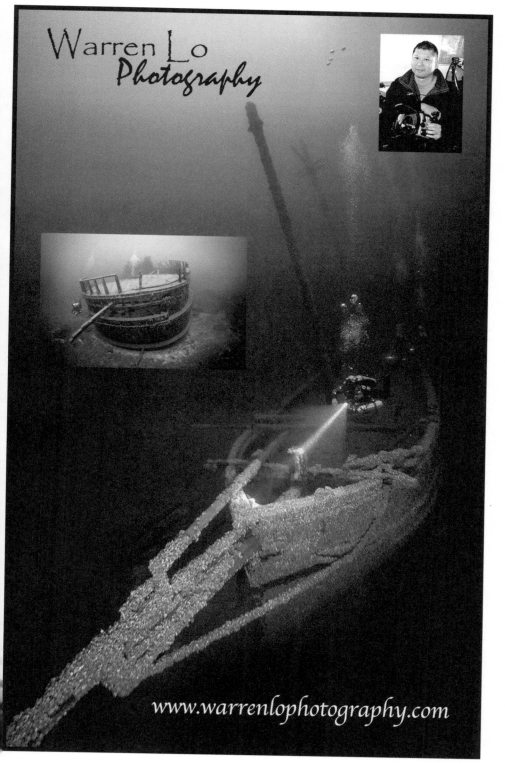

4. MUNSON (UPDATE -- *GLDG2* p. 91-92)

DEPTH: 93 to 112 feet   LEVEL: Advanced
COORDINATES: 44.208881N/-76.607632W

The *Munson*, a local dredge that sank in 1890, remains popular as a shipwreck destination for scuba divers. More of this unregistered vessel's early history is being unearthed.

For a small dredge lost in 1890, the **Munson** *carried considerable machinery. The bucket and hinged arm* (**right**) *remain very visible on the wreck site.* (VIDEO FREEZE-FRAMES BY JOAN FORSBERG)

5. CORNWALL (UPDATE -- *GLDG2* p. 95, 98)

DEPTH: 73 feet   LEVEL: Advanced
COORDINATES: 44° 08.179′N/076° 37.151′W
44.137780N/-76.619069W

The *Cornwall* and the nearby *Comet* continue to be popular among scuba divers because they can do a rare thing: explore TWO sidewheel paddle steamers on the same day.

The steamer, Cornwall, *still displays an upright paddle wheel,* **left,** *and its enormous boiler,* **right,** *is surrounded by wooden hull debris.* (PHOTOS BY WARREN LO)

6. 'GLENDORA' (UPDATE -- *GLDG2* p. 99)

DEPTH: 80 feet   LEVEL: Advanced
COORDINATES: 44° 08.557′N/076° 38.051′W
44.142630N/-76.634199W

No ship named the 'Glendora' was ever a Great Lakes vessel or a Great Lakes shipwreck, and it has long been known that that appellation is a nickname given by scuba divers to an unidentified, likely abandoned hull near Kingston, ON.

Some sources state that this shipwreck is that of the large (166-foot-long), wooden schooner named the *Glenora* (not *Glendora*), launched in 1882 at Kingston, Ontario. But that vessel's name was changed to *Hector* in 1896, two years before it and the *Kildonen*, plus their tow vessel, the steamer, *James A. Walker*, were all lost at Nicholson Island, Lake Ontario, on October 25, 1898. Besides, this 'Glendora' shipwreck has a huge propeller -- not something you would find on a vintage schooner. Obviously, more research is needed.

7. COMET (UPDATE -- *GLDG2* p. 94)

> **DEPTH: 90 feet   LEVEL: Advanced**
> **COORDINATES: 44° 08.320′N/076° 35.041′W**
> **44.138802N/-76.58451W**

8. GEORGE T. DAVIE (UPDATE -- *GLDG2* p. 93)

> **DEPTH: 105 feet   LEVEL: Advanced**
> **COORDINATES: 44° 06.791′N/076° 34.782′W**
> **44.113581N/-76.580069W**

The bulk freight barge named the *George T. Davie*, which foundered in 1945, had worked with the wrecking tug, *Salvage Queen* (see p. 34) during its 47-year-long career.

9. GEORGE A. MARSH (UPDATE -- *GLDG2* p. 96-97)

> **DEPTH: 70 to 85 feet   LEVEL: Advanced**
> **COORDINATES: 44.126831N/-76.602799W**

The relatively intact schooner named the *George A. Marsh,* which was lost with severe loss of life in August 1917, is an exploration target for many scuba divers. A strong appeal of this shipwreck lies in the mystery behind it, namely the fact that the master of the vessel, Captain John Smith, presumed for many years to have been one of the 12 people from the 14 on board this ship who were lost, secretly survived the sinking and disappeared as far away from water as he could get to start his life anew.

We (Cris and Joan) tracked down this Great Lakes captain's tale by driving to a little town called Harrah, Oklahoma, in 2002. There, many history-minded individuals shared with us much information about this man's time in Harrah from 1917 to his death in 1927. He was known to them only as "J. Smith," and local historians knew nothing about his Great Lakes connections. We were able to make contact with an elderly lady who remembered him, as he had been one of her father's best friends. A chapter called "The Dead Captain's Secrets" in the 2004 book, *Shipwreck Tales of the Great Lakes*, by Cris Kohl, told his story. A subsequent trip we made to Harrah in 2008 yielded more fascinating information about "our man." But we also added to our list of questions; our searches continue.

Left: *Joan Forsberg glides past the* **George A. Marsh's** *upright bowsprit, support chains still in place.* **Right:** *A diver prepares to "steer the* **Marsh."** (VIDEO FREEZE-FRAME AND PHOTO BY CRIS KOHL)

10. CITY OF SHEBOYGAN (UPDATE -- *GLDG2* p. 102-103)

> **DEPTH: 90 to 105 feet   LEVEL: Advanced**
> **COORDINATES: 44° 04.559′N/076° 44.069′W**
> **44.075969N/-76.734469W**

11. *KATIE ECCLES* (UPDATE -- *GLDG2* p. 109-110)

> DEPTH: 102 feet   LEVEL: Advanced
> COORDINATES: 44° 0′ 34.801″N/076° 44′ 31.801″W
> 44.009669N/-76.742169W

12. *OLIVE BRANCH* (UPDATE -- *GLDG2* p. 112)

> DEPTH: 90 to 101 feet   LEVEL: Advanced
> COORDINATES: 44.930501N/-76.737169W

The schooner, **Olive Branch,** *lost with all hands in 1880, is amazingly intact, from a hawse pipe and chain* (left) *to a dramatic reminder that people died here* (right).   (PHOTOS BY CRIS KOHL)

13. *ALEXANDRIA* (UPDATE -- *GLDG2* p. 119-120)

> DEPTH: To 10 feet   LEVEL: Novice
> COORDINATES: 43° 43′ 44.46″N/079° 12′ 40.68″W
> 43.729019N/-79.211304W

14. *SLIGO* (UPDATE -- *GLDG2* p. 121)

> DEPTH: 67 feet   LEVEL: Advanced
> COORDINATES: 43° 36.899′N/079° 27.090′W

The schooner-barge, **Sligo,** *lost off Toronto in 1918 during a fierce storm, displays an anchor on the bow and the ship's wheel at the stern.*   (PHOTOS BY WARREN LO)

15. 'TILLER WRECK' (UPDATE -- *GLDG2* p. 122)

> DEPTH: 116 feet   LEVEL: Advanced
> COORDINATES: 43° 14.733′N/070° 17.062′W
> 43.246150N/-79.284585W

A Great Lakes Sidebar

Burning Ships as Public Spectacles

People have always been attracted to anything that is burning, like proverbial moths to a flame. In the Great Lakes, old, unseaworthy ships, though usually abandoned in some out-of-the-way bayou, or sunk in deep water, were sometimes put to the torch in a very public way. This occurred in places as varied as Chicago and Port Arthur, Ontario, as well as Niagara Falls, Manitowoc, Detroit, and elsewhere.

But no place on the Great Lakes appeared more excited about burning ships than Toronto in the late 1920's-early 1930's. It began when the 22-year-old, 95-foot-long steamer, *Missisiquoi* (which had rescued the crew of the burning *Schoolcraft* in 1920 -- see p. 13) was intentionally burned in August 1928. This was followed by the public torching at Sunnyside (Toronto's waterfront amusement park that could hold many more spectators) of the 45-year-old ferry *John Hanlan* (71' x 16' x 6') on July 19, 1929, the 45-year-old steamer *Jasmine* (112'4" x 21'9" x 7'4") on August 2, 1929, and the 40-year-old ferry *Clark Brothers* (80' x 16'2" x 5'5") on July 1, 1930. Each event saw increased, more dramatic advertising ("Superb Spectacle of the Torpedoing and Burning of the Steamer *Jasmine*!") and each burning drew larger and larger crowds. But the main attractions were yet to come: the *Julia B. Merrill* and *Lyman M. Davis*.

The John Hanlan *ablaze, the* Jasmine, *and the* Clark Brothers. (KOHL-FORSBERG ARCHIVES)

16. *JULIA B. MERRILL* (UPDATE -- *GLDG2* p. 120)

> **DEPTH: 60 feet   LEVEL: Intermediate-Advanced**
> **COORDINATES: 43° 37.131'N/079° 26.760'W**
> **43.618981N/-79.445719W**

A classic Great Lakes schooner, the *Julia B. Merrill* (128' x 26'5" x 8'4"), built at Wenona, Michigan, in 1872, hauled grain and lumber. The ship was sold to Canadian interests in 1910, and was an incredible 59 years old when the vessel was burned at Toronto's Sunnyside Park as a public spectacle on July 21, 1931. Letters of outrage over the burning appeared in Toronto newspapers, mostly over the destruction of history, but one practical person, aware that the Great Depression was in progress, argued that the lumber from the *Merrill* would have kept many families warm that winter.

Left: *The* Julia B. Merrill *was on display prior to the actual burning.* (KOHL-FORSBERG ARCHIVES) **Right:** *The hull's frames and deck support posts remain recognizable.* (PHOTO BY WARREN LO).

17. LYMAN M. DAVIS (UPDATE -- *GLDG2* p. 120)

DEPTH: 135 feet   LEVEL: Technical
COORDINATES: 43.602202N/-79.416599W
43° 36′ 7.91″N/079° 24′ 59.75″W

By the spring of 1934, it had been three years since the last ship burning in Toronto, and promoters were getting restless. Finally, in 1934, another suitable candidate was located -- it turned out to be the last, commercial Great Lakes schooner in existence.

The 225-gross-ton *Lyman M. Davis* (123′ x 27′2″ x 9′4″), launched at Muskegon,

The classic **Lyman M. Davis** *cut a fine figure under sail, right down to her final days.* **Davis** *commemorative pin buttons were sold to the crowds. Ads for the spectacle became more descriptive than ever, this one appearing in the Toronto* **Globe** *on June 24, 1934.*
(ALL ITEMS ARE FROM THE KOHL-FORSBERG ARCHIVES)

Amusements   Amusements

SUNNYSIDE BEACH
TONIGHT AT MIDNIGHT
The Spectacle of the
LYMAN M. DAVIS
BURNING

The feature of Toronto's Centennial Year that will be talked of when all else is forgotten. A 128-foot, 400-ton schooner, last of over a thousand vessels that have plied the Great Lakes. Famed as the most graceful of all at the peak of the Canvas Era. Loaded with oil, wood and a variety of rockets, bombs and sprays. Visible across the lake. Postponement for nothing but rain or a gale. Motorists should secure parking space early.

8.15 P.M.—FREE ATTRACTION
NITE CLUB SWEETHEARTS REVUE
8 TO 11.50 P.M.—
WALLACK'S CIRCUS Continuous Performance

MONDAY AFTERNOON AT 4 O'CLOCK
COMIC OLD CAR PARADE
Tens of Thousands have witnessed this greatest of all outdoor comedies in the past. It is still the most laughable exhibition in Canada. *

Michigan, in 1873, as a lumber schooner, was sold to Canadian interests at Kincardine, Ontario, in 1913, and eventually ended up being owned in Kingston.

When it came time to publicize the burning of the *Lyman M. Davis* at Sunnyside Park, promoters implied that the spectacle was part of the City of Toronto's centennial celebrations that year, which the city vehemently denied while denouncing the planned burning as a "shameful deed." The destruction of the obsolete, Toronto ferry boats in 1929 and 1930 had been one thing, but people now felt a historic need to save this last schooner. C.H.J. Snider, author of a maritime column and an editor of the *Toronto Telegram*, led the charge to save the *Davis*. Thousands of people signed petitions to rescue the ship. But nothing worked.

Her timbers soaked in oil, dry wood piled on her deck, rockets and fireworks attached to her rigging, the *Lyman M. Davis* was ignited and set adrift on June 29, 1934, while thousands watched from shore. This "grand light" served only to show Sunnyside's dark side.

The last Great Lakes schooner, the **Lyman M. Davis**, *sank in deep water off Toronto after being torched as a public spectacle. While the invasive species known as zebra mussels and quagga mussels have filtered the water clean, divers now have clear views of shipwrecks completely covered in multiple layers of mussels, like tattered carpeting concealing ship details.* (PHOTOS BY WARREN LO)

3. Niagara River

While the word "Niagara" is universally recognized as one of the most famous waterfalls in the world (not to mention THE traditional place to go for a honeymoon), the river that runs just before and continues just after the falls, despite being lesser known, is also quite historic. Here are some shipwrecks associated with "Niagara."

Left: The 71-foot, sidewheel steamer, Caroline, formerly the Carolina, built in New York City in 1822, became a dramatic victim of Niagara Falls when Canadian rebels, fearing an American invasion, torched this ship at Schlosser, NY, on the Niagara River, and cast it adrift on December 29, 1837. But this painting is over-dramatized and unreal: the ship was unmanned, so no victims could have fallen off the bow of the plunging vessel, as depicted, and most sources indicate that the ship stranded above the falls, burned itself out, and broke up before going over the falls. (KOHL-FORSBERG ARCHIVES)

Millions of visitors to Niagara Falls have taken one of the daring boats from a downriver dock right up to the misty foot of mighty Niagara Falls. The very first Maid of the Mist operated from 1846 until 1854, while the second one ran from 1854 to 1860. After a 25-year hiatus, a new, 71-foot-long, wooden, propeller-driven Maid of the Mist (left) was built in 1885, followed in 1892 by a 76-foot-long running mate, Maid of the Mist II. Trapped for their entire careers as tourist boats in that narrow strip of the Niagara River between the falls and the whirlpool rapids, these two ships, the longest-running of a long line of "Maids of the Mist," burned to total losses on April 22, 1955, while being fitted out for the new season (right). (KOHL-FORSBERG ARCHIVES)

Right: The most visible and the most viewed shipwreck in Niagara is the steel scow that has been wedged in the rocks just above the edge of Niagara Falls for about 100 years. On August 6, 1918, this scow broke loose from its towing tug, the Hassayampa (1910-1934), after the tug stranded about a mile upstream. The two Buffalo, NY, men on board the scow, Gustav Luffberg and James Harris, stopped the scow's drift to the falls by dropping an anchor and opening the dumping doors. During their rescue, breeches buoy lines became snarled, but William "Red" Hill untangled them, allowing the two men to reach shore safely. (PHOTO BY CRIS KOHL)

CORONA (NEW)

> **DEPTH: To 20 feet   LEVEL: Novice-Intermediate**
> **COORDINATES: : 43° 02.971'N   078° 54.9465'W**

The steamer, **Corona.** (KOHL-FORSBERG ARCHIVES)

LOCATION: The shipwreck is situated off northeast Grand Island, New York, in the Niagara River, just off the island's shore near the mouth of Gun Creek.

The 470-gross-ton, wooden sidewheel steamer, *Corona* (172' x 45'5" x 11'), built in 1870 at Manitowoc, Wisconsin, burned to a total loss near Tonawanda, New York, on November 18, 1898.

This wreck can be seen from the surface, with the smokestack still jutting out of the water very close to shore.

Some Other Shipwrecks in the Niagara River

IDLE HOUR -- The double-decked excursion steamer, *Idle Hour* (140' x 32' x 17'), built at Buffalo, New York, in 1893, burned to a total loss in the middle of the night on December 8, 1901, at the start of her winter lay-up at Grand Island, New York.

MASSASOIT -- This huge, twin-masted schooner (189'6" x 34'5" x 18'2"), launched as the *Jessie Linn* at Gibraltar, Michigan, in 1874, and renamed *Massasoit* in 1882, stranded on the Niagara River above the falls on Nov. 25, 1904, on the waterworks intake crib, and sank. Too old to salvage and positioned too dangerously to abandon, the wreck was dynamited in 1905, a process which also damaged the crib and the water works building.

The **Idle Hour.** (KOHL-FORSBERG ARCHIVES)

BUFFALO -- Launched in 1871 at Gibraltar, Michigan, as the 216-foot-long, wooden schooner-barge *Brunette* (and perhaps best-known as the only surviving ship in the storm-wrecked threesome at Tobermory, Ontario, in late 1901, that destroyed the steamer, *W. L. Wetmore* and the schooner-barge, *James C. King),* this ship, renamed the *Buffalo* in 1902, was abandoned in 1915 by its owner, shipping magnate James O'Connor, at Tonawanda, New York.

The **Massasoit.** (KOHL-FORSBERG ARCHIVES)

We will also mention the wooden, sidewheel ferry named the *Alliance* (87' x 16'1" x 6'1"), built by Bidwell & Banta at Buffalo, NY, in 1857, that broke its mooring on November 23, 1869, and went over Niagara Falls (no lives lost), and the tale of the three men who accidentally went over Niagara Falls in 1842 in a small boat loaded with barrels of whiskey (three lives lost).

No one ever said that working on a boat around Niagara Falls was easy!

The **Buffalo.** (KOHL-FORSBERG ARCHIVES)

4. Lake Erie

"NEW SHIPWRECKS" refers to those that are not in the book, *The Great Lakes Diving Guide,* second edition, 2008 (*GLDG2*), either because they had not yet been discovered, or because the authors had not yet learned about their locations.

NEW SHIPWRECKS

A. 'Long Point Schooner'
B. *Belle Mitchell*
C. *H. A. Barr?*
D. *Theodore Perry*
E. *C. B. Lockwood*
F. *Plymouth* ('Cleveland Tiller Wreck')
G. *Riverside*
H. *Sultan*
I. *Sun*
J. *Ivanhoe*
K. *Alva B.*
L. *Commodore*
M. *Argo*

N. *Smith & Post*
O. *May Flower*
P. *Mount Vernon*
Q. *Zadock Pratt*
R. *City of London*
S. *N. J. Nessen*
T. *Charles B. Packard*
U. *Fox*
V. *Manhattan*
W. Colchester Light Ship?
X. *William Case*
Y. 'Jana's Wreck'
Z. Unidentified (ex-*Comet*)

"UPDATED SHIPWRECKS" refers to ones that are in the book, *The Great Lakes Diving Guide* (shortened to *GLDG2* when referenced in this chapter). The UPDATED information about each of these shipwrecks could be new or corrected GPS coordinates, additional maritime history, and/or modern-day news about that particular wreck.

UPDATED SHIPWRECKS

1. *W. C. Richardson*
2. *Dacotah*
3. *Raleigh*
4. *C. B. Benson*
5. *J.G. McGrath* ('Stone Wreck')
6. *Washington Irving*
7. 'Schooner C?' 'Brigantine C?'
8. *Carlingford*
9. *Caledonia* aka 'Admiralty Wreck' and 'Schooner G'
10. *George C. Finney*
11. *Niagara*
12. 'Barge F'
13. *George Whelan*
14. *Brown Brothers*
15. *Wilma*

16. '17-Fathom Wreck'
17. *Siberia*
18. *C. W. Elphicke*
19. *St. James*
20. *Trade Wind*
21. 'Crystal Wreck'
22. *Majestic*
23. *Barge No. 3* or *No. 4*
24. *James H. Reed*
25. *John B. Lyon*
26. *Louie O'Neill*
27. *Dawn*
28. The 1916 Storm Wrecks: *Merida, James B. Colgate, Marshall F. Butters, D. L. Filer*
29. *Lycoming*

30. *Colonial*
31. *Little Wissahickon*
32. *George Stone*
33. *Specular*
34. *Northern Indiana*
35. *Tioga*
36. *Tasmania*
37. *Jay Gould*
38. *Dominion*
39. *Clarion*
40. *Willis*
41. *David Vance*
42. *George Dunbar*
43. *(Gen.) Anthony Wayne*
44. *Success*

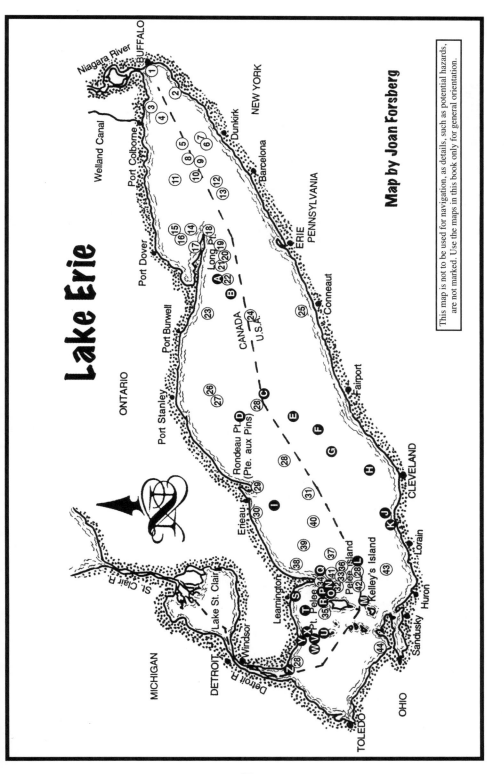

This map is not to be used for navigation, as details, such as potential hazards, are not marked. Use the maps in this book only for general orientation.

Map by Joan Forsberg

A. 'LONG POINT SCHOONER' (NEW)

> **DEPTH: 49 feet   LEVEL: Intermediate**
> **COORDINATES: 42° 26.902'N/080° 24.062'W**

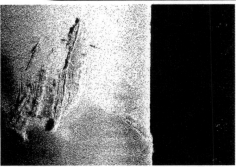

LOCATION: This unidentified shipwreck lies approximately eight miles due south of the entrance to Long Point, Ontario.

This 19th-century schooner is quite intact and in surprisingly good shape, despite being considerably embedded in the lake bottom. Underwater visibility here can often top 50 feet, which is superb for Lake Erie.

Sidescan sonar image of the unidentified 'Long Point Schooner.' (COURTESY OF ROY PICKERING)

B. *BELLE MITCHELL* (NEW)

> **DEPTH: To 70 feet   LEVEL: Advanced**
> **COORDINATES:**

LOCATION: This wreck is located approximately six miles southwest of the 'Long Point Schooner' described above.

The 320-gross-ton, gaff-rigged schooner, *Belle Mitchell* (136'7" x 25'6" x 11'4"), built and launched at Algonac, Michigan, in 1874, foundered in a severe storm on October 14, 1886, with the loss of all 8 hands.

So intact it retains the ship's bell, this wreck's location coordinates remain a secret.

Right: *The* **Belle Mitchell** *resembled the two-masted, 140-foot-long schooner,* **Albany** *(1872-abandoned 1907)* (KOHL-FORSBERG ARCHIVES)

C. *H. A. BARR?* THE REAL ONE? (NEW)

In 2015, well-known shipwreck hunter, Mike Fletcher, teamed up with accomplished Lake Superior shipwreck hunters Jerry Eliason and his team, for some boating on Lake Erie, and by coincidence they found the remains of a large schooner-barge in the middle of the lake. With remnants of a cargo steam engine and a boiler on the bow, this vessel could prove to be the *H. A. Barr* (225' x 35' x 17'), lost in a storm on Aug. 24, 1902 (more details are in *GLDG2*, p. 167). For more than 30 years, divers thought that the bow half of a large shipwreck off Rondeau was the *H. A. Barr,* but perhaps they were wrong, in which case, what is the identity of the shipwreck on which they have been diving for so many years?

D. *THEODORE PERRY* (NEW)

> **DEPTH: 81 feet   LEVEL: Advanced**
> **COORDINATES: 42° 14.451'N/081° 22.684'W**

LOCATION: This wreck lies in Canadian waters about 25 miles east of Rondeau.

Built at Buffalo, New York, in 1855 by Bidwell & Banta, the three-masted schooner, *Theodore Perry* (137'4" x 25'8" x 10'7"), enjoyed a very long career on the Great Lakes, which, unfortunately, included the replacement of comparatively small sailing ships by much larger, faster, and more efficient steam-powered vessels. By the 1880's, the schooner *Theodore Perry* had been demoted to a bulk cargo barge towed behind a steamer. On July 22, 1887, while in tow of the steamer, *D. W. Powers* (built 1871, abandoned 1910), and third in a line of four tows that included the *B. B. Buckhout* (built 1873, wrecked in Lake Huron, 1912), *Senator Blood* (built 1863, wrecked in Lake Huron, 1896), and, behind the oldest ship, the *Perry,* the *Wyandotte* (built 1856, abandoned 1909). High seas in a storm broke the tow line just ahead of the *Perry* and, while the *Wyandotte* fared well on its own, the starboard seams of the *Perry* opened, and the ship and its heavy coal cargo sank in five minutes, taking with it 5 of the 7 people on board. The captain and mate, clinging to wreckage, were picked up 11 hours later. The press denounced the *Perry* as a "floating coffin."

The wreck site features intact railings, two pumps, mast remnants, the coal cargo, a windlass with chain, the impressive starboard anchor, and the ship's wheel.

Left: *The schooner,* Southampton (1860-1901; 134'5" x 23'7" x 11'8"), *was very similar in appearance to the* Theodore Perry (KOHL-FORSBERG ARCHIVES). Middle: *The* Perry's *loss was reported in the* Chatham *(Ontario)* Tri-Weekly Planet *on July 27, 1887* (KOHL-FORSBERG ARCHIVES). Right: *Roy Pickering shines a light on the* Theodore Perry's *wheel.* (VIDEO FREEZE-FRAME BY CRIS KOHL)

www.clueshipwrecks.org

THERE'S SOMETHING ABOUT ERIE -- DISAPPEARING ACTS

E. *C. B. LOCKWOOD* (NEW)

> **DEPTH: 75 feet, plus 15 feet more below lake bottom**
> **COORDINATES: 41° 56.000495′N/081° 23.499′W**

Lake Erie is the smallest and the shallowest of the five Great Lakes, yet it contains far more shipwrecks (at least 1,700) than any one of the other four. It seems odd, in light of the average shipwreck density per square mile that must exist, and the large number of people searching for shipwrecks, that comparatively few wrecks have been located.

This mystery was finally, unquestionably, solved in 2010 by the Cleveland Underwater Explorers (CLUE). Member Jim Paskert, a longtime Lake Erie wreck diver and maritime historian, presented CLUE's findings at the annual "Shipwrecks!" Show in Welland, Ontario, on April 2, 2011. He recalled diving, back in 1985, where the Lake Erie wreck of the propeller, *C. B. Lockwood*, was supposed to be, but only a couple of lifeboat davits could be seen above the lake floor. Soon even those davits were gone. It appeared that the heavy ship had sunk naturally, in its entirety, into one of Lake Erie's underwater "valleys" of soft sediment, totally out of sight! CLUE members visited the site with a sub-bottom profiler, which gives a readout of large objects that lie buried in the lake bottom, and, sure enough, they scored a shipwreck discovery where no shipwreck could be seen by scuba divers!

The immense, 2,139-gross-ton, wooden steamer, *C. B. Lockwood* (285′2″ x 45′ x 18′9″), built in Cleveland in 1890, foundered in a storm on October 13, 1902, with the loss of 10 of its 19 lives, plus the wheat cargo. The crew had left the sinking ship in their two lifeboats; one reached shore safely, while the other did not.

The wreck of the *C. B. Lockwood* was found within days of its sinking, and its location was charted and marked with buoys. Then the wreck was forgotten.

But CLUE proved that out of sight does not necessarily mean out of mind.

N
↑

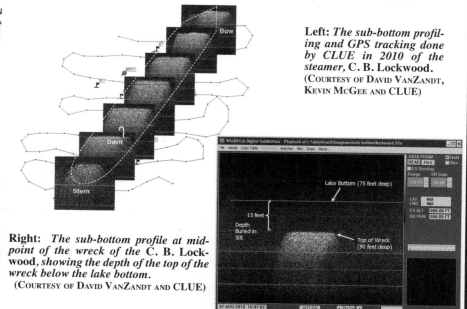

Left: *The sub-bottom profiling and GPS tracking done by CLUE in 2010 of the steamer,* C. B. Lockwood.
(COURTESY OF DAVID VANZANDT, KEVIN MCGEE AND CLUE)

Right: *The sub-bottom profile at midpoint of the wreck of the* C. B. Lockwood, *showing the depth of the top of the wreck below the lake bottom.*
(COURTESY OF DAVID VANZANDT AND CLUE)

F. PLYMOUTH ('CLEVELAND TILLER WRECK') (NEW)

DEPTH: 75 feet   LEVEL: Advanced
COORDINATES: 41° 49.121′N/081° 44.510′W

LOCATION: This shipwreck is located approximately 20 miles off Cleveland.

In June, 1996, Rob Ruetschle located this wreck of a vintage sailing ship, the presence of a tiller designating the vessel as having been built prior to the 1850's, when ship's wheels replaced tillers for steering larger sailboats. Thus, for years, this unidentified shipwreck was nicknamed the 'Cleveland Tiller Wreck.' Suspicions were that the vessel could be the schooner *Mackinaw*, lost off Cleveland in 1851, but in 2013, Jim Paskert, maritime historian with CLUE, thinking the location incorrect to be the *Mackinaw*, researched it and concluded that it had to be the schooner *Plymouth*.

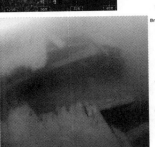

The two-masted *Plymouth* (106' x 23'4" x 8'9"), built at Huron, Ohio, in 1847, sank after a collision with the sidewheel steamer, *Northern Indiana* (see p. 72 of this book, and p. 185-186 of *GLDG2*), on June 23, 1852, with the subsequent court case establishing the legal right of way of sail vessels over powered vessels.

Left: *Side scan sonar image of the* **Plymouth.** (DAVID VAN ZANDT/CLUE)

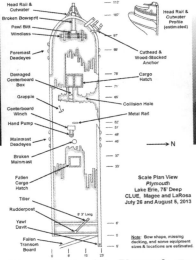

The wreck site of the **Plymouth.** (BY KEVIN MCGEE AND CINDY LAROSA/CLUE)

Above: *The* **Plymouth's** *tiller, which gave it the early nickname, 'Cleveland Tiller Wreck.'*

Below: *The windlass, with chain, on the bow of the* **Plymouth.**

(BOTH PHOTOS BY DAVID VAN-ZANDT, COURTESY OF DAVID VANZANDT/CLUE)

Above: *The collision damage that sank the* **Plymouth** *is very evident.*

Below: *The bow of the* **Plymouth.**

(BOTH PHOTOS BY DAVID VAN-ZANDT, COURTESY OF DAVID VANZANDT/CLUE)

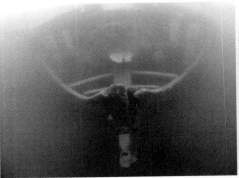

G. RIVERSIDE (NEW)

LOCATION: The wreck lies about 25 miles off Cleveland, Ohio.

Launched as a two-masted (a third mast was added in the 1880's) schooner on April 9, 1870, at Oswego, New York, the *Riverside* (133' x 25'8" x 10') foundered in a storm off Cleveland on Friday, the 13th of October, 1893, with the loss of all seven people on board. The ship had stranded earlier on Pilot Island between Lake Michigan and Green Bay, on October 15, 1887, and given up as a total loss, but was recovered a year later and towed to Green Bay, Wisconsin, on October 18, 1888, for repairs. It lasted only five more years.

The *Riverside* was located by Cleveland divers Leroy Meermans and Jerry Metzler in the 1980's, and relocated by CLUE (Cleveland Underwater Explorers) on Oct. 6, 2007.

The intact wreck, in 75 feet, is complete with the ship's wheel, brass bell, a hinged bow (the bowsprit is missing), windlass and chain, and the stern cabin with all of its portholes.

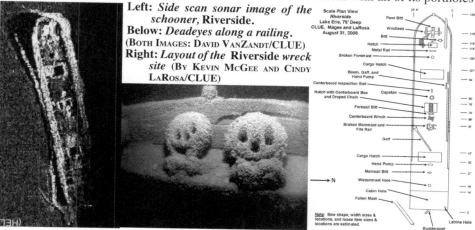

Left: *Side scan sonar image of the schooner,* **Riverside.**
Below: *Deadeyes along a railing.* (BOTH IMAGES: DAVID VANZANDT/CLUE)
Right: *Layout of the* **Riverside** *wreck site* (BY KEVIN MCGEE AND CINDY LAROSA/CLUE)

H. SULTAN (NEW)

LOCATION: This ship capsized and sank in 48 feet of water off Euclid, Ohio.

Built at Chicago in 1848, the two-masted brigantine, *Sultan* (127' x 24' x 9'4"), foundered on September 24, 1864, with its cargo of grindstones and lumber. The first mate was the sole survivor; two sailors were lost with their lifeboat, and the other four dropped, one by one due to the cold, from the tops of the masts.

The *Sultan* was located and identified by CLUE (Cleveland Underwater Explorers) in 2011. Features of this site include two deck pumps, two anchors, and the grindstones.

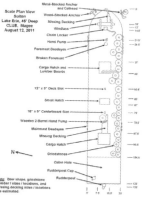

Left: *Side scan sonar image of the wreck of the brigantine,* **Sultan.** **Middle:** *Part of the cargo of grindstones, which made identification of this shipwreck easy.* (BOTH IMAGES: DAVID VANZANDT/ CLUE). **Right:** *Layout of the* **Sultan** *wreck site* (BY KEVIN MCGEE AND CINDY LAROSA/CLUE)

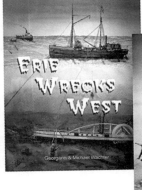
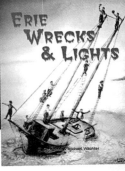

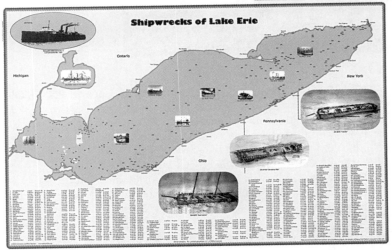

I. Sun (NEW)

DEPTH: 60 feet   LEVEL: Advanced
COORDINATES: 42° 08.550′N/081° 58.220′W

LOCATION: The *Sun* lies about eight miles southwest of Rondeau Point, Ontario.
Accidentally located on Aug. 10, 2008, by Mike and Georgann Wachter as they were crossing the lake back to Ohio, the *Sun* foundered in a storm on July 12, 1874, after her seams opened. Her three tow barges reached the Detroit River on their own, while the schooner *Lillie Pratt* rescued the *Sun's* crew. The *Sun* (191′11″ x 28′6″ x 12′) was built at Buffalo, NY, in 1854. The site includes the engine, boiler, anchors, and much hull wood.

Far left: *The* **Sun** *resembled this steamer, the* **Fountain City.**
(Kohl-Forsberg Archives)

Left: *Diver Gary Smith follows the* **Sun's** *keel and frames.* (Video freeze-frame by Cris Kohl)

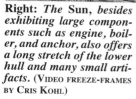

Right: *The* **Sun,** *besides exhibiting large components such as engine, boiler, and anchor, also offers a long stretch of the lower hull and many small artifacts.* (Video freeze-frames by Cris Kohl)

J. Ivanhoe (NEW)

DEPTH: 58 feet   LEVEL: Intermediate
COORDINATES: 41° 33.312′N/082° 02.825′W

LOCATION: This wreck lies off Vermilion, Ohio.
Located in 2012 by Tom Kowalczk and CLUE (Cleveland Underwater Explorers), the 238-ton, coal-laden schooner, *Ivanhoe* (110′ x 26′ x 9′), built at Buffalo, NY, in 1848, sank in a midnight collision with the schooner, *Arab*, on October 4, 1855. No lives were lost.

K. Alva B. (NEW)

DEPTH: 12 feet   LEVEL: Novice
COORDINATES: 41° 30.769′N/082° 01.895′W

LOCATION: One mile west of Avon Lake, Ohio.
Her wooden hull dried out from inactivity, the tug, *Alva B.* (73′6″ x 18′5″ x 10′6″), built at Buffalo in 1890, stranded and broke up in a storm on November 1, 1917. The boiler, propshaft, and wooden pieces remain.

Left: *The tug,* **Alva B.,** *lies about 300 feet off shore.* **Below, right:** *The tow barge,* **Commodore.** (Both: Kohl-Forsberg Archives)

L. Commodore (NEW)

LOCATION: Midlake north of Lorain, Ohio.
Lying in 65 feet of water near **41° 42.788′N/082° 18.895′W,** the 38-year-old tow barge, *Commodore* (176′5″ x 34′ x 12′2″) was lost in the same storm on June 17, 1918, as the steamer towing it, the *Jay Gould* (see p. 72 in this book, plus *GLDG2* p. 188.)

M. *ARGO* (NEW)

> **DEPTH: 46 feet   LEVEL: Intermediate**
> **COORDINATES: 41° 38′ 21″N/082° 29′ 35″W**

LOCATION: Four miles northeast of Kelley's Island Shoals.

On a windy Sunday evening, October 17, 1937, Capt. J. E. McQueen of Amherstburg, Ontario, gazed at five derelict ships sunk in the Detroit River's Callam's Bay -- the sailing vessels *American Giant* and the *L. S. Hammond*, the tugs *Energy* and *Helen*, and the huge steam-barge, *Bulgaria* -- imagining how he would go about his next job. He had just been awarded the contract to remove those eyesores. As he pondered the matter, he noticed a strange tug and the even stranger vessel it was towing duck into Amherstburg harbor to escape the heavy weather.

This tug, the *Syosset*, and its tow, the 120-foot-long, 26-year-old, steel tank barge named the *Argo*, were heading back to New York City after picking up a 200,000-gallon cargo (100,000 gallons each of crude light oil and benzol) in Detroit. By the 1930's, transporting oil products was big business; Cramp's shipyard in Philadelphia, which had closed in 1927 after 97 years in business, reopened in 1937 to produce only welded steel tank barges.

The *Syosset* and the *Argo* waited two days at Amherstburg without the autumn gales subsiding, but grew impatient and decided to risk the run to Buffalo at the other end of Lake Erie. The *Argo*, not built for inland waters and possibly operating illegally on Lake Erie, sank on Oct. 20, its two crew members being rescued with difficulty. The U.S. Coast Guard cutter, *Tahoma*, located the wreck on Oct. 21, but declared it "no menace to navigation," environmental concern being a thing of the future. Vague 1970 and 1985 reports hint that divers found the wreck with its oil leaking, but did nothing.

On August 28, 2015, Tom Kowalczk and CLUE found the *Argo* and, because of oil visibly coating the surface, contacted NOAA and the Coast Guard. Mild media frenzy followed in both the USA and Canada, but by December 3, 2015, most of the *Argo's* remaining cargo had been removed.

In November, 1937, Capt. McQueen decided to remove Amherstburg's derelict ships with dynamite (but the large *Bulgaria* would have to be cofferdammed, pumped, raised, and scrapped piecemeal in the spring), with the wood from the dynamited wrecks hauled to shore and used as fuel for the welfare families of Amherstburg. It is unlikely that his thoughts drifted to the wreck of the *Argo*.

Left: *The* **Argo** *resembled this typical East Coast tank barge.*

Right, top: *The wreck was not considered a threat in 1937.* (BOTH OF THE ABOVE: KOHL-FORSBERG ARCHIVES)

Right, bottom: *The side scan image of the* **Argo** *clearly reveals the typical, rectangular shape of a barge.* (TOM KOWALCZK/CLUE)

Missing Oil Barge Is Believed Found

CLEVELAND, Oct. 21—(A. P.) —Capt. Henry G. Fisher, commander of the Cleveland District Coast Guard, said tonight that the crew of the cutter Tahoma believed that they had found the

N. SMITH & POST (NEW)

> **DEPTH:** 38 feet   **LEVEL:** Novice-Intermediate
> **COORDINATES:** 41° 49.240′N/082° 27.622′W

LOCATION: At Southeast Shoal off Point Pelee, Ontario.

Built at Oakville, Ontario, in 1866, the two-masted schooner named the *Smith & Post* (118′ x 23′6″ x 9′11″) was chartered in July, 1901, by the Lake Carriers Association in Cleveland as a temporary lightship in Pelee Passage when it caught on fire on August 18, 1901. With its many barrels of oil used for illumination, the old vessel burned quickly to the waterline and sank. The passing steamer, *Codorus*, rescued the crew with difficulty due to the nearby shoal water. The ship was dynamited later that month to clear the wreckage after hardhat diver Quinn recovered the anchors and chain, being paid $400 for that job.

Left: *The* Smith & Post *resembled the 116-foot-long schooner, L. D. Bullock* (KOHL-FORSBERG ARCHIVES).   Right: *A side scan image of the dynamited wreckage.* (COURTESY OF ROY PICKERING)

O. *MAY FLOWER* (NEW)

LOCATION: Broken up on Grubb's Reef, just southwest of Point Pelee, Ontario.

The *May Flower* was one of several, elegant, passenger sidewheel steamers built in the 1840's-1850's to carry passengers from one end of Lake Erie to the other end prior to the construction of a railroad. Others included the *Northern Indiana* (see p. 72 in this book, and p. 185-186 in *GLDG2*), *America* (p. 194 in *GLDG2*), and the *Atlantic* (p. 154 in *GLDG2*).

The double-decked *May Flower* (283'2" x 35'8" x 13'10"), built at Detroit in 1849, set speed records, e.g. Detroit to Buffalo in under 17 hours. But in a dense fog on November 20, 1854, the ship stranded on rocks on Grubb's Reef, and before the ship could be recovered, it began to break up, soon becoming a total loss. The machinery was removed for use in another ship in 1855, and, years later, much of the cargo of railroad iron was salvaged.

Above, left to right: *The elegant* May Flower *in 1850's art* (KOHL-FORSBERG ARCHIVES). *Stranded in 1851 (but later recovered), the* May Flower *was photographed; this reputedly is the earliest known Great Lakes shipwreck photograph* (KOHL-FORSBERG ARCHIVES). *Side scan sonar image of the nearly flattened shipwreck* (COURTESY OF ROY PICKERING). Below: *Detailed, ornate china from the* May Flower *shows the opulence of Lake Erie steamer travel in the 1850's.* (PHOTOS BY CRIS KOHL)

P. *MOUNT VERNON* (NEW)

> **DEPTH: 26 feet   LEVEL: Novice-Intermediate**
> **COORDINATES: 41° 51.483′N/082° 30.404′W**
> **COORDINATES: 41° 51.563′N/082° 30.546′W**

LOCATION: Just east of the old "dummy" light location, off Point Pelee, Ontario.

Launched in 1854 at Huron, Ohio, the double-decked propeller (178' x 29'4" x 11'8"), *Mount Vernon's* boiler exploded on Oct. 9, 1860, with two lives lost. Before it could be dynamited, this wreck caused the loss of the scow *Ottoca* and the *Zadock Pratt* (see p. 59)

Left: *The steamer,* Mount Vernon, *resembled the* John R. *(1873-scrapped 1914)* (KOHL-FORSBERG ARCHIVES)

Right: *Side scan sonar image of the* Mount Vernon. (COURTESY OF ROY PICKERING)

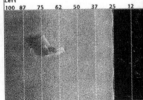

Q. ZADOCK PRATT (NEW)

> **DEPTH: 26 feet   LEVEL: Novice-Intermediate**
> **COORDINATES: 41° 52.025′N/082° 28.690′W**

LOCATION: Just east of the old "dummy" light location, off Point Pelee, Ontario.

The schooner, *Zadock Pratt* (133′ x 26′ x 10′), built in 1855 at Buffalo, NY, sank on Nov. 20, 1860, with a cargo of grain from Chicago after striking the wreck of the *Mount Vernon* (see p. 58). Only five years old, the *Pratt* was insured for $8,000, a high sum at that time.

Left: *The* **Zadock Pratt** *looked like this schooner, the* **Star of the North** *(1854-1903, wrecked on Lake Michigan).* (KOHL-FORSBERG ARCHIVES)

R. CITY OF LONDON (NEW)

> **DEPTH: 31 feet   LEVEL: Novice-Intermediate**
> **COORDINATES: 41° 51.404′N/082° 35.796′W**

LOCATION: 1.5 miles southwest of Point Pelee, Ontario.

This wooden propeller, built in 1891 at West Bay City, MI, and sunk in a collision with the steamer *Joe E. Morrow* on Sept. 30, 1913, was dynamited in 1914.

Left: *The* **City of London.** (KOHL-FORSBERG ARCHIVES). **Right:** *Side scan image of the* **City of London.** (COURTESY OF ROY PICKERING)

S. N. J. NESSEN (NEW)

LOCATION: Some is buried in Lake Erie at Leamington, some is on a nearby farm.

The wooden propeller, *N. J. Nessen* (148'6" x 37' x 11'5"), launched as the *H. Louella Worthington* at Lorain, Ohio, on July 14, 1880, stranded at Leamington, Ontario, in a gale on October 21, 1929, all the sailors being rescued by the Point Pelee Life Saving crew.

Some of this shipwreck was accidentally dredged up in 1984 during construction at approximately 42.025181N/-82.597079W near the Leamington Municipal Marina and Waterfront Promenade. History-minded Robert McCracken generously offered his farm as a temporary resting place for the dredged-up wreckage until a public memorial/exhibit could be arranged by local maritime groups. These remains were moved to another local farm for further temporary storage in 2013.

Left: *The N. J. Nessen stranded off Leamington, Ontario, in 1929.* (KOHL-FORSBERG ARCHIVES). **Right:** *Robert McCracken poses with* Nessen *wreckage on his farm in 2012.* (PHOTO BY CRIS KOHL)

T. CHARLES B. PACKARD (NEW)

DEPTH: 35 feet   LEVEL: Novice-Intermediate
COORDINATES: 41° 55.852'N/082° 41.504'W

LOCATION: This wreck lies near the *Armenia* wreck off Colchester Reef, Ontario.

This wreck, discovered in July 2010, is probably the REAL *Packard*. The one described in *GLDG2* p. 195, is now called 'The False Packard.' Perhaps 'The False Packard' is really the steamer, *Forest Queen* (161' x 25'4" x 9'9"), built in 1852 at Cleveland and sunk by ice in December, 1868, near "the Clay Banks" (Colchester); failed efforts to locate the wreck of the *Forest Queen* in 1869 resulted in newspaper statements such as "The ice... has doubtless pretty much broken her up" and the ship "has entirely disappeared."

Left: *The wooden, steam-powered propeller,* Charles B. Packard.
(KOHL-FORSBERG ARCHIVES)
Right: *Side scan image of the* Charles B. Packard. *This wreck is very intact compared to the one that was initially thought to be the* **Packard!** (COURTESY OF ROY PICKERING)

U. FOX (NEW)

COORDINATES: 41° 50.873'N/082° 50.771'W

LOCATION: In 25 feet at North Harbour reef, one mile north of East Sister Island.

This 405-ton brigantine, built at Buffalo, NY, in 1852, stranded on Oct. 16, 1867, a total loss. Her equipment and the staves cargo were recovered from the uninsured ship.

V. MANHATTAN (NEW)

DEPTH: 32 feet   LEVEL: Novice-Intermediate
COORDINATES: 41° 55.165'N/082° 54.207'W

LOCATION: At Colchester Reef, Ontario, half a mile from the shipping channel.

The relatively modern, 310-ton dredge named the *Manhattan*, measuring 100 feet long and 36 feet wide, sank on November 19, 1978.

W. COLCHESTER LIGHT SHIP? (NEW)

DEPTH: 16 feet   LEVEL: Novice
COORDINATES: 41.982247N/-82.932193W

LOCATION: Near Colchester Reef, Ontario.

Since Colchester Reef has long been viewed as one of the most dangerous navigational hazards in Lake Erie, efforts to warn sailors of it have long been attempted. A lightship was used for decades before a lighthouse was built there. The oft-damaged and oft-repaired Colchester Lightship (60' x 17' x 5'), believed first built in 1848 at Amherstburg, Ontario, foundered on November 11, 1883, with the loss of the captain. It is believed that the unidentified wreckage at this location could be of that tragic, historic vessel.

X. *WILLIAM CASE* (NEW)

DEPTH: 23 feet   LEVEL: Novice-Intermediate
COORDINATES: 41° 59.113'N/082° 51.130'W

LOCATION: This wreck lies north-northeast of the Colchester Shoal Light.

The very old schooner, *William Case* (136'9" x 26'7" x 10'8"), built in 1855 at Cleveland, sprang a leak during a storm on July 26, 1906, and foundered with no lives lost.

Left: *The 137-foot-long* **William Case** *strongly resembled this 140-foot-long schooner, the* **H. C. Winslow** *(1853-1905).* (KOHL-FORSBERG ARCHIVES). **Right:** *Side scan image of what is believed to be the wreck of the* **William Case.** (COURTESY OF ROY PICKERING)

Y. 'JANA'S WRECK' (NEW)

DEPTH: 16 feet   LEVEL: Novice
COORDINATES: 41.982247N/-82.932193W

LOCATION: Right at the entrance to the harbour at Colchester, Ontario.

This unidentified but interesting wreck, at first thought to be only some sort of a debris field, but definitely identified as a shipwreck in 2012 by Colchester dive shop owner Mike Drexler and nicknamed after his wife, has had its artifacts dated to the 1850's, but the identity of this vessel remains elusive, hard to believe in light of its estimated length of 200 feet. This size ship would not have gone unnoticed in the 1850's! Clues indicate that the wreck was probably a sidewheel steamer.

Below: *Mike Drexler at Colchester Reef. His goal is to identify 'Jana's Wreck.'* (PHOTO BY CRIS KOHL)

Below and right: *Clear images of 'Jana's Wreck,' specifically the 1850's capstan with diver Rich Synowiec, taken under the ice.* (PHOTOS BY ANDY MORRISON)

Z. UNIDENTIFIED (EX-*COMET*) (NEW)

> **DEPTH: 5-6 feet   LEVEL: Novice**
> **COORDINATES: 42° 01.108′N/083° 00.308′W**

LOCATION: This wreckage is located approximately 5 miles from the Detroit River.
Identifying a shipwreck can prove challenging, especially in a crowded field with only minimal keel and frames to assist. Current thinking is that the wreck is the *Comet* (64′ x 18 x 5′), the 1857 scow schooner built at Algonac, Michigan, and which sank due to hull failure on September 11, 1866. But a problem arises from this November 1866 newspaper article:

> **VESSEL RAISED. -- The scow, *Comet*, which sunk** [sic] **during the summer with a cargo of coal, at Bar Point, has been raised and taken to Malden for repairs. She is completely uninjured, while the most of her sails and outfit are in good condition.**

Work will continue to identify this little shipwreck.   (COURTESY OF ROY PICKERING)

1. *W. C. RICHARDSON* (UPDATE -- See *GLDG2* p. 136)

> **DEPTH: 40 feet   LEVEL: Intermediate**
> **COORDINATES: 42° 51.074′N/078° 54.776′W**

2. *DACOTAH* (UPDATE -- *GLDG2* p. 138)

> **DEPTH: 20 to 25 feet   LEVEL: Novice**
> **COORDINATES: 42° 42.286′N/078° 59.477′W**

3. *RALEIGH* (UPDATE -- *GLDG2* p. 138)

> **DEPTH: 33 feet   LEVEL: Novice-Intermediate**
> **COORDINATES: 42.865429N/-79.154228W**

4. *C. B. BENSON* (UPDATE -- *GLDG2* p. 139)

> **DEPTH: 87 feet   LEVEL: Advanced**
> **COORDINATES: 42.771028N/-79.243485W**

The date that the *C. B. Benson* was lost in a violent storm was October 14, 1893.

5. *J. G. MCGRATH* ('STONE WRECK') (UPDATE -- *GLDG2* p. 140)

> **DEPTH: 90 feet   LEVEL: Advanced**
> **COORDINATES: 42.667933N/-79.396333W**

6. *WASHINGTON IRVING* (UPDATE -- *GLDG2* p. 142)

> **DEPTH: 120 feet   LEVEL: Advanced**
> **COORDINATES: 42° 32.365′N/079° 27.641′W**

See underwater photos of the *Washington Irving* on the next page!

The small schooner, Washington Irving, *proves to be quite photogenic.* (Photos by Vlada Dekina)

7. 'Schooner C' ('Brigantine C'?) (UPDATE -- *GLDG2* p. 142)

DEPTH: 115 feet   LEVEL: Advanced
COORDINATES: 42° 33.232′N/079° 27.186′W

It is unclear at this point if this unidentified sailing vessel was a schooner or a brigantine.

Left: *A diver prepares to photograph a capstan on the deck of the unidentified wreck labeled 'Schooner C' or 'Brigantine C.'* **Right:** *An anchor on the bow rail.* (Photos by Vlada Dekina)

8. *CARLINGFORD* (UPDATE -- *GLDG2* p. 143)

> **DEPTH: 90 to 105 feet   LEVEL: Advanced**
> **COORDINATES: 42.654799N/-79.476618W**

9. *CALEDONIA?* ('ADMIRALTY WRECK,' 'SCHOONER G')
(UPDATE -- *GLDG2* p. 144)

> **DEPTH: To 170 feet   LEVEL: Technical**
> **COORDINATES: 42° 34.610′N/079° 35.000′W**

This beautiful, little shipwreck has sparked considerable controversy. If it is, indeed, the *Caledonia*, as one group of investors (who want to raise the wreck and exhibit it in Buffalo) believe, then it was a British-built-in-1807 brig from Amherstburg, Ontario, captured by Americans at the start of the War of 1812, used in the Battle of Lake Erie in 1813, and lost long after the war. New York state has denied permission to raise this delicate wreck.

10. *GEORGE C. FINNEY* (UPDATE -- *GLDG2* p. 144)

> **DEPTH: 100 feet   LEVEL: Advanced**
> **COORDINATES: 42.668122N/-79.604169′W**

This three-masted schooner sank about 15 miles south of Port Maitland, Ontario, in a late-1891 storm with a cargo of wheat. Tragically, all seven sailors on board perished.

The George C. Finney *displays her wheel and numerous deadeyes.* (PHOTOS BY VLADA DEKINA)

11. *NIAGARA* (UPDATE -- *GLDG2* p. 144)

> **DEPTH: 90 feet   LEVEL: Advanced**
> **COORDINATES: 42.738500N/-79.604750W**

12. 'BARGE F' (UPDATE -- *GLDG2* p. 146)

This unidentified barge lies in 145 feet of water about 12 miles north of Barcelona, NY.

'Barge F' rewards visitors with views of her windlass and wheel. (PHOTOS BY VLADA DEKINA)

13. GEORGE WHELAN (UPDATE -- _GLDG2_ p. 147)

> **DEPTH: 150 feet**   **LEVEL: Technical**
> **COORDINATES: 42° 25.570'N/079° 44.000'W**

Located about eight miles northwest of Barcelona, New York, the 220-foot-long, steel freighter, _George Whelan,_ built in 1910, foundered in 1930 with the loss of 15 lives. The wreck, found in 2005, lies 3/4 over on her port side, more upside-down than rightside-up.

Left: _Fully trained and prepared divers can penetrate the wreck of the_ George Whelan. **Right:** _A lifeboat lies to one side of the wreck._ **Below:** _An anchor and the propeller are wreck highlights._ (PHOTOS BY VLADA DEKINA)

14. BROWN BROTHERS (UPDATE -- *GLDG2* p. 151)

> **DEPTH: 120 feet   LEVEL: Advanced**
> **COORDINATES: 42.627540N/-80.015200W**

15. WILMA (UPDATE -- *GLDG2* p. 151)

> **DEPTH: 74 feet   LEVEL: Intermediate-Advanced**
> **COORDINATES: 42.702333N/-80.034473W**

16. '17-FATHOM WRECK' (UPDATE -- *GLDG2* p. 151-152)

> **DEPTH: 106 feet   LEVEL: Advanced**
> **COORDINATES: 42.651720N/-80.052420W**

17. SIBERIA (UPDATE -- *GLDG2* p. 152)

> **DEPTH: 19 feet   LEVEL: Novice**
> **COORDINATES: 42° 34.600'N/080° 07.856'W**

18. C. W. ELPHICKE (UPDATE -- *GLDG2* p. 153, 155)

> **DEPTH: 22 feet   LEVEL: Novice**
> **COORDINATES: 42° 32.184'N/080° 03.977'W**

Despite what some books about the Great Storm of 1913 tell you, the *C.W. Elphicke*, which stranded on Long Point prior to the storm, was not rendered unsalvagable by that storm. The ship had already broken its spine and was declared a total loss before the storm started.

The wooden steamer, **C. W. Elphicke,** *wrecked at Long Point, Ontario.* (**KOHL-FORSBERG ARCHIVES**)

19. ST. JAMES (UPDATE -- *GLDG2* p. 156-157)

> **DEPTH: 164 feet   LEVEL: Technical**
> **COORDINATES: 42° 27.100'N/080° 07.328'W**

The probable date of loss of this upright schooner in deep water off Long Point, Ontario, is October 24, 1870.

20. TRADE WIND (UPDATE -- *GLDG2* p. 158)

> **DEPTH: 120 feet   LEVEL: Advanced**
> **COORDINATES: 42.425268N/-80.200933W**

This three-masted bark (1853-Dec. 1, 1854) sank in a collision during a snowstorm.

21. 'CRYSTAL WRECK' (UPDATE -- *GLDG2* p. 158)

> **DEPTH: 119 feet**   **LEVEL: Advanced**
> **COORDINATES: 42.452489N/-80.275481W**

22. *MAJESTIC* (UPDATE -- *GLDG2* p. 161)

> **DEPTH: 55 feet**   **LEVEL: Intermediate-Advanced**
> **COORDINATES: 42° 22.470'N/080° 25.100'W**

23. *BARGE NO. 3* OR *NO. 4* (UPDATE -- *GLDG2* p. 161)

> **DEPTH: 60 feet**   **LEVEL: Intermediate-Advanced**
> **COORDINATES: 42° 29.465'N/080° 41.610'W**

24. *JAMES H. REED* (UPDATE -- *GLDG2* p. 162)

> **DEPTH: 76 feet**   **LEVEL: Advanced**
> **COORDINATES: 42° 16.172'N/080° 47.777'W**

The correct dimensions of this huge ship, sunk in a collision on the foggy night of April 27, 1944, are 455'2" x 52'2" x 24'9", making it the largest shipwreck in Lake Erie.

25. *JOHN B. LYON* (UPDATE -- *GLDG2* p. 162)

> **DEPTH: 52 feet**   **LEVEL: Intermediate-Advanced**
> **COORDINATES: 42° 02.369'N/080° 33.757'W**

This 256-foot-long, wooden freighter sank in a storm (the tail end of the horrible Galveston Hurricane) on Sept. 11, 1900, with nine of the 15 lives on board lost.

26. *LOUIE O'NEILL* (UPDATE -- *GLDG2* p. 164)

> **DEPTH: 72 feet**   **LEVEL: Advanced**
> **COORDINATES: 42° 25.444'N/081° 10.312'W**

The *Louie O'Neill*, launched in 1862 as the steamer *S. D. Caldwell*, underwent a propulsion change when it was converted to a schooner-barge in 1884. The most information about this ship/shipwreck ever published appeared as a 3,400-word article entitled "Lake Erie's Surprising Mystery Shipwreck" in *Wreck Diving Magazine*, issue #19 (2009).

Above, l. to r.: *The steamship* S. D. Caldwell *later became the schooner-barge* Louie O'Neill, *similar to this ship* (KOHL-FORSBERG ARCHIVES). *The* O'Neill's *deck pump.* **Left:** *a fork from the wreck engraved* "J. D. Caldwell," *which, ironically, had nothing to do with the name* S. D. Caldwell. (PHOTOS BY CRIS KOHL; FORK COURTESY OF WAYNE WINEGARDEN)

27. DAWN (UPDATE -- *GLDG2* p. 166)

> **DEPTH: 67 feet**   **LEVEL: Advanced**
> **COORDINATES: 42° 25.251′N/081° 21.502′W**

The 105-foot-long schooner, *Dawn*, built at Milan, Ohio, in 1847, sank in a collision with the steamer, *New York* (today a Lake Huron wreck; see p. 123), on October 21, 1859.

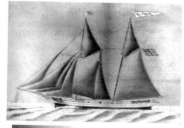

Left: The schooner, Dawn, was similar to this ship, the Hyphen (KOHL-FORSBERG ARCHIVES). *Roy Pickering examines the Dawn's windlass* (right) *and deck features* (below). (VIDEO FREEZE-FRAMES BY CRIS KOHL)

28. THE 1916 STORM WRECKS
(UPDATE -- *GLDG2* p. 165, 166-167, 168, 181, 200)

One of the most destructive storms to hit Lake Erie occurred on October 20, 1916, with its centennial commemorated in 2016. Named "The Black Friday Storm," it sank four ships: the steel freighter, *Merida,* lost with all 22 hands; the steel whaleback, *James B. Colgate*, with only the captain surviving by clinging to a raft for 37 hours; the wooden steamer, *Marshall F. Butters,* with no lives lost; and the wooden schooner-barge, *D. L. Filer,* with only the captain surviving by clinging desperately to a mast until rescued.

The freighter, **Merida** (KOHL-FORSBERG ARCHIVES). **Middle:** *Cracks appear in the steel hull.* **Right:** *This plate and a half-full whiskey bottle came from the captain's cabin.* (PHOTOS BY CRIS KOHL)

The whaleback, **James B. Colgate,** *in a Louis Pesha photo* (KOHL-FORSBERG ARCHIVES). *A diver inches along the overturned hull until reaching the propeller* (**right**). (FREEZE-FRAMES BY CRIS KOHL)

The **Marshall F. Butters** (KOHL-FORSBERG ARCHIVES). *The wreck is badly broken up, exposing decking supports; invasive gobies cluster and feed on top of the boiler.* (FREEZE-FRAMES BY CRIS KOHL)

Left: *The D. L. Filer, with an ice coating* (KOHL-FORSBERG ARCHIVES). *This shipwreck, located near the mouth of the Detroit River, is mostly broken up and embedded in the lake bottom.*

STRS. MERIDA AND COLGATE
FOUNDER IN LAKE ERIE

Only One Man in Two Crews Rescued---
Black Friday's Death Toll Now Mounts
to Four Ships and 47 Men

One of the many storm headlines on Oct. 23, 1916. (KOHL-FORSBERG ARCHIVES)

29. *LYCOMING* (UPDATE -- *GLDG2* p. 169)

> **DEPTH: 28 feet**   **LEVEL: Novice-Intermediate**
> **COORDINATES: 42.251285N/-81.889829W**

30. *COLONIAL* (UPDATE -- *GLDG2* p. 171)

> **DEPTH: 13 to 22 feet**   **LEVEL: Novice**
> **COORDINATES: 42.253161N/-82.071820W**

This wreck is a NOVICE, not an ADVANCED, dive, as erroneously printed in *GLDG2*.

31. LITTLE WISSAHICKON (UPDATE -- *GLDG2* p. 173-174)

> **DEPTH: 68 to 80 feet**   **LEVEL: Advanced**
> **COORDINATES: 41° 54.222′N/081° 56.786′W**

The schooner-barge, *Little Wissahickon* (146′4″ x 29′4″ x 12′), was launched as the *Edward Kean* in 1869 at Marine City, Michigan, with its name changed in the spring of 1882. The *Little Wissahickon*, one of four barges being towed by the steamer, *James P. Donaldson*, sprang a leak and foundered with three lives lost on July 10, 1896.

The schooner-barge, Little Wissahickon, *resembled this vessel, the 148-foot-long* Narragansett *(1861-1901, sunk in Lake Huron).* (KOHL-FORSBERG ARCHIVES). *Roy Pickering shines his light on the ship's wheel.* (VIDEO FREEZE-FRAME BY CRIS KOHL)

32. GEORGE STONE (UPDATE -- *GLDG2* p. 184)

> **DEPTH: 32 to 42 feet**   **LEVEL: Novice-Intermediate**
> **COORDINATES: 41.887448N/-82.553995W**

33. SPECULAR (UPDATE -- *GLDG2* p. 184)

> **DEPTH: 37 feet**   **LEVEL: Novice-Intermediate**
> **COORDINATES: 44.822879N/-82.536171W**

34. NORTHERN INDIANA (UPDATE -- *GLDG2* p. 185-186)

> **DEPTH: 20 to 25 feet   LEVEL: Novice-Intermediate**
> **COORDINATES: 41.897980N/-82.509979W**

The tragic *Northern Indiana* is the second-closest shipwreck to Point Pelee's actual point (only the wooden propeller, *Conemaugh* -- see p. 190-191 of *GLDG2* -- lies closer.)

After the beautiful passenger-and-freight paddlewheel steamer, the **Northern Indiana,** *caught on fire and sank at Point Pelee with severe loss of life on July 17, 1856,* Frank Leslie's Illustrated Newspaper *commissioned artwork* (KOHL-FORSBERG ARCHIVES). *Lying near Point Pelee, the wreck, in shallow water, is severely broken up and creates a large debris field.*   (PHOTOS BY CRIS KOHL)

35. TIOGA (UPDATE -- *GLDG2* p. 186)

> **DEPTH: 40 feet   LEVEL: Intermediate**
> **COORDINATES: 41.884303N/-82.588980W**

36. TASMANIA (UPDATE -- *GLDG2* p. 186-187)

> **DEPTH: 38 to 40 feet   LEVEL: Intermediate**
> **COORDINATES: 41.788331N/-82.496499W**

37. JAY GOULD (UPDATE -- *GLDG2* p. 188)

> **DEPTH: 36 to 44 feet   LEVEL: Intermediate**
> **COORDINATES: 41.858830N/-82.4101129W**

38. DOMINION (UPDATE -- *GLDG2* p. 189)

> **DEPTH: 45 feet   LEVEL: Intermediate**
> **COORDINATES: 41.995838N/-82.445171W**

This steam-powered dredge, sunk in 1892, sits five miles south of Wheatley, Ontario.

Left: *Diver Roy Pickering examines the wreck of the* **Dominion**. **Middle:** *Most of this wreck site consists of many pieces of broken hull and decking.* **Right:** *Diver Cris Kohl gets set to photograph the wreck, with its distinctive boiler in the background.* (VIDEO FREEZE-FRAMES BY JOAN FORSBERG)

39. CLARION   (UPDATE -- *GLDG2* p. 189)

> **DEPTH: 58 to 77 feet   LEVEL: Advanced**
> **COORDINATES: 41.954330N/-82.271670W**

This 1909 wreck produced one of the most daring and heroic maritime rescues ever of six remaining crewmembers! The complete story appeared in a 3,950-word article in *Wreck Diving Magazine*, Issue #35, with the very first photos of this shipwreck ever published.

Left: *The* **Clarion** *in its home port of Erie, PA* (FROM A GLASS NEGATIVE PLATE IN THE KOHL-FORSBERG ARCHIVES). **Right:** *The approach for the final rescue attempt* (KOHL-FORSBERG ARCHIVES). **Below:** *Roy Pickering explores the* **Clarion's** *interior.* (VIDEO FREEZE-FRAMES BY CRIS KOHL)

40. WILLIS   (UPDATE -- *GLDG2* p. 190)

> **DEPTH: 60 to 73 feet   LEVEL: Intermediate-Advanced**
> **COORDINATES: 41.931331N/-82.161170W**

41. DAVID VANCE   (UPDATE -- *GLDG2* p. 194)

> **DEPTH: 42 feet   LEVEL: Intermediate**
> **COORDINATES: 41° 51.724′N/082° 31.440′W**

The correct date of sinking is July 20, 1893, not July 20, 1873.

42. GEORGE DUNBAR   (UPDATE -- *GLDG2* p. 196)

> **DEPTH: 42 to 45 feet   LEVEL: Intermediate**
> **COORDINATES: 41° 40.627′N/082° 33.891′W**

This wooden propeller, lost on June 29, 1902, was built in 1867 at Allegan, Michigan.

43. (GEN.) ANTHONY WAYNE   (UPDATE -- *GLDG2* p. 181)

> **DEPTH: 50 feet   LEVEL: Intermediate**
> **COORDINATES: 41° 31.666'N/082° 23.090'W**

This was an early paddlewheel steamer lost in an explosion in 1850, killing 22.

Left: The Gen. Anthony Wayne
*was built at Perrysburg,
Ohio, in 1837* (KOHL-FORSBERG
ARCHIVES).
*Right: Identifiable portions of a
paddlewheel remain in place*
(PHOTO BY ANDY MORRISON).

44. SUCCESS   (UPDATE -- *GLDG2* p. 198)

> **DEPTH: 15 feet   LEVEL: Novice**
> **COORDINATES: 41° 31.319'N/082° 54.703'W**

This Australian convict ship sailed the world earning millions of dollars at exhibitions.

Left: *The* Success *on
tour; thousands of sou-
venirs made of copper,
allegedly from this ship,
were sold* (KOHL-FORS-
BERG ARCHIVES). **Right:**
*The ship burned on July
4, 1946* (PHOTO COURTESY
OF HAROLD V. COOLEY)

LAKE ERIE'S WAR OF 1812 BICENTENNIAL (2012-2014)

Many events were held around the Great Lakes to commemorate the bicentennial of the War of 1812, the last time the USA and Great Britain/Canada were at war. Events included land battle reenactments, special concerts, countless presentations and educational programs, shoreline fireworks, and tall ships visiting from saltwater coastlines to help relive those ancient days of 200 years ago.

Despite the seriously violent nature of warfare at sea, none of the 15 ships (9 American and 6 British) was actually sunk in the Battle of Lake Erie in 1813. A total of 68 combatants were killed, 27 from the U.S. side and 41 from the British. Dead officers were buried on land at Put-in-Bay, while the common seamen were buried "at sea" in Lake Erie. Scuba divers today would be lucky to find even so much as a cannonball as evidence that a major battle took place on these waters.

The Battle of Lake Erie has been depicted by many artists in numerous renditions over two centuries. This art, from 1856, clearly shows, in the center, the pounding suffered by the **Lawrence,** *Commodore Perry's initial flagship.* (KOHL-FORSBERG ARCHIVES)

The 1912-1914 centennial of the War of 1812, according to the many newspaper and photographic accounts, appears to have been celebrated with greater zeal and energy, and better attendance, than the recent bicentennial. Perhaps that war really is being forgotten!

Left: *At the height of the Battle of Lake Erie, Perry ordered his men to row him to his newly-designated flagship, the* **Niagara,** *because the* **Lawrence** *was in tatters.* (KOHL-FORSBERG ARCHIVES)
Right: *The* **Lawrence,** *being raised in 1875 from where it had been abandoned at Erie, PA, after the Battle of Lake Erie, was displayed at Philadelphia in 1876 for the USA's centennial. But it was destroyed when its exhibition building burned that year.* (KOHL-FORSBERG ARCHIVES)

SOME LATE ADDITIONS

The coordinates to the wreck of the *Charles Spademan* (see *GLDG2*, p. 200) a 134-foot-long schooner that sank in 32 feet of water off South Bass Island near Put-in-Bay on December 10, 1909, after ice punctured its hull, are: **41° 37.379′N/082° 50.142′W**

The coordinates to the wreck of the *St. Lawrence* (see *GLDG2*, p. 180), a 137-foot-long schooner stranded and wrecked on November 21, 1900, near Lorain, Ohio, are **41° 28.42′N/082° 10.12′W**

The coordinates to the wreck of the *Quito* (see *GLDG2*, p. 180), a 204-foot-long, wooden steamer which grounded and broke up near Lorain, Ohio, on November 25, 1902, are **41° 28.37′N/082° 10.19′W**

5. Detroit River

The Detroit River, like the St. Clair River, has been a "bottleneck" to Great Lakes maritime traffic for centuries. Because the river is narrow, contains numerous islands and shoals, and includes a brisk current, navigation is far more dangerous than on the open lakes. Not surprisingly, the result has been shipwrecks. What may come as a surprise is that, of the thousands of times that ships stranded or sank in the Detroit River, more than 95% of them were recovered and returned to service.

However, scuba diving on shipwrecks in these high-traffic, murky waters can be dangerous, and Detroit has long had laws banning swimming and diving in the Detroit River within its city limits; more recently, Windsor enacted similar laws within its city limits. That still leaves a lot of river to explore beyond those two cities.

The most visible shipwreck in the Detroit River is the canaler, Queenston *(261' x 43'3" x 20') (left;* KOHL-FORSBERG ARCHIVES), *formerly the* Lachinedoc, *launched in Sunderland, England, in 1927, and which sailed immediately for service out of Montreal. Decommissioned in 1961, and with its cabins removed, the steel hull was purposely sunk to provide an extension to the ferry dock on Canada's Bob-lo (formerly Bois Blanc) Island in the Detroit River.* (PHOTO BY CRIS KOHL)

Some Shipwrecks in the Detroit River

ERIE -- This twin-decked, wooden steamer (120'4" x 18' x 7'2"), built at Detroit in 1836 (and not to be confused with the steamer, *Erie*, that sank with the loss of more than 100 lives on Lake Erie on August 9, 1841), exploded and burned on the Detroit River on March 9, 1844.

The wrecked Nile.
(KOHL-FORSBERG ARCHIVES)

NILE -- This wooden propeller (190' x 28'2" x 12'8"), launched in Ohio in 1852, exploded in the Detroit River just below Belle Isle on May 21, 1864, killing eight crew.

INTERNATIONAL -- This 27-gross-ton tug, built at Tonawanda, NY, in 1871, burned to a total loss at Amherstburg, Ontario, on December 8, 1892.

TOPEKA -- This bulk freighter (228'3" x 28' x 19'2"), launched in 1889 at Milwaukee, Wisconsin, sank at Sandwich, Ontario, on August 15,

The wrecked Topeka.
(KOHL-FORSBERG ARCHIVES)

1916, after colliding with the steamer, *Christopher.* It was dynamited four months later.

JOHN PLANKINTON -- Sunk after colliding with the steamer, *Detroit,* on May 9, 1917, with the loss of one life, this 28-year-old wooden ship (267' x 40'9" x 21') was launched at West Bay City, Michigan.

MINNIE MORTON -- This 55-foot-long tug did not sink in the Detroit River in 1881 (as has been published), but was swept into Lake Erie in a log raft before sinking; however, it was found and raised in 1886.

The **John Plankinton.**
(KOHL-FORSBERG ARCHIVES)

Some Ships Abandoned in the Detroit River

Left: *Half a dozen shipwrecks are marked on the chart of Stony Island.*
Right: *The small bay opposite the south end of Bois Blanc (Bob-lo) Island was a derelict ship dumping ground; see page 56.* (CHART PORTIONS COURTESY OF NOAA)

MILTON D. WARD -- This sidewheel steamer (182'5" x 28'5" x 7'8"), built at Marine City, Michigan, in 1870, carried silver ore from Lake Superior and served as a hospital ship for two years (1892-1894) during Detroit's cholera epidemic, but burned on August 16, 1894, and was never repaired. The engine was removed and the hull was abandoned at Waterworks Park in Detroit.

CITY OF SANDUSKY -- Launched as the *Jay Cooke* at Detroit in 1868, this sidewheel steamer (162'8" x 25'7" x 9') was renamed *City of Sandusky* in 1888. The hull was abandoned in 1905 at Detroit's 24th Street boneyard, but was moved in 1908 to Windmill Point near Lake St. Clair to serve as a breakwall against ice build-up.

MELITTA -- Once a 'Christmas Tree Ship' on Lake Michigan, this 71-foot-long schooner, built in 1881, was abandoned in 1924 at the foot of Dubois Street in Detroit.

<u>NOTE</u>: Very few of the Detroit River shipwrecks/abandoned ships are marked on the charts.

Left: *The* **Milton D. Ward** *appeared majestic while underway, but* (right) *looked forlorn as an abandoned vessel. As part of a long and varied career, the* **Ward** *nearly sank after striking the wreck of the* **Nile** *in 1877.* (KOHL-FORSBERG ARCHIVES)

The **City of Sandusky** *once serviced the Lake Erie Islands* (above, left), *but was abandoned at Windmill Point in 1908* (above, middle, extreme right hull) (KOHL-FORSBERG ARCHIVES). *Above, right: Shipboard silverware, embossed 'City of Sandusky,' serves to remind us of this fine vessel today.* (KOHL-FORSBERG ARCHIVES)

6. Lake St. Clair

Lake St. Clair, roughly round in shape with a 25-mile diameter, is a very shallow segment (averaging only about 12 feet in depth, but with a deeper channel for ships dredged diagonally across it) of the interconnecting waterway system between Lake Huron to the north and Lake Erie to the south. The St. Clair River flows into Lake St. Clair from Lake Huron, and the Detroit River flows out of Lake St. Clair towards Lake Erie. A geographical aberration places the southernmost peninsula in Canada just below Lake St. Clair, very unusually positioning that part of Canada south of the United States; geographically, Windsor, Ontario is just south of Detroit, Michigan.

Lake St. Clair has a soft bottom, so the shipwrecks there are, for the most part, embedded, and because the silt and mud stir up easily, destroying underwater visibility, the lake is not particularly popular as a scuba diving destination.

Some Shipwrecks in Lake St. Clair

EMILY -- This two-masted schooner (54'4" x 15' x 4'9"), built at Detroit in 1826, capsized and sank on November 15, 1830, with the loss of all seven hands. The poem, "The Loss of the *Jules LaPlante*," was based on this tragic sinking.

ALEXANDER -- Built in Sandusky, Ohio, in 1865, as the *General Sherman*, and renamed in 1873, this wooden steamer (104'3" x 23'4" x 5'6") caught on fire and burned to a total loss near Belle River, Ontario, on October 4, 1879, with no lives lost.

ST. JOSEPH -- This 90-foot-long barge, built at Toledo, Ohio, in 1868, was lost in a storm on October 31, 1883.

ALPENA -- This wooden steambarge (154'4" x 30'4" x 10'8"), launched at Gibraltar, Michigan, in 1874, burned to a total loss about three miles below the St. Clair Flats canal on October 26, 1891. Locals reportedly scavenged the ship's cargo of lumber as it washed ashore.

The Alanson Sumner.
(KOHL-FORSBERG ARCHIVES)

GEORGE N. BRADY -- This large, 1865 tug (102'4" x 20' x 10'8") from Detroit, caught on fire and sank while towing a log raft about three miles above Grosse Point, Michigan, on August 24, 1892. No lives were lost.

ALANSON SUMNER -- Another large tug (127' x 24'2" x 11'1"), built at Oswego, NY, in 1872, sank on December 6, 1898, one mile southeast of the St. Clair Flats canal.

POINT ABINO -- On November 14, 1905, this 112-foot-long barge, built in 1872 at Buffalo, NY, sprang a leak and was beached a mile from the St. Clair Flats canal, where a subsequent storm broke it apart.

The Point Abino
(KOHL-FORSBERG ARCHIVES)

FANNIE TUTHILL -- This tug (60'3" x 14'5" x 6'9"),

launched at East Saginaw, Michigan, in 1873, was struck by the wooden steamer, *D. C. Whitney*, on October 1, 1905, and was totally destroyed with one life lost.

GEORGE NELSON -- Ice punctured the hull and sank this little tugboat (65' x 17'4" x 8') while it tried to force its way into the mouth of the Thames River on December 7, 1910.

Built in 1886 at Saugatuck, Michigan, this abandoned wreck reportedly sank in 24 feet of water.

ELMER -- This tug (60' x 16' x 6'), built at Mt. Clemens, Michigan, in 1882, foundered on August 13, 1916. No lives were lost.

The tug, **Elmer.**
(KOHL-FORSBERG ARCHIVES)

The tug, **George Nelson.**
(KOHL-FORSBERG ARCHIVES)

Blazing Spectacles on Lake St. Clair

In the 1950's, Lake St. Clair experienced pyromania similar to that which heated up the blood of Toronto residents in the late 1920's-early 1930's (see pages 42-43 in this book.) While the following two ships did not actually sink to the bottom of Lake St. Clair, this was the site of each vessel's dramatic demise -- before being scrapped. These stories are told here for the historical record of this lake.

PUT-IN-BAY -- This popular excursion steamer simply grew too old. With its wooden superstructure built atop a steel hull, the ship (227' x 46' x 17'3"), launched in 1911 at Wyandotte, Michigan, and capable of carrying 2,539 passengers, transported hundreds of thousands of summer excursionists on pleasant day trips between Detroit and Port Huron, with numerous stops at a variety of resorts along the way. But the new prosperity after World War Two -- which featured homes and cars, as well as television sets and numerous other social distractions -- did not include day trips across local lakes and rivers on board old-fashioned steamers. In a widely-viewed public spectacle, the venerable *Put-in-Bay* was set ablaze in Lake St. Clair on October 3, 1953, and then scrapped at nearby River Rouge.

The regal, "mile-long" **Put-in-Bay,** *not so regal the day after the fire.* (KOHL-FORSBERG ARCHIVES)

EASTERN STATES -- This much larger excursion vessel (350' x 45'3" x 19'6"), built in 1902 at Wyandotte, Michigan, as a steel-hulled paddlewheel steamer, was burned as a public spectacle in Lake St. Clair on December 12, 1956 and scrapped in 1957 at Hamilton Ontario.

The **Eastern States,** *photo by Louis Pesha.* (KOHL-FORSBERG ARCHIVES)

FINALLY: Hoping to solve the greatest mystery of Lake St. Clair, one group of researchers is searching for War of 1812, cannon-laden ships captured on the Thames River in October, 1813, from the fleeing British under Proctor by American forces under Harrison, but which sank in the soft-bottomed lake between the Thames River and the Puce River while on their way back to Detroit. Stay tuned!

7. St. Clair River

The St. Clair River is the heart of the "Bluewater" tourist region, and the water is amazingly clean as it attempts to squeeze itself from broad Lake Huron into the narrow funnel that is this river. It is only about 30 miles downstream, at the wide, multiple fingers of the shallow St. Clair Flats where the river empties itself into Lake St. Clair, that it becomes dirty with suspended sediment. Nonetheless, being considered a "bottleneck" in the navigation of the Great Lakes, this river has been crowded with maritime traffic over the past two centuries that often resulted in shipwrecks. Here are a few more to go along with the 26 St. Clair River shipwrecks in *GLDG2* (p. 209-220), and the many in the 1987 book, *Shipwreck Tales: The St. Clair River (to 1900)*:

GLENIFFER -- The captain's wife and a sailor from Windsor, Ontario, were drowned when the Canadian tow-barge, *Gleniffer* (134' x 26'1" x 11'5") sank after a nighttime collision with the steamer, *Admiral*, off the Star Island House in the St. Clair Flats on June 2, 1902. The *Gleniffer*, built in 1873 at Port Robinson, Ontario, was dynamited later that month. The wreck sits in 47 feet of water.

Left: *The schooner-barge,* **Gleniffer**, *was sunk in a collision with another ship.*   (KOHL-FORSBERG ARCHIVES)

JAMES FISK, JR. -- This 914-ton, wooden, bulk freighter (213' x 32'6" x 12'3"), built at Buffalo, NY, in 1870 and used mainly in the lumber trade, burned to the waterline at Muir's Landing in the Southeast Bend of the St. Clair River at 5 P.M. on November 14, 1906, before settling in 23 feet of water.

Right: *The lumber carrier,* **James Fisk, Jr.**, *was traveling light (empty) when she burned to a total loss. No lives were lost.* (KOHL-FORSBERG ARCHIVES)

The **Tampa,** *sunk in one river, abandoned in another.*   (KOHL-FORSBERG ARCHIVES)

TAMPA -- The steambarge, *Tampa* (291'6" x 41' x 19'8"), built in 1890 at West Bay City, Michigan, sank when the steamer, *John W. Gates,* collided with her in the Detroit River at the Hiram Walker Distillery at Walkerville, Ontario, on July 18, 1911. Raised in 1914 and taken to Marine City, Michigan, the ship was again abandoned, blocking the Belle River entrance. In November 1914, the wreck drifted to the head of Fawn Island. It was later reportededly scrapped, but may have been used as a breakwall at Marine City.

GEORGE T. BURROUGHS -- Built at Chicago in 1881 (ten years after the Great Fire), this steambarge (109' x 24'2" x 8'7"), while hauling a cargo of gravel from Port Huron, MI, to Windsor, ON, sank in a collision with the steamer, *C. F. Bielman*, on May 31, 1905. With the machinery removed and the hull dynamited as a hazard to navigation, what remains today sits in 33 feet of water near the old Trautz dock in the St. Clair Flats.

The Wreck of the *Sidney E. Smith, Jr.* -- Updates

At approximately 2:00 A.M. on June 5, 1972, the 532-foot-long steel freighter, *Parker Evans*, collided with the 489-foot-long steel freighter, *Sidney E. Smith, Jr.*, just south (downstream) of the Bluewater Bridge at Port Huron/Point Edward/Sarnia. The quick actions of a local pilot boat captain and his deckhand probably saved many lives in a dramatic rescue.

The 66-year-old, upbound *Smith,* fighting the strong current, had angled too much and caught her bow, the forceful water swinging the ship's nose right into the course of the 64-year-old *Evans,* itself being pushed downstream with great force. The long shriek of steel-on-steel abruptly caught Capt. Robert Campbell's attention. He jumped from the pilot office on the Canadian shore and quickly activated his little boat, the *Sally M.* Along with deckhand, James Chadwick, he removed 31 of the 34 men on board (the remaining three had launched the *Smith's* work skiff and reached shore safely).

The *Evans,* her bow damaged but not leaking, proceeded to a nearby dock, but the *Smith,* her starboard bow pierced, took on water quickly, settled in 35 feet, and took on a severe list. The bow section hung over a drop-off that was 55 feet deep, and several days later, the ship cracked in half, eventually breaking completely in two. The salvage was longer and costlier than anyone imagined.

Left: *The collision was drawn by Canadian artist Marcel Blanchette in 1997 for the 25th anniversary commemoration* (COURTESY OF MARCEL BLANCHETTE). **Right:** *On April 27, 1973, the salvaged bow section of the* **Smith** *was towed to Sarnia for use as a dock and land fill. This remains the only part of the shipwreck that is visible above water today. Removing the fuel and the two halves of the* **Sidney E. Smith, Jr.** *became the costliest salvage in Great Lakes history.* (PHOTO BY CRIS KOHL)

Above: *In a formal ceremoney at Detroit's Selfridge Air Force Base on June 27, 1973, Capt. Robert Campbell and deckhand James Chadwick received Medals of Honor for their part in the rescue of the* **Smith's** *crew. Capt. Campbell lived out the rest of his days enjoying the panoramic view of the St. Clair River from his residence in Sarnia.* (1997 PHOTOS BY CRIS KOHL)

Left: *The City of Sarnia honored Capt. Campbell by placing a historic marker along the waterfront where the sinking of the* **Sidney E. Smith, Jr.** *occurred -- a reminder of heroic actions during the last commercial ship sinking in the St. Clair River.* (PHOTO BY CRIS KOHL)

A Great Lakes Sidebar

Maritime Photographer: *Louis Pesha*

The St. Clair River region produced one of the most productive and best-known maritime photographers in the Great Lakes.

Louis Pesha, born on August 11, 1868 in Euphemia Township (near Shetland), Ontario, southeast of Sarnia, farmed the land until 1895, when he, with the blessings of his wife, Lena, whom he had married on August 29, 1892, turned to professional photography. After moderate success with portrait studios in the Ontario towns of Oil Springs and Alvinston, he moved everything to Marine City, Michigan, in 1901. By 1906, he had established the Pesha Postcard Company to take advantage of the popularity of postcards in this penny-post, golden age.

Pesha's postcard subjects included buildings and street scenes in Michigan and Ontario towns (of which he produced approximately 7,000 postcards), but it was his roughly 1,500 ship photos that proved most popular. *The Photographic Times* magazine in 1910 called Pesha "one of the most popular photographers of the year." He was so successful that he was able to purchase a luxury White model MM steam car for $4,000 (at a time when the popular model-T Ford cost only a few hundred dollars).

A quirk to which many photographers can relate, preferring to be <u>behind</u> the camera rather than <u>in front of</u> it, was a chief characteristic of the "camera-shy" Louis Pesha. This is the only known picture of this man, taken while he worked photographing a passing steamer on the St. Clair River. (KOHL-FORSBERG ARCHIVES)

But on October 1, 1912, Louis Pesha met his untimely death in the vehicle that he loved so much. One newspaper account provided details:

Louis Pesha, aged 45 [sic], a leading photographer, of Marine City, Mich., and a former resident of Euphemia Township, was instantly killed at the family homestead... when by mistake he put his foot on the reverse lever of his auto, thinking it was the service brake, and the car shot backwards over a steep embankment, and turning over, landed wheels upward in the ditch. Mr. Pesha was pinned under the steering wheel and was dead when taken out....His skull was terribly fractured.

SOME EXAMPLES OF LOUIS PESHA'S WORK:

Left: *The popular Detroit excursion steamer,* Tashmoo, *sank in the Detroit River on June 18, 1936.*
(KOHL-FORSBERG ARCHIVES)

Right: *Another popular excursion steamer, the* North West, *lost its bow half in Lake Ontario on November 28, 1918.*
(KOHL-FORSBERG ARCHIVES)

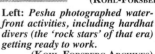

Left: *Pesha photographed waterfront activities, including hardhat divers (the 'rock stars' of that era) getting ready to work.*
(KOHL-FORSBERG ARCHIVES)

Right: *The schooner,* Azov, *was wrecked in Lake Huron on Oct. 22, 1911.* (KOHL-FORSBERG ARCHIVES)

Other examples of the maritime photos taken by Louis Pesha appear in this book on pages 70 and 79.

Louis Pesha, the country boy from Canada, had a lighter, often impish, side to him, and this was reflected in some of his "trick photography" postcards created in his darkroom, such as the excursion steamer Tashmoo *about to go over Niagara Falls, and a whaleback steamer being towed by one of those newfangled inventions of the time, a biplane.* (KOHL-FORSBERG ARCHIVES)

Mr. Pesha had only arrived a few minutes before the accident, having enjoyed the trip over in company with his wife and 11-year-old daughter. They had intended spending a few days with Mr. Pesha's father, whom they had not seen for some time.

Another account a day later pronounced Pesha's legacy:

The death of Louis Pesha, the well-known photographer, came as a distinct shock to his many friends in Sarnia. Mr. Pesha was the best marine photographer on the lakes, and perhaps the best in the United States.

Hundreds of pictures of the vessels which pass up and down the St. Clair River have been taken by him, many in Sarnia and Port Huron....

Lena Pesha kept her late husband's business operating, moving it to Detroit, but real-photo postcards gradually fell out of fashion, forcing her to give it up in 1921. To make ends meet, she sold most of her husband's glass-plate negatives to a window manufacturer because the glass was worth more than the photos! Louis Pesha's post-cards, however, remain popular today and are highly-sought by collectors.

Left and middle: Louis Pesha purchased this luxury steam car from the White Company in 1910. It is shown here parked in front of Pesha's Marine City studios. An unusual feature was its right-hand steering. Pesha had electric headlights and taillights added to it. (KOHL-FORSBERG ARCHIVES)
Right: Louis Pesha's headstone in the family plot at Shetland, Ontario. (PHOTO BY CRIS KOHL)

Ten months after Pesha's untimely death, an unusual accident occurred on the St. Clair River. The American whaleback steamer, Atikoken, *recently sold to Canadian interests, lost its steering mechanism while underway on August 17, 1913, and ended up in the most embarrassing position possible for any ship, running far ashore at Marine City, Michigan. Fortunately, no one was killed or injured, but a number of buildings were destroyed -- including Louis Pesha's Marine Photo Gallery building. Was this divine retribution for his biplane postcard?* (KOHL-FORSBERG ARCHIVES)

8. Lake Huron

"NEW SHIPWRECKS" refers to those that are not in the book, *The Great Lakes Diving Guide,* second edition, 2008 (*GLDG2*), either because they had not yet been discovered, or because the authors had not yet learned about their locations.

NEW SHIPWRECKS

A. *Malta* and *Lynda Hindman*
B. The Goderich 'Boneyard'
C. *Erie Belle*
D. *Africa* and *Severn*
E. *Kincardine*
F. *Dan Proctor*
G. *Nancy*
H. *Tecumseth*
I. *C. C. Martin* and *Albatross*
J. *Charles A. King*
K. *E. B. Hale*
L. *John L. Shaw*
M. *Corsair*

N. *Francis Berriman*
O. *Egyptian*
P. *Keystone State*
Q. *New York*
R. *Marion Egan*
S. *Hydrus*
T. Shallow wrecks: Alpena
U. *Mary Woolson*
V. *Corsican*
W. *M. F. Merrick*
X. *Etruria*
Y. Shallow wrecks: Rogers City
Z. *Hope*

"UPDATED SHIPWRECKS" refers to ones that are in the book, *The Great Lakes Diving Guide* (shortened to *GLDG2* when referenced in this chapter). The UPDATED information about each of these shipwrecks could be new or corrected GPS coordinates, additional maritime history, and/or modern-day news about that particular wreck.

UPDATED SHIPWRECKS

1. *Sweetheart*
2. *Province* and Ghost Ships
3. *Wexford*
4. *General Hunter*
5. *Sweepstakes*
6. *City of Grand Rapids*
7. *John Walters*
8. *James C. King*
9. *Arabia*
10. *Forest City*
11. *Niagara II*
12. *Lady Dufferin*
13. a. *San Jacinto*
    b. *City of Cleveland*
14. *Michigan*
15. *Mary Ward*
16. *Emma*
17. *Atlantic*
18. *Jane McLeod*

19. *Seattle*
20. *Metamora*
21. *India*
22. *Hiawatha*
23. *B. B. Buckhout*
24. *Emma E. Thompson*
25. *Alberta M.*
26. *Burlington*
27. *Joyland*
28. *Rome*
29. *Sport*
30. *Charles A. Street*
31. *New York*
32. *Col. A. B. Williams*
33. *Glenorchy*
34. *Anna Dobbins*
35. *Troy*
36. *Detroit*
37. *Daniel J. Morrell*

38. *Argus*
39. *Minnedosa*
40. *W. C. Franz*
41. Sport diving wrecks: Alpena
42. *W. H. Gilbert*
43. *Pewabic*
44. *Viator*
45. *D. R. Hanna*
46. *Defiance*
47. *Typo*
48. *Florida*
49. *Norman*
50. *C. B. Windiate*
51. *Kyle Spangler*
52. *Northwestern*
53. *Cedarville*
54. *William Young*

Lake Huron

This map is not to be used for navigation, as details, such as potential hazards, are not marked. Use the maps in this book only for general orientation.

Map by
Joan Forsberg

Not on this map:

These Lake Huron shipwrecks are not on the above map or in *GLDG2*:

The **'BAYFIELD DREDGE'** -- This wreck lies in 88 feet of water about 7.5 miles west of Bayfield, Ontario. Its technical name is *Public Works Dredge Q and R No. 1* and it reportedly sank in June, 1932 while being towed by the government tug, *Peel*. All eleven people on board the barge were saved. When discovered in the 1990's, this wreck was initially hoped to be the *Wexford* (see page 112 in this book and page 224-225 in *GLDG2*).

Coordinates: 43° 32′ 48.0010″N/081° 49′ 36.0011″W.

The wreck of the steamer *Asia,* the worst loss-of-life maritime disaster ever to take place on Lake Huron (123 people perished, with only two survivors, on September 14, 1882), reportedly lies in about 100 feet of water off Byng Inlet, in northeastern Georgian Bay. However, there has been no evidence to verify this claim; searches reportedly continue in efforts to find the historic wreck of the *Asia.*

A. *Malta* and *Lynda Hindman* (NEW)

> **DEPTH: Shallow and/or above water**
> **COORDINATES: 43.566324 N/-81.706726 W**

LOCATION: Both of these very different shipwrecks lie off Bayfield, Ontario.

The barkentine, *Malta* (137'5" x 23'5" x 8'2"), launched by famous shipbuilder Louis Shickluna at St. Catharines, Canada West (Ontario), in 1853, was storm-wrecked on November 23, 1882. The ship carried salt bound for Goderich (before Goderich mined salt!)

Left: *No lives were lost when the* **Malta** *was stranded and wrecked at Bayfield.*
Right: *For years, the hulk of the* **Malta** *served as a changehouse for beach visitors. In 1974, the rudder/rudder post washed ashore; local residents, with much difficulty, set it up in front of their Bayfield home.* **Malta** *wreckage can often be seen in the sand or in the shallow water.* (BOTH KOHL-FORSBERG ARCHIVES)

Tourists gazing down at Lake Huron from their clifftop perch at Pioneer Park in Bayfield often wonder about what violent tragedy befell the broken shipwreck visible in the shallows below them. We have heard many tales, including that this wreck was from the Great Storm of 1913! The truth, however, is not quite as dramatic as that.

The large tug, *William A. McGonagle* (110' x 28' x 15'3"), built at Lorain, Ohio, in 1908, and much later renamed the *Lynda Hindman*, was about to be scrapped in Goderich in 1973 when a Bayfield resident purchased the old hulk for use as a breakwall off his waterfront property. But she was scuttled too far off shore; subsequent winters broke her up.

Left: *The 1908 steel fire tug,* **William A. McGonagle,** *was renamed the* **Lynda Hindman** *in 1965.*
(KOHL-FORSBERG ARCHIVES)

Right: *One can gaze at the* **Lynda Hindman** *and meditate on the meaning of life.*
(PHOTO BY CRIS KOHL)

B. THE GODERICH 'BONEYARD' (NEW)

> **DEPTH: to 18 feet   LEVEL: Novice**
> **COORDINATES: 43° 44' 16.0189"N/081° 43' 59.9989"W**

LOCATION: A number of abandoned hulls lie about 600 feet off the arch at Rotary Beach. Because they lie together in shallow water, they are all badly broken up and virtually unidentifiable.

This wreckage includes: the tug *Harold B. Phillips* (59' x 16' x 8'), built in 1882 as the *George W. Lormer* (below, left); the 1874 steambarge, *Abercorn* (126'1" x 26'1" x 11'), burned at the Goderich dock on September 5, 1904; the 1873 schooner-barge, *Scotia* (210'9" x 34'5" x 15'), abandoned in 1928 (below, middle); the 1881 schooner-barge, *Olga* (137' x 30'4" x 10'), wrecked three miles above Goderich on November 26, 1905; and the 1873 steamer *Tecumseh* (213' x 29'9" x 13'2"), burned at Goderich Jan 16, 1909 (below, right).   (ALL IMAGES KOHL-FORSBERG ARCHIVES)

The Great Storm of 1913 Centennial

The Great Storm of 1913, the worst storm in recorded Great Lakes history, claimed a dozen ships and approximately 250 sailors' lives. Most of the destruction occurred on lower Lake Huron.

In November, 2013, a spectacular variety of 100th anniversary commemorative events was set up in both Michigan and Ontario, particularly in the southern half of Lake Huron.

Port Huron saw, among several other events, the auctioning of numerous items, mostly bottles with remnants of scotch, champagne, and ketchup, from the wreck of the Canadian steel freighter, the *Regina,* lost with all hands in that 1913 storm just off Port Sanilac, Michigan. A special commemorative coin was also minted for this event.

But the bulk of commemorative activities took place at or near Goderich, Ontario, on the side of Lake Huron where nearly all of the bodies recovered from those 1913 Storm shipwrecks washed ashore.

An ambitious, weekly, pre-event series of nine guest speakers sharing their experiences and wisdom on topics ranging from the history of the Goderich lighthouse

Joan Forsberg reads the story of the Great Storm of 1913 as told on the memorial marker at the point where Lake Huron flows into the St. Clair River. From here, one has a panoramic overview of the area hardest hit by that storm.
(PHOTO BY CRIS KOHL)

and Goderich harbour in postcards, to details of the actual Storm of 1913, culminated on the weekend of November 8-10, 2013 (coincidentally the exact dates of the actual storm in 1913!), with musicians (such as Lee Murdock and David MacAdam) singing their new songs about the Great Storm, well-known presenters such as Paul Carroll, Dennis Hale, Dave Trotter, Mike & Georgann Wachter, Ric Mixter, and Cris Kohl & Joan Forsberg, captivating audiences with their lively presentations, and live stage presentations of the new play, "White Hurricane" (calling this storm by its new, 21st-century name). People in Goderich even produced not one, but TWO, new books about the 1913 Storm!

For information about some of the Great Storm of 1913 shipwrecks, please turn to pages 101, 112, and 126.

Left and right: *On November 9, 2013, at Goderich, Ontario, Jo-Anne Homan, a member of the Storm of 1913 committee, unveiled the impressive 1913 Storm memorial designed by her husband, Keith.*
(PHOTOS BY CRIS KOHL)

Left: *A memorial service took place at Goderich at the grave of five unidentified sailors washed up in the Great Storm of 1913.*

Right: *In keeping with the event, massive waves broke over the Goderich harbour light that day.*
(PHOTOS BY CRIS KOHL)

C. ERIE BELLE (NEW)

LOCATION: On a sandy beach about two miles south of Kincardine, Ontario.

A massive, contorted mound of thick, broken steel mars an otherwise idyllic shoreline of white sand beach along Lake Huron's blue waters. This out-of-place object is apparently the only thing left of the wooden steamer, *Erie Belle* (120'5" x 20'5" x 9'1"), after that ship exploded on November 21, 1883. A mid-November storm had stranded the schooner, *J. N. Carter,* at this location, and the powerful *Erie Belle,* dispatched from Windsor, Ontario, and attempting to free the ship, pushed its steam engine to the limit. The resulting boiler explosion blew the ship into little pieces and killed two engineers and two firemen from the crew of twelve. The survivors were pulled out of the freezing water by the volunteer lifeboat crew from Kincardine. One deckhand was blinded, the cook was severely scalded, and another survivor reportedly became mentally unbalanced and died a few years later.

The freight and passenger steamer, **Erie Belle.** (KOHL-FORSBERG ARCHIVES)

The stranded *J. N. Carter*, pulled free by another tug in the summer of 1884, enjoyed ten more years of life before being wrecked off the southwest shore of Manitoulin Island in northern Lake Huron on September 15, 1894.

Built as the *Hector* in Cleveland, Ohio, in 1862, by Peck & Masters, this ship was sold to Canadian interests in 1879 and renamed the *Erie Belle,* operating between Windsor, Leamington, and Pelee Island. The vessel had been rebuilt by the Jenkins Brothers in Windsor in 1882.

Left: *High and dry on a sandy beach, the boiler from the* **Erie Belle** *has become a popular landmark.*

Right: *A historic marker was set up at the tree line near the boiler.*

(PHOTOS BY CRIS KOHL)

D. AFRICA AND SEVERN (NEW)

LOCATION: Off Bradley Harbour, Ontario, about four miles north of Lyal Island.

The steam barge, *Africa,* towing the schooner-barge, *Severn*, both came to grief off the west side of the Bruce Peninsula on October 7, 1895, during a violent storm. Both ships

were coal-laden from Ashtabula, Ohio, for Owen Sound, Ontario, at the time of loss.

While the *Africa* was seen disappearing into the depths of Lake Huron about 20 miles off the Bruce Peninsula coast, the *Severn* was blown east by the wind until the ship stranded about half a mile off shore north of Bradley Harbour. A fishing boat from Stokes Bay daringly rescued the entire

Left: *The steamer,* **Africa,** *sank a fair distance off shore.* (KOHL-FORSBERG ARCHIVES)

crew of six men and the female cook from the *Severn*. While the *Africa* carried $9,000 worth of insurance, about three-quarters of the value of the ship, the *Severn* was not insured at all.

Bodies and wreckage from the *Africa* came ashore near the community of Stokes Bay, Ontario. An unfortunate court battle was fought between the *Severn's* captain and the fisherman who had rescued him and his crew -- over ownership of the many items that the fisherman had salvaged from the wreck of the *Severn*!

The *Africa* (148' x 26' x 13'), launched at Kingston, Ontario, in 1873, operated for a time between Montreal and Chicago, but burned during winter layup at Owen Sound in 1886 before being rebuilt in 1887, with the passenger cabins removed, as a freight steamer in the lumber and coal trade.

The *Severn* (151' x 27'5" x 12'7"), launched at Welland, Ontario, in 1872, worked mostly in the lumber trade her entire life.

While there are only rumors that the wreck of the *Africa* has been found off shore, at least one charter boat operator has been taking scuba divers to the wreck of the *Severn*, reportedly lying in about 30 feet of water north of Stokes Bay, Ontario.

ARE THEY ALL LOST?

CANADIAN STEAMER AFRICA FOUND-
ERS ON LAKE HURON.

REPORTS INDICATE THAT ELEVEN
SOULS ARE GONE.

A SLIGHT HOPE THAT THEY MAY
HAVE ESCAPED.

Her Boats and Life Preservers Found
on Loyal Island.

Stokes Bay, Ont., October 9.—Reports indicate that the steamer Africa, of Owen
Sound, is lost with all on board. Following is a complete list of her crew: Capt.
H. P. Larsen, Toronto; Mate William An-
derson, Owen Sound; Chief Engineer Has

The Oct. 10, 1895 Detroit Free Press *reported the losses.* (KOHL-FORSBERG ARCHIVES)

E. KINCARDINE (NEW)

LOCATION: On the shore about 1.3 miles west of Wingfield Basin, at the base of West Bluff, part of the Niagara Escarpment.

Launched on June 7, 1871, at Port Dalhousie, Ontario, the 343-gross-ton, wooden steamer, *Kincardine* (107' x 20' x 9'), after three previous strandings as well as three earlier sinkings/recoveries, stranded a final time in November, 1892, at this location near Cabot Head, and broke up. No lives were lost. In 1896, the tug, *Saucy Jim* (see *GLDG2*, p. 262) salvaged the engine and some other items.

The location of the boiler, the only part of this wreck remaining on the beach, is **45.244731 N/-81.319754 W**; the easiest access is by boat.

The wooden steamer, **Kincardine.**
(KOHL-FORSBERG ARCHIVES)

F. DAN PROCTOR (NEW)

DEPTH: To 30 feet   LEVEL: Novice-Intermediate
COORDINATES: 44.585688 N/-80.935335 W

LOCATION: This site is about 650 feet off the Owen Sound (Ontario) Wastewater Treatment Plant near the harbor.

Three wrecks, apparently abandoned next to each other, were found at Owen Sound in

the spring of 2015; the middle one (and the largest) is likely the remains of the wooden steamer, *Dan Proctor*. Launched in 1893 at West Bay City, Michigan, as the *Ed McWilliams* (200' x 34' x 14'), the ship was renamed after an official of the Keenan Brothers Lumber Company when they acquired the ship in 1922. It was stripped and abandoned in 1937. The site is currently being professionally surveyed.

Left: *The* **Dan Proctor.** (KOHL-FORSBERG ARCHIVES)

G. NANCY (NEW)

COORDINATES: 44.519390 N/-80.020072 W

LOCATION: This historic shipwreck is in a museum on Nancy Island in the Nottawasaga River at Wasaga Beach, Ontario.

The schooner, *Nancy,* built at Detroit in 1789 as a merchant vessel, served the British forces in the War of 1812 as a supply ship (food, clothing, armaments) for their garrison at Mackinac Island. But the *Nancy* was trapped in the Nottawasaga River by three American ships and, after a seven-hour battle on August 14, 1814, and aware that they were greatly outnumbered, the British set their vessel on fire and allowed it to sink. With time, an increasingly larger island formed around this shipwreck. In 1927, the hull was excavated and placed into a newly-constructed museum building which opened to the public on August 14, 1928. In 1985, a protective glass enclosure was built around the hull. History is kept alive here through a variety of educational programs and special events.

This is a famous Great Lakes shipwreck that anyone can visit without getting wet!

Left: *The schooner,* Nancy *under sail* (ART BY GEORGE CUTHBERTSON). **Middle and right:** *A modern and informative museum houses the remains of the* Nancy's *hull.* (PHOTOS BY CRIS KOHL)

H. TECUMSETH (NEW)

COORDINATES: 44.804999 N/-79.931859 W

LOCATION: In Discovery Harbour village/museum at Penetanguishene, Ontario.

The 76-foot-long, two-masted schooner named the H. M. S. *Tecumseth,* built in 1815 at Chippewa, Upper Canada (Ontario), on the upper Niagara River, was acquired by the British in 1817 just after the War of 1812, and stationed at Penetanguishene. While docked "in ordinary" (meaning no longer in actual use), the ship sank due to hull failure in 1828. More than a century later, in 1953, the shipwreck remains were raised and placed on the open shoreline, where they stayed for about ten years before being moved under a large, protective roof. Finally, in 2014, these ancient, delicate hull timbers were carefully moved into a modern, climate-controlled building. Her sister ship, the H. M. S. *Newash,* similarly abandoned in the 1820s, has not been raised from the harbor.

Left: *A contemporary drawing of the* Tecumseth *under construction* (KOHL-FORSBERG ARCHIVES) **Middle:** *Prior to 2014, when the indoor, climate-controlled H. M. S.* Tecumseth *Centre was opened, the wreck was housed outdoors under a simple roof.* **Right:** *Discovery Harbour at Penetanguishene, Ontario, recreates living conditions as they were in the War of 1812 era, complete with a 124' replica of the H. M. S.* Tecumseth *at the dock.* (PHOTOS BY CRIS KOHL)

I. *C. C. MARTIN* AND *ALBATROSS* (NEW)

COORDINATES: (Wikipedia) 45.51555 N/-81.07027 W
These numbers are highly unlikely, as they indicate a mid-Georgian-Bay location halfway between Lonely Island and Pointe au Baril, more suited to be the location of the long-lost *ASIA!*

LOCATION: Somewhere between Key Harbour and Byng Inlet, north Georgian Bay. On August 21, 1911, two vessels, the five-year-old tug, *C. C. Martin,* towing the 40-year-old barge, *Albatross* (136'6" x 26'3" x 11'9"), towards the French River, met with disaster. In darkness at 11 P. M. during a storm, the barge began to sink from a leak. All seven

Left: *The 69-ton, 70-foot-long tug,* Erastus Day, *was similar in size and appearance to the lost, 78-ton, 71-foot-long* **C.C. Martin.** **Right:** *The barge,* **Albatross.** (BOTH KOHL-FORSBERG ARCHIVES)
Below, left and right: *A large number of Great Lakes newspapers, including the* **Duluth Herald** *and the* **Toledo Blade,** *reported this tragic story.* (KOHL-FORSBERG ARCHIVES)

MARINE

TEN ARE LOST; NINE SAVED

Steamer C. C. Martin Believed to Have Gone Down With All Hands.

Crew of Barge Albatross Reaches Lighthouse Near Midland.

Midland, Ont., Aug. 25.—The steamer C. C. Martin of Midland, with a crew of ten, was probably lost in the storm on Georgian bay Monday night. The barge Albatross, in tow of the Martin, sank during the storm, but her crew reached during the storm, but her crew reached

people (two men, three women, and two infants, the women and children dressed only in night clothes) somehow made it into their crowded yawl boat before the barge sank. Meanwhile, the lights had gone out on the tug, and it was lost from view, but before long, the seven from the *Albatross* found the tug's yawl adrift, secured it, and balanced their numbers between the two 13-foot boats. They reached the French River Light 36 hours later. But the *Martin,* its captain, his wife, and eight sailors were missing.

The first body from the *Martin* was found in remarkably good condition 17 days after the sinking. Near the body was a raft, and further searching recovered two more bodies, all of them located on shoals at Black Bill Island, quite a distance south of the place where the tug and barge had gone down. Two more bodies from the *Martin* were located on September 20th, for a total of five. No others were found. The raft, made up of doors from the *Martin,* suggested that the tug, which had lost its yawl boat in the storm, did not sink immediately, giving the crew time to build this raft. What happened after that is a mystery. But a horrifying fact is that the five recovered bodies had not drowned or died from exposure -- they had all starved to death.

GALE IN GEORGIAN BAY DROWNS TEN

The Tug C. C. Martin Lost—Barge Albatross Also Goes Under.

CREW OF ALBATROSS ESCAPE IN YAWL

No Word From Martin—Woman Was One of the Company.

By the Associated Press.
Midland, Ont., August 25.—The tug C. C. Martin, of Midland, with a crew of 10, was probably lost in the storm on Georgian Bay Monday night. The barge Albatross, in tow of the Martin, sank during the storm, but her crew reached the lighthouse at the mouth of the French river—

The carefully-crafted raft, consisting of six doors, a flagpole, rope, and spikes, had not been built in haste. (KOHL-FORSBERG ARCHIVES)

J. CHARLES A. KING (NEW)

DEPTH: 215 feet **LEVEL: Technical**
COORDINATES:

LOCATION: Approximately ten miles northeast of Point aux Barques, Michigan.

Maritime historian, Julius E. Wolff, wrote in his Lake Superior shipwrecks book, "The weather in the last week of September, 1895, was atrocious," and while he wrote that in reference only to Lake Superior shipwrecks, it applied equally to ships on two other lakes.

On Lake Huron, the 32-year-old schooner, *Charles A. King* (139'8" x 26' x 9'), built at Cleveland during the middle of the Civil War, succumbed to the powerful violence of this long storm on September 26, 1895. No lives were lost, all six having been rescued by the steam barge, *E. C. Pope*, which had stood by for two hours, but the coal cargo from Toledo would never reach Bay City. Captain James Glenn had just purchased the *King* five days earlier, and he had not yet arranged any insurance for his acquisition.

Also lost on Lake Huron were the barge *Lady Franklin*, and the schooners, *C.H. Johnson* and *Elvina Hunter*. On Lake Michigan, the losses included the schooners *E.R. Williams* (see *GLDG2*, p.485), *Skylark*, and *Queen City*. Lake Superior saw these losses: the steamer *Kershaw* (see *GLDG2*, p. 516), the barges *A.W. Comstock* and *Elma* (*GLDG2*, p. 513), and the scow schooner, *Richard J. Carney*. Surprisingly, few lives were lost in these sinkings.

The wreck of the *Charles A. King* was located by the U.S.E.P.A.ship, *Lake Guardian*, on June 21, 2008, and was first explored and identified by the Harbor Beach Explorers.

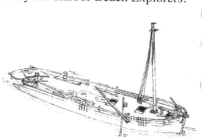

Left: *The two-masted schooner,* **Grace Whitney**, *closely resembled the* **Charles A. King**. (KOHL-FORSBERG ARCHIVES)   Middle: *These headlines, from the* **Duluth News Tribune**, *dated September 28, 1895, summarized the* King's *dramatic sinking.* (KOHL-FORSBERG ARCHIVES)   Right: *The wreck of the* **Charles A. King** *sits upright in deep water.* (ARTWORK BY ROBERT McGREEVY)

K. E. B. HALE (NEW)

LOCATION: In deep waters of Saginaw Bay, off Pointe aux Barques, Michigan.

Launched on June 11, 1874, at Cleveland, Ohio, the steamer, *E. B. Hale* (217'7" x 34'8" x 17'9"), sprang a leak and foundered in raging seas on October 8, 1897, with a cargo of 1,186 tons of steel billets. A passing steamer, the *Nebraska*, rescued the entire crew.

This is one of the many shipwrecks found in this area by Dave Trotter and his team.

The wooden freighter, **E. B. Hale**, *sank with no lives lost in 1897.* (KOHL-FORSBERG ARCHIVES)

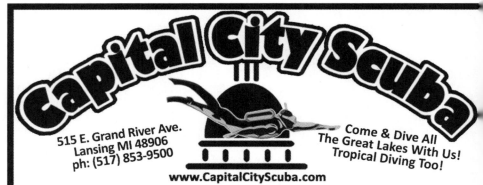

L. JOHN SHAW (NEW)

> **DEPTH: 128 feet   LEVEL: Advanced**
> **COORDINATES: 44° 37.000′N/083° 08.000′W**

LOCATION: In a straight line directly off Greenbush, Michigan.

In July 2007, local commercial fisherman, John Gauthier, while setting his nets, detected this shipwreck, which turned out to be the enormous, three-masted schooner-barge named the *John Shaw*. Launched on October 28, 1885, by James Davidson (well-known for

building huge, wooden ships!) at West Bay City, Michigan, the *Shaw* (205′7″ x 37′1″ x 14′3″), in tow of the steam barge, *John F. Eddy,* foundered during a blinding snowstorm on November 13, 1894. The crew took to the yawl boat at 3 A.M. after they found seven feet of water in the holds, and drifted for two hours before being rescued by the steamer, *H. E. Runnels.* In July 1896, a salvage tug located this wreck, but plans for recovery of either the wreck or its Chicago-bound coal cargo fizzled.

The **John Shaw.** (KOHL-FORSBERG ARCHIVES)

M. CORSAIR (NEW)

> **DEPTH: 182 feet   LEVEL: Technical**
> **COORDINATES: 44° 46.922′N/083° 07.426′W**

LOCATION: This wreck lies north of Harrisville, Michigan, off Sturgeon Point.

Launched on April 21, 1866, at Oswego, NY, the two-masted schooner, *Corsair* (133′ x 26′3″ x 11′), hauling a heavy cargo of iron ore from Lake Superior towards Oswego, encountered increasing gales on Saturday evening, September 28, 1872. At 4:15, the leaking ship suddenly sank, taking five of the seven crew with her. The two survivors drifted in a damaged lifeboat for 36 hours before the *City of Boston* picked them up.

N. FRANCIS BERRIMAN (NEW)

LOCATION: In about 200 feet of water, ten miles off Sturgeon Point, Michigan.

Two of the ten people on board the five-year-old, three-masted schooner, *Francis Berriman* (183′5″ x 33′ x 13′9″), perished when their ship collided with the steamer, *David Rust,* on May 7, 1877, due to a passing error. The *Berriman,* Buffalo-bound, had loaded wheat at Milwaukee; the *Rust* picked up the eight survivors.

Dave Trotter and his team located this shipwreck in 2012.

The **Francis Berriman** *resembled the 180-foot-long* **Ogarita,** *which burned and sank north of the* **Berriman** *on October 25, 1905.* (KOHL-FORSBERG ARCHIVES)

O. EGYPTIAN (NEW)

> **DEPTH: 230 feet   LEVEL: Technical**
> **COORDINATES:**

LOCATION: North of Sturgeon Point and south of Alpena, Michigan.

This wooden steamer (232′4″ x 36′2″ x 14′), built at Lorain, Ohio, in 1873, caught on fire and sank on December 1, 1897, the crew rescued by a passing steamer.

This wreck was found by NOAA Thunder Bay and a U. of Texas team in 2010.

P. KEYSTONE STATE (NEW)

DEPTH: 175 feet **LEVEL: Technical**
COORDINATES:

LOCATION: Approximately 30 miles northeast of Harrisville, Michigan.

Ships that sink leaving no survivors become silent mysteries that are difficult to solve, and their remains are more challenging to locate than others, but, in early July 2013, Dave Trotter and his team, after many years of searching, found the tragic, historic sidewheel steamer, *Keystone State*.

The wooden, twin-smokestacked *Keystone State* (288'3" x 35'8" x 14'1") left Detroit in haste on Friday, November 8, 1861, with 33 people on board (most residing in Buffalo, as opposed to being westbound immigrants), heading towards Milwaukee, but the ship, overtaken by a violent storm off Michigan's "thumb," foundered. Lifeboats had been left behind in Detroit because of the hasty departure, so everyone on board prayed desperately for the ship to remain afloat. People on shore near Port Austin were the last to see the vessel and the troubles it began to experience as it plowed north into the storm. For that reason, it was assumed that this steamer sank shortly thereafter. In actuality, as proven when the wreck was found, the *Keystone State* made it much farther north than anyone anticipated! This ship, lost early during the Civil War, was built in Buffalo, New York, in 1849, plied mostly between Buffalo and Chicago, and was under command of a captain from Buffalo at the time of loss. Reportedly this 12-year-old vessel was "terribly in need of repairs."

The *Keystone State's* twin paddlewheels remain in place and upright, as are the vintage "walking beam" steam engine and the ship's boilers. Divers, the first people to explore this ship in 152 years, were disappointed by the lack of any cargo -- which was reportedly iron farm equipment that might have been thrown overboard by the worried crew and the frantic

KEY STONE STATE
288 x 35 x 14

Built 1849, Bidwell & Banta, Buffalo N.Y.
Large side wheeler lost in Lake Huron during
the Civil War Nov 9, 1861. A violent storm claimed
the ship and entire 33 man crew
discovered July 2013 by David Trotter and
Undersea Research Associates

Illustrations by Marine Artist Robert McGreevy

(ARTWORK COURTESY OF ROBERT McGREEVY)

passengers over the course of many desperate miles during the storm to help keep the vessel afloat. On November 19, 1861, a wheel house and other parts of a steamer came ashore above Forestville, while upper cabins and stanchions washed up near White Rock, and several captains reported floating debris off Pointe aux Barques. North winds must have blown consistently, because shipwreck flotsam/jetsam appeared as far south as Lexington, 70 miles from where the wreck is now known to sit! No body was ever found, but clues to this ship's loss might be discovered in a large debris field near the shipwreck.

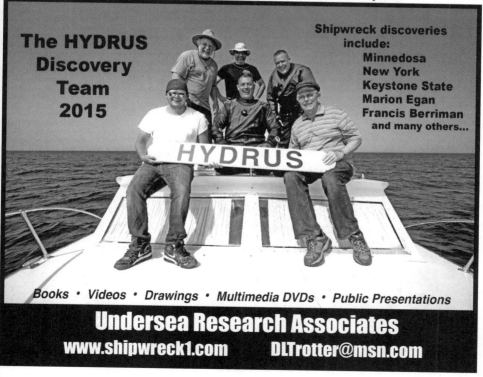

Q. *New York* (NEW)

DEPTH: 240 feet   **LEVEL: Technical**
COORDINATES:

LOCATION: About 25 miles northwest of Harrisville, Michigan, south of Alpena.

Dave Trotter and his team found this deep wreck in May 2012, considerably south of where it was reported to have gone down. The wooden steamer, *New York* (268′9″ x 36′9″ x 16′2″), built at Buffalo, New York, in 1879, the longest vessel on the lakes at that time and the first to be built with steel straps instead of wood arches, foundered in a severe storm on October 1, 1910. The ship's 14 crew members in two yawl boats were rescued by the passing steamer, *Mataafa*, which was towing the whaleback barge, *Alexander Holley,* at the time. The *New York* was enroute from Detroit to Owen Sound, Ontario, with 2,200 tons of coal; the ship and cargo were worth at least $75,000 (in 1910 dollars, of course!)

(Artwork courtesy of Robert McGreevy)

R. *Marion Egan* (NEW)

> **DEPTH: 200+ feet**   **LEVEL: Technical**
> **COORDINATES:**

LOCATION: Approximately 17 miles southeast of Thunder Bay Island, Michigan.

The 14-year-old, two-masted schooner, *Marion Egan* (134'8" x 25' x 10'9"), carrying coal from Erie, PA, towards Chicago, encountered the downbound, wheat-laden schooner, *E. R. Williams* (see *GLDG*, p. 485), at midnight on September 22-23, 1875. The two vessels collided nearly head-on, the *Egan* losing two sailors, one being the captain's son. Termed "an old vessel" by one newspaper, the *Egan*, valued at $8,500 but having received a low rating from the underwriters, carried no insurance. The *Williams'* bow was quite damaged, but the ship did not sink.

The **J. F. Card** *closely resembled the* **Marion Egan.** (Kohl-Forsberg Archives)

The *Marion Egan* sits upright, with both tall masts reaching high towards the surface.

S. *Hydrus* (NEW)

> **DEPTH: Just under 200 feet**   **LEVEL: Technical**
> **COORDINATES:**

LOCATION: In mid-lake, 32 miles off Alpena, Michigan, at Six Fathom Bank.

Definitely one of the most exciting finds in the past few years is Dave Trotter's discovery of the wreck of the *Hydrus* (416' x 50' x 28'), a steel freighter that was one of eight huge ships that disappeared on Lake Huron with the loss of all crews in the Great Storm of November 8-10, 1913, the worst storm in lakes history, the one that sank vessels with all hands in four of the five Great Lakes.

This leaves three more shipwrecks lost with all hands in that storm still to be located: the 550-foot-long *James Carruthers,* in 1913 a newly-launched Canadian freighter, in Lake Huron (indications suggest that it could lie in the deep Manitoulin Basin, in 400 to 500 feet of water); the *Leafield* in Lake Superior, and, in Lake Michigan, the *Plymouth.*

HYDRUS
Loa 436 x 50 x 28
Built 1903, American Sb Co. Lorian Ohio
The Hydrus and her sister ship Argus were lost during the
Great Storm of Nov 1913. The wreck of the Hydrus with
her cargo of iron ore was located in mid Lake Huron,
July 2015 by David Trotter and members of
his Undersea Research Associates.

Illustrations by Marine Artist Robert McGreevy

(Artwork courtesy of Robert McGreevy)

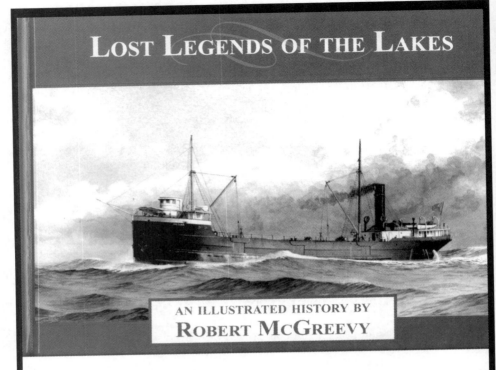

*The **Hydrus**, identified mainly by its dimensions and its iron ore cargo, is the second 1913 Storm wreck located by Dave Trotter; in 1985, his team found the **John A. McGean** (see GLDG, p. 318, 320). Of the seven Lake Huron 1913 Storm wrecks found, the **Hydrus** is only the second one that is not upside-down.* (Photos courtesy of Dave Trotter and Undersea Research Associates)

T. SHALLOW WRECKS NEAR ALPENA (NEW and UPDATES)

These shallow shipwrecks are presented in this book in geographical order following the Michigan shoreline from south to north. In a small boat on a good day, someone could visit many of these wrecks; most are visible from the surface. The NOAA Thunder Bay researchers have made great progress in identifying and publicizing the shipwrecks here!

NORTHERN LIGHT (NEW)

> **DEPTH: 2 feet   LEVEL: A wade or a snorkel**
> **COORDINATES: 44° 39.616′N/083° 17.209′W**

LOCATION: At the northwest end of the marina at Harrisville, Michigan.

Launched at Cleveland on March 25, 1858, this sidewheel steamer (209′4″ x 30′3″ x 19′), converted to a barge in 1875, stranded and became a total loss in August 1881.

DETROIT (NEW)

> **DEPTH: 10 feet   LEVEL: Novice**
> **COORDINATES: 44° 35.171′N/083° 18.686′W**

LOCATION: Between Greenbush and Harrisville, Michigan.

The steamer-turned-barge, *Detroit* (240′ x 34′8″ x 12′5″), built at Buffalo in 1859, was wrecked in a botched salvage on September 29, 1872. Frames and keelsons remain.

MARINE CITY (NEW)

> **DEPTH: 5 feet   LEVEL: Snorkel**
> **COORDINATES: 44° 46.237′N/083° 17.366′W**

LOCATION: Approximately one mile north of Sturgeon Point Lighthouse.

This popular paddle wheeler burned while southbound on August 29, 1880, with the tragic loss of about 20 lives. The tug, *Vulcan*, the fishing boat, *Grayling*, and the Sturgeon Point Life Saving crew rescued most of the 158 on board. Built at Marine City, Michigan, in 1866, the *Marine City* (192′1″ x 27′9″ x 10′18″) wreck site features boiler fragments, some machinery, and charred, lower wooden hull structure.

Left: *The **Marine City**, under way in this modern painting.* (Artwork courtesy of Robert McGreevy)

Right: *The flaming demise of the **Marine City**, as depicted by a contemporary artist.* (Kohl-Forsberg Archives)

CITY OF ALPENA (NEW)

> **DEPTH: 9 feet**   **LEVEL: Snorkel**
> **COORDINATES: 44° 47.268'N/083° 17.664'W**

LOCATION: About two miles north of Alcona, Michigan, and 1/2 mile off shore.
This 1874 tug boat (71'5" x 16'7" x 10'2") burned to the waterline on August 9, 1880. Ice and waves inverted the hull; the stern is intact, with the four-bladed propeller in place.

ISHPEMING (NEW)

> **DEPTH: 12 feet**   **LEVEL: Novice**
> **COORDINATES: 44° 48.589'N/083° 16.650'W**

LOCATION: This 1872 schooner broke up on Black River Island on Nov. 29, 1903. Most of the 3-masted *Ishpeming* (139'7" x 26'4" x 11'8") lies broken and scattered.

LORETTA (NEW)

> **DEPTH: 7 feet**   **LEVEL: Snorkel**
> **COORDINATES: 44° 48.903'N/083° 16.955'W**

LOCATION: At the Alger, Smith and Company dock, Black River, Michigan.
The steamer, *Loretta* (140' x 30'5" x 8'8"), built in 1892 at Sebewaing, Michigan, burned on Oct. 7, 1896. The bow and superstructure are gone, but the stern is complete.

ALVIN BUCKINGHAM (NEW)

> **DEPTH: 8 feet**   **LEVEL: Snorkel**
> **COORDINATES: 44° 50.459'N/083° 17.123'W**

LOCATION: Just off shore, one mile below Black River Island, Michigan.
This two-masted schooner, built at Perrysburg, Ohio, in 1853, sprang a leak during a storm on October 15, 1870, and it was run aground. Only the lower hull remains.

WILLIAM H. STEVENS -- NOT THE NELLIE GARNER! (UPDATE)

> **DEPTH: 10 feet**   **LEVEL: Novice**
> **COORDINATES: 44° 53.773'N/083° 19.653'W**

LOCATION: Just north of South Point, between Scarecrow and Bird Islands
Misidentified as the *Nellie Garner* (not *Gardner*; see *GLDG*, p. 325-326), this wreck has been identified as the 2-masted schooner, *William H. Stevens* (117' x 32'), which stranded and broke up here on November 15, 1863. The complete lower hull lies flattened.

JOHN F. WARNER (NEW)

> **DEPTH: 9 feet**   **LEVEL: Snorkel**
> **COORDINATES: 45° 03.050'N/083° 26.128'W**

LOCATION: This two-masted schooner lies near the mouth of Thunder Bay River. Built at Cleveland in 1855 and wrecked here in a storm on October 13, 1890, the *Warner* (124' x 26' x 11') spent years carrying lumber to England. The lower hull remains.

SHAMROCK (UPDATE -- GLDG2 p. 324)

> **DEPTH: 11 feet**   **LEVEL: Novice**
> **COORDINATES: 45° 03.077'N/083° 26.052'W**

HARVEY BISSELL (UPDATE -- *GLDG2* p. 324)

> **DEPTH: 15 feet**   **LEVEL: Novice**
> **COORDINATES: 45° 03.287′N/083° 25.603′W**

BAY CITY (NEW)

> **DEPTH: 11 feet**   **LEVEL: Novice**
> **COORDINATES: 45° 03.369′N/083° 25.605′W**

LOCATION: The ship was wrecked on the piers at the harbor of Alpena, Michigan. This brig-converted-to-a-schooner-barge (140′2″ x 29′ x 10′4″), built in 1857 at East Saginaw, Michigan, was abandoned after a gale pounded it onto the piers on November 29, 1902. The lower hull frames, keel, and some planking remain in place.

JAMES H. HALL (NEW)

> **DEPTH: 6 feet**   **LEVEL: Snorkel**
> **COORDINATES: 45° 03.444′N/083° 25.764′W**

LOCATION: In front of the Alpena Yacht Club, Alpena, Michigan.
The two-masted schooner, *James H. Hall* (91′7″ x 22′ x 7′), launched on November 17, 1884, sank with a full cargo of hardwood lumber after striking a stone crib on the south side of the Thunder Bay River on November 6, 1916. In 1989, a local historic preservation group refloated this wreckage to its current, safer location.

WILLIAM P. REND (UPDATE -- *GLDG2* p. 324)

> **DEPTH: 17 feet**   **LEVEL: Novice**
> **COORDINATES: 45° 03.742′N/083° 23.555′W**

HEART FAILURE (NEW)

> **DEPTH: 18 feet**   **LEVEL: Novice**
> **COORDINATES: 45° 03.726′N/083° 22.653′W**

LOCATION: This scattered wreckage is in Isaacson Bay, east of Alpena, Michigan.
This barge worked in the first decade of the 1900's on dredging, setting breakwalls, and other harbor improvements before being abandoned here in about 1910.

S. H. LATHROP (NEW)

> **DEPTH: 3 to 7 feet**   **LEVEL: Snorkel**
> **COORDINATES: 45.050571N/-83.358443W**

LOCATION: This "Gilchrist Fleet" lies in Isaacson Bay, off Whitefish Point.
Three ships were abandoned by F. W. Gilchrist. On May 14, 1902, the 1856 schooner barge, *S. H. Lathrop* (137′ x 26′1″ x 10′3″), became the first to be stripped and left here.

LIGHT GUARD (NEW)

This two-masted schooner (142′6″ x 26′6″ x 10′8″), built in 1866 at Detroit, after a long career with numerous strandings and collisions, was abandoned on July 22, 1903.

KNIGHT TEMPLAR (NEW)

Launched at Oswego, New York, in 1865, this schooner-barge (136′ x 26′2″ x 11′6″) was abandoned on July 25, 1903.

HALTINER BARGE (NEW)

> **DEPTH: 13 feet**   **LEVEL: Novice**
> **COORDINATES: 45° 02.091′N/083° 19.595′W**

LOCATION: Two miles west of the southeast tip of North Point, 1/2 mile off shore.
This work vessel, wrecked or abandoned in about 1929, likely did dredging and similar marine work. It measures 80 feet long, with a beam of 33 feet.

EMPIRE STATE (NEW)

> **DEPTH: 12 feet**   **LEVEL: Novice**
> **COORDINATES: 44° 00.853′N/083° 15.377′W**

LOCATION: Two miles west of the southeast tip of North Point, 1/2 mile off shore.
Built by famous Canadian shipbuilder, Louis Shickluna, at St. Catharines, Canada West (Ontario), in 1862, this schooner (136′5″ x 25′8″ x 12′7″) was storm-wrecked, breaking in two, on November 8, 1877, with its iron ore cargo. The rudder lies to the west.

MONOHANSETT (UPDATE -- *GLDG2* p. 328)

> **DEPTH: 18 feet**   **LEVEL: Novice**
> **COORDINATES: 45° 01.996′N/083° 11.988′W**

MAID OF THE MIST (UPDATE -- *GLDG2* p. 328)

> **DEPTH: 7 feet**   **LEVEL: Snorkel**
> **COORDINATES: 45° 06.971′N/083° 19.044′W**

NEW ORLEANS (UPDATE -- *GLDG2* p. 328)

> **DEPTH: 15 feet**   **LEVEL: Novice**
> **COORDINATES: 45° 02.579′N/083° 14.425′W**

LOCATION: Off Sugar Island, Michigan.
The sidewheel steamer, *New Orleans* (185′4″ x 26′8″ x 12′10″), is the oldest wreck in the Thunder Bay NOAA Sanctuary. Built in 1838 in Detroit as the *Vermillion*, and rebuilt/renamed after a damaging fire in 1842, it stranded on a reef in fog on June 13, 1849. Everyone was safely transferred to Thunder Bay Island, but nature destroyed the ship.

(ARTWORK COURTESY OF ROBERT MCGREEVY)

'SPUD BARGE' (NEW)

> **DEPTH: 1 foot/above water**   **LEVEL: A wade**
> **COORDINATES: 45° 02.194′N/083° 16.067′W**

LOCATION: This wreckage lies off the end of North Point, near Alpena, Michigan.
Very little is known about this wooden barge, other than the fact that it served as a dock for the U. S. Coast Guard in the late 1930's, but is now broken and scattered.

GALENA (UPDATE -- *GLDG2* p. 327)

> **DEPTH: 16 feet**   **LEVEL: Novice**
> **COORDINATES: 45° 00.460′N/083° 14.990′W**

B. W. BLANCHARD (UPDATE -- *GLDG2* p. 327)

> **DEPTH: 9 feet   LEVEL: Snorkel**
> **COORDINATES: 45° 01.271'N/083° 15.763'W**

The steamer, *B. W. Blanchard* (212'3" x 32'4" x 12'2"), was towing the barges, *John T. Johnson* (171' x 31' x 10'5") and *John Kilderhouse,* when a blinding snowstorm caused them to run aground on November 29, 1904. The *Kilderhouse* was recovered, but the others' wreckage lies broken and intermixed.

Left: *The wrecked* **Blanchard.** (KOHL-FORSBERG ARCHIVES)

JOHN T. JOHNSON (UPDATE -- *GLDG2* p. 327)

> **DEPTH: 7 feet   LEVEL: Snorkel**
> **COORDINATES: 45° 01.299'N/083° 15.721'W**

BENJAMIN FRANKLIN (NEW)

> **DEPTH: 15 feet   LEVEL: Novice**
> **COORDINATES: 45° 01.934'N/083° 11.529'W**

LOCATION: Broken up and scattered just off Thunder Bay Island, near Alpena, MI.
The sidewheel steamer, *Benjamin Franklin* (135' x 19'10" x 9'), built in 1842 at Buffalo, New York, stranded on October 8, 1850, becoming a total wreck. No lives were lost.

WILLIAM MAXWELL (NEW)

> **DEPTH: 12 feet   LEVEL: Novice**
> **COORDINATES: 45° 01.990'N/083° 11.493'W**

LOCATION: This wreck lies off the southeast end of Thunder Bay Island, MI.
The fish tug, *William Maxwell* (66'7" x 17' x 6'9"), was wrecked in a storm on September 19, 1908. Only stern deadwood and broken propeller and shaft remain of this ship.

PORTSMOUTH (UPDATE -- *GLDG2* p. 330)

> **DEPTH: 8 feet   LEVEL: Snorkel**
> **COORDINATES: 45° 11.870'N/083° 20.030'W**

PORTLAND (NEW)

> **DEPTH: 6 feet   LEVEL: Snorkel**
> **COORDINATES: 45° 14.929'N/083° 24.450'W**

LOCATION: At Bell Bay, near Presque Isle, Michigan.
The 1863, two-masted schooner, *Portland* (150' x 24'), was wrecked with a cargo of salt on Oct. 17, 1877. The starboard side and bilge remain, with other pieces scattered.

ALBANY (NEW)

> **DEPTH: 5 feet   LEVEL: Snorkel**
> **COORDINATES: 45° 19.396'N/083° 27.508'W**

LOCATION: This wooden, lower hull wreckage lies near Presque Isle, Michigan.
The 1846, Detroit-built steamer, *Albany* (202' x 29' x 11'8"), sought harbor shelter on November 26, 1853, but was stranded and wrecked. Machinery was salvaged in 1854.

U. MARY WOOLSON (NEW)

> **DEPTH: 180 feet**   **LEVEL: Technical**
> **COORDINATES:**

Scuba divers have reportedly been exploring the 1888 schooner-barge, *Mary Woolson* (179'1" x 34'8" x 13'2"), which sank on July 18, 1920, after colliding with her towing steamer, the *Charles H. Bradley*, about 8 miles northeast of Sturgeon Point, Michigan.

V. CORSICAN (NEW)

> **DEPTH: 160 feet**   **LEVEL: Technical**
> **COORDINATES: 44° 54.760'N/083° 03.300'W**

LOCATION: This 1862 ship sank off Thunder Bay Island, near Alpena, Michigan.

The two-masted schooner, *Corsican* (112'4" x 25'4" x 10'), built at Olcott, NY, sank in a collision with the steamer, *Corsica*, on June 2, 1893, with the loss of all six hands.

W. M. F. MERRICK (NEW)

> **DEPTH: 310 feet**   **LEVEL: Technical**
> **COORDINATES:**

LOCATION: This 1863, two-masted schooner lies off Presque Isle, Michigan.

The *M. F. Merrick* was run down by the steamer, *R. P. Ranney,* in dense fog on May 17, 1889, sinking immediately with five lives lost. The *Merrick* was built in Clayton, NY.

Left and right: *Inside the* **M. F. Merrick,** *showing collision damage at left.*
(PHOTOS BY JOHN JANZEN)

Below: *John Scoles approaches the* **Merrick's** *stern, where the ship's wheel remains in place.*
(PHOTOS BY JOHN JANZEN)

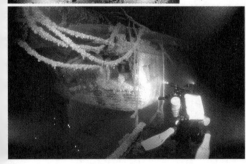

MESSENGER (NEW)   (Not on the Map,...But Better LATE Than NEVER!)

> **DEPTH: 194 feet**   **LEVEL: Technical**
> **COORDINATES: 45° 24.613'N/083° 45.983'W**

LOCATION: In deep water approximately four miles off Rogers City, Michigan.

The steam barge, *Messenger* (136'2" x 29'2" x 9'4"), built at Cleveland in 1866, was cut free from a dock when it caught on fire at Rogers City on November 11, 1890, and it drifted far out into the lake before sinking.

The upright hull displays the engine, anchors, rudder, and propeller.

X. *ETRURIA* (NEW)

> **DEPTH: 310 feet**   **LEVEL: Technical**
> **COORDINATES:**

LOCATION: Approximately 10 miles off Presque Isle, Michigan.

Launched at West Bay City, Michigan, in 1902, the steel freighter, *Etruria* (414' x 50' x 24'), sank in a collision with the 505-foot-long *Amasa Stone* in fog on June 18, 1905, while enroute with coal from Toledo, Ohio, to Superior, Wisconsin. All crew members were rescued by the steamer *Maritana*. Like the *M. F. Merrick,* the *Etruria* was found in July, 2011, by five high school students working with the Thunder Bay National Marine Sanctuary during "Project Shiphunt."

Right: *The steamer,* **Etruria.** (KOHL-FORSBERG ARCHIVES)   **Below, left:** *The upside-down wreck.*   (PHOTO BY BECKY KAGAN SCHOTT)
Below, right: *Sue Smith inside the wreck.*   (PHOTO BY JOHN JANZEN)

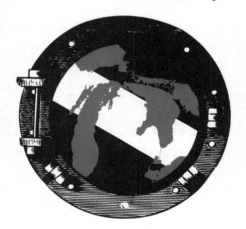

Y. Shallow Wrecks near Rogers City (NEW and UPDATES)

Numerous shipwrecks lie between Forty Mile Point and Presque Isle, Michigan:

Racer (NEW)

DEPTH: 11 feet	LEVEL: Novice
COORDINATES: 45° 34.900′N/084° 08.919′W	

Built at Buffalo in 1856, this two-masted brig (130′ x 28′3″ x 11′), hauling iron ore, was blown ashore in a violent storm on November 17, 1869. The lower hull lies intact.

Reindeer (NEW)

DEPTH: 16 feet	LEVEL: Novice
COORDINATES: 45° 24.620′N/083° 45.986′W	

Built at Clayton, NY, in 1860, this schooner (111′ x 24′4″ x 10′7″) was storm-destroyed while loading at a dock on October 6, 1895. The lower, double-framed hull remains.

L. M. Mason (NEW)

DEPTH: 5 to 17 feet	LEVEL: Novice
COORDINATES: 45° 20.776′N/083° 29.604′W	

Thunder Bay National Marine Sanctuary has cautiously identified the wreck formerly known as the "North Bay wreck" as likely being the two-masted schooner, *L. M. Mason* (125′ x 26′ x 11′), built at Port Huron in 1853 and lost in a storm with its grain cargo on October 22, 1861, with no lives lost. Eight other schooners were blown ashore in this area in this same storm, but only two of those (*L. M. Nelson* and *Dardanelles*) became total losses. The intact port side of the *L. M. Mason* lies in the deepest part.

Duncan City (UPDATE -- *GLDG2* p. 342)

DEPTH: 15 feet	LEVEL: Novice
COORDINATES: 45° 24.787′N/083° 45.733′W	

W. G. Mason (UPDATE -- *GLDG2* p. 342)

DEPTH: 13 feet	LEVEL: Novice
COORDINATES: 45° 24.639′N/083° 44.833′W	

American Union (UPDATE -- *GLDG2* p. 342)

DEPTH: 10 feet	LEVEL: Novice
COORDINATES: 45° 21.412′N/083° 35.368′W	

Joseph S. Fay (UPDATE -- *GLDG2* p. 338)

DEPTH: 17 feet	LEVEL: Novice
COORDINATES: 45° 29.317′N/083° 54.600′W	

Z. *Hope* (NEW)

LOCATION: In Detour Passage on a heading to Fort St. Joseph.

The British ship, H.M.S. *Hope,* one of the earliest vessels to sail on Lake Huron, stranded and broke up on October 4, 1805, while on a resupply mission from Fort Malden (Amherstburg) to Fort St. Joseph in Upper Canada (presentday Ontario). One life was lost. The ship's cargo and all nautical components were recovered shortly thereafter. Today, only huge fragments of frame and keel remain very broken and scattered over a large area.

1. SWEETHEART   (UPDATE -- *GLDG2* p. 222)

DEPTH: 30 feet   LEVEL: Novice-Intermediate
COORDINATES: 42° 36' 55"N/082° 30' 59"W

The two-masted schooner-barge, *Sweetheart* (175'4" x 32'6" x 13'4"), built at Detroit in 1867, burned and sank on July 6, 1913, 3.25 miles NNE of the St. Clair River's mouth.

2. GHOST FLEET WRECK -- *SACHEM* (UPDATE -- *GLDG2* p. 222-224)

DEPTH: To 68 feet   LEVEL: Advanced
COORDINATES: 43° 09.90'N/082° 18.36'W

A team led by Jim Stayer and Cris Kohl in 1993 found and identified several ship-wrecks in Lake Huron that had mysteriously disappeared from the St. Clair River.

Image Credits

Left: PHOTO BY CRIS KOHL.

Right: COURTESY OF THE MOORE MUSEUM, MOORETOWN, ON.

Left: *Burned beams and scorched hanging knees helped us identify the* **Sachem** *in 1993.*
Right: *The wreck in this "mystery photo," long unidentified, is the* **Province,** *a 1923 shipwreck that became part of the Ghost Fleet of the St. Clair River.*

3. WEXFORD   (UPDATE -- *GLDG2* p. 224-225)

DEPTH: 62 to 75 feet   LEVEL: Advanced
COORDINATES: 43° 24.080'N/081° 53.322'W

Found several miles off Grand Bend, Ontario, this steel freighter is one of eight that disappeared with all hands in lower Lake Huron in the Great Storm of 1913.

Above, left: *A 1913 Storm victim, the steamer,* **Wexford.**   (COURTESY OF ARTIST ROBERT MCGREEVY)
Above, right: *Roy Pickering explores hatches on the deck of the* **Wexford.**   (PHOTO BY CRIS KOHL)

Left: *A fallen set of steps and other debris inside the* **Wexford.**

Right: *Roy Pickering shines his light on an artifact inside the* **Wexford.**

(PHOTOS BY CRIS KOHL)

4. GENERAL HUNTER (UPDATE -- *GLDG2* p. 230)

The brig, *General Hunter* (54′ x 18′ x 8′), nearly identical to the *Hope* (see p. 111), was built at Amherstburg, Upper Canada (later Ontario) in 1806, following the loss of the *Hope*. The *General Hunter* was captured by U.S. forces in the Battle of Lake Erie in 1813 during the War of 1812. Sold to private interests after the war, the ship's name was shortened to *Hunter*. It stranded and wrecked on a Lake Huron wilderness shoreline in a storm on August 19, 1816, the eight crew and two passengers taking a week to reach Detroit in their yawl boat. In 2001, shifting sands uncovered part of the *Hunter* on a busy beach at Southampton, Ontario. Archaeologists uncovered and surveyed the wreck in 2004-2005, then buried it again for preservation. A small work barge (from the 1870's?) also lies under the sand, almost touching, on the north side of the *Hunter*. Artifacts, such as a cannon, from the *Hunter* are displayed at Southampton's Bruce County Museum and Cultural Centre.

NOTE: On the map of Tobermory shipwrecks on page 233 of *GLDG2*, the wrecks of "11. *Philo Scoville*" and "12. *Newaygo*" should be switched to read "11. *Newaygo*" and "12. *Philo Scoville*."

5. SWEEPSTAKES (UPDATE -- *GLDG2* p. 236)

> **DEPTH: 8 to 20 feet   LEVEL: Novice**
> **COORDINATES: 45° 15.315′ N/081° 40.855′ W**
> **COORDINATES: 45.255268 N/-81.680901 W**

LOCATION: At the end of Big Tub Harbour, Tobermory, Ontario.

Left: *The schooner,* **Sweepstakes,** *is the most visited shipwreck in the Great Lakes; many tour boats, kayakers, and scuba divers appear daily from June to September.* (PHOTO BY CRIS KOHL)
Right: *The wreck of the* **City of Grand Rapids** *lies near the* **Sweepstakes.** (PHOTO BY CRIS KOHL)

6. CITY OF GRAND RAPIDS (UPDATE -- *GLDG2* p. 236-237)

> **DEPTH: To 15 feet   LEVEL: Novice**
> **COORDINATES: 45° 15.295′ N/081° 40.845′ W**
> **COORDINATES: 45.254916 N/-81.680766 W**

7. JOHN WALTERS (UPDATE -- *GLDG2* p. 241)

> **DEPTH: To 15 feet   LEVEL: Novice**
> **COORDINATES: 45° 15.595′ N/081° 42.185′ W**
> **COORDINATES: 45.259984 N/-81.703106 W**

8. JAMES C. KING (UPDATE -- *GLDG2* p. 244)

> **DEPTH: 22 to 93 feet   LEVEL: Intermediate-Advanced**
> **COORDINATES: 45.267534 N/-81.708282 W**

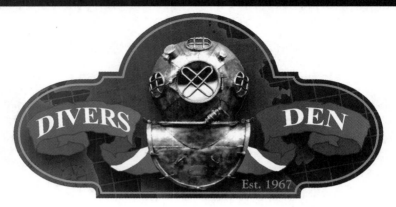

9. *ARABIA* (UPDATE -- *GLDG2* p. 246, 248)

> **DEPTH: 97 to 117 feet   LEVEL: Advanced**
> **COORDINATES: 45° 18.713′ N/081° 40.444′ W**

LOCATION: Off the northeast side of Echo Island, north of Tobermory, Ontario.

The *Arabia* (1853-1884) was converted from a barque rig to a schooner rig in 1876. One fact generally swept under the carpet by Chicago historians is that the *Arabia*, in 1855, became the very first ship to reach Chicago with a cargo of goods it brought over directly from England. The most detailed account of the *Arabia* ever published appeared as a two-part article in *Wreck Diving Magazine,* issues #27 and #28, in 2012.

The schooner, **Arabia,** *lost in a storm in 1884, is an amazingly intact shipwreck at Tobermory, but it is also one of the deeper ones. While no lives were lost in the sinking, ten scuba divers have died on this wreck since 1971 -- more than on any other Great Lakes shipwreck!* (PHOTOS BY CRIS KOHL)

10. *FOREST CITY* (UPDATE -- *GLDG2* p. 248-249)

> **DEPTH: 60 to 150 feet   LEVEL: Advanced to Technical**
> **COORDINATES: 45° 18.909′N/081° 33.422′W**

Left: *The wrecked* **Forest City.** (KOHL-FORSBERG ARCHIVES)
Below: *The deep stern of the* **Forest City,** *which lies on a steep slope in 60 to 150 feet of water.* (PHOTO BY WARREN LO)

11. *NIAGARA II* (UPDATE -- *GLDG2* p. 254)

DEPTH: 48 to 98 feet   LEVEL: Intermediate-Advanced
COORDINATES: 45° 15.050′N/081° 36.032′W

LOCATION: This wreck lies several miles east of Tobermory, Ontario.

The 182-foot-long steel freighter, *Niagara II*, named the *Rideaulite* when launched in England in 1930, was purposely sunk to create a new shipwreck dive site in May 1999.

Left: *The* Niagara II *in the 1980's.* (KOHL-FORSBERG ARCHIVES) **Other photos:** *Divers, including Joan Forsberg, explore many of the interesting parts of the* Niagara II.   (PHOTOS BY CRIS KOHL)

12. *LADY DUFFERIN* (UPDATE -- *GLDG2* p. 255)

DEPTH: From 40 to 200+ feet   LEVEL: All levels to Technical
COORDINATES:

LOCATION: Many pieces of this broken wreck run down a long, steep slope about 1.5 miles east of Little Cove, just past Driftwood Cove. Built in 1872 at Port Burwell, Ontario, this three-masted schooner (135′ x 23′7″ x 11′10″) was wrecked on October 24, 1886.

13a. *SAN JACINTO* (UPDATE -- *GLDG2* p. 256)

DEPTH: To 80 feet   LEVEL: Advanced
COORDINATES: 45° 24.273′N/081° 47.722′W

LOCATION: This schooner, lost in 1881, lies NW of Yeo Island, north of Tobermory.

Left: *Its sides collapsed, the* San Jacinto's *deck dropped to the bottom of the hull.*

Right: *Windlass and anchor chain on the* San Jacinto.

(PHOTOS BY WARREN LO)

13b. CITY OF CLEVELAND (UPDATE -- *GLDG2* p. 280-281)

> **DEPTH: 10 to 30 feet   LEVEL: Novice**
> **COORDINATES: 45.464131 N/-81.850074 W**

LOCATION: While only nine miles from South Baymouth on Manitoulin Island, the scuba charter boats leave from Tobermory, 18 miles away. This 256-foot-long, wooden steamer (the largest shipwreck in the Tobermory area!), lying in a maximum of only 30 feet of water, is an absolutely amazing shipwreck site and dive experience, despite being difficult to reach.

Left: *The* **City of Cleveland's** *huge propeller.*   (PHOTO BY ANDY MORRISON)

14. MICHIGAN (UPDATE -- *GLDG2* p. 280)

> **DEPTH: To 25 feet   LEVEL: Novice**
> **COORDINATES: 45.530601 N/-81.710402 W**

LOCATION: This abandoned schooner lies in Rattlesnake Harbour, Ontario.

15. MARY WARD (UPDATE -- *GLDG2* p. 260)

> **DEPTH: To 10 feet   LEVEL: Novice**
> **COORDINATES: 44° 33.665' N/080° 19.714' W**
> **COORDINATES: 44.56086 N/-80.32844 W**

LOCATION: The many rocky reefs could make reaching this site confusing. But this steamship wreck from 1872 is visible from the surface. In recent years, a couple of Collingwood boats have been taking families on snorkel trips to this interesting wreckage.

Left: *A historic marker in Craigleith Provincial Park relates the tale of the* **Mary Ward** *shipwreck.*

Right: *Only the keel and lower frames remain of the* **Ward's** *hull.*

Below, left and right: *Joan Forsberg explores the stern area, which includes its large propeller.*

(PHOTOS BY CRIS KOHL)

16. *EMMA* (UPDATE -- *GLDG2* p. 270-271)

> **DEPTH: 4 to 20 feet   LEVEL: Novice**
> **COORDINATES: 45.234161 N/-80.224374 W**

LOCATION: In the midst of the Boyd Group of islands, SW of Parry Sound, ON.

Left: *The beautiful excursion steamer,* Emma, *built in 1894, burned at this remote site on July 4, 1912.*   (KOHL-FORSBERG ARCHIVES)
Below: *The broken hull of the* Emma, *mostly in wooden slabs, shows signs of the fire that destroyed this popular ship.*   (PHOTOS BY CRIS KOHL)

17. *ATLANTIC* (UPDATE -- *GLDG2* p. 273)

> **DEPTH: 6 to 50 feet   LEVEL: Novice-Intermediate**
> **COORDINATES: 45° 20.036′ N/080° 15.652′ W**
> **COORDINATES: 45.33380 N/-80.26076 W**

LOCATION: This wreck lies just north of Spruce Island, west of Parry Sound, ON.

Steamer Atlantic Burned.

The steamer Atlantic was burned to the water's edge about nine o'clock on Tuesday morning about fourteen miles from Parry Sound. The crew escaped in the boats and reached Parry Sound in safety although a heavy gale was blowing. The Atlantic was on a special trip from Collingwood to Byng Inlet, part of her cargo consisting of 140 barrels of coal oil and five tons of hay. The origin of the fire is not yet stated but in a short time after it broke out the whole

Above, left: *The steamer,* Atlantic, *and a news report of its demise.*   (KOHL-FORSBERG ARCHIVES)
Above, right: *The rudder; Joan Forsberg heads down the sloping wreck.*   (PHOTOS BY CRIS KOHL)

18. JANE MCLEOD   (UPDATE -- *GLDG2* p. 274)

DEPTH: 20 to 25 feet   LEVEL: Novice
COORDINATES: 45.354281 N/-80.310065 W

LOCATION: The wreck lies off the rocky, southwest part of McLeod Island, ON.

When a wooden schooner (left) such as the Jane McLeod is wrecked on a rocky shoreline, the results (right) can be devastating for the structural integrity of the hull. Nonetheless, the wreck is fascinating! (LEFT: KOHL-FORSBERG ARCHIVES. PHOTO ON RIGHT BY CRIS KOHL)

19. SEATTLE   (UPDATE -- *GLDG2* p. 275-276)

DEPTH: 15 to 25+ feet   LEVEL: Novice-Intermediate
COORDINATES: 45.395788 N/-80.453023 W

LOCATION: In the Mink Islands, just west of Green Island, well off shore, Ontario.

20. METAMORA   (UPDATE -- *GLDG2* p. 276)

DEPTH: To 15 feet   LEVEL: Novice
COORDINATES: 45.530596 N/-80.409084 W

LOCATION: In the Shawanaga Inlet, 700 feet west of Turning Island, Ontario.

21. *INDIA* (UPDATE -- *GLDG2* p. 281)

DEPTH: 20 to 30 feet   LEVEL: Novice
COORDINATES: 45.973042 N/-81.762310 W

LOCATION: This steamer, burned in 1928, lies 8 miles east of Little Current, ON.

22. *HIAWATHA* (UPDATE -- *GLDG2* p. 282)

DEPTH: 5 to 30 feet   LEVEL: Novice
COORDINATES: 45.987562 N/-81.934171 W

23. *B. B. BUCKHOUT* (UPDATE -- *GLDG2* p. 282)

DEPTH: To 40 feet   LEVEL: Novice-Intermediate
COORDINATES: 45.990790 N/-81.982245 W

LOCATION: This schooner-barge, wrecked in 1912, lies just west of Narrow Island.

24. *EMMA E. THOMPSON* (UPDATE -- *GLDG2* p. 283-284)

DEPTH: To 30 feet   LEVEL: Novice
COORDINATES: 46° 04' 05.7610"N/082° 19' 27.0010"W
COORDINATES: 46.06769 N/-82.31699 W

LOCATION: This steamer, burned in 1914, lies off the northeast side of Innes Island.

25. *ALBERTA M.* (UPDATE -- *GLDG2* p. 285)

DEPTH: 2 to 15 feet   LEVEL: Novice
COORDINATES: 45.915617 N/-83.089330 W

26. *BURLINGTON* (UPDATE -- *GLDG2* p. 286-287)

DEPTH: To 30 feet   LEVEL: Novice
COORDINATES: 45.892910 N/-83.224493 W

LOCATION: In a bay just to the north of Mississagi Straits Lighthouse.

27. *JOYLAND* (UPDATE -- *GLDG2* p. 287-288)

DEPTH: To 18 feet   LEVEL: Novice
COORDINATES: 45.823074 N/-82.940375 W

LOCATION: This land-visible wreck is off the SE shore of Burnt Island Harbour.

The Joyland *wreckage offers Joan Forsberg many interesting sights.* (PHOTOS BY CRIS KOHL)

28. ROME   (UPDATE -- *GLDG2* p. 290)

> **DEPTH: 15 feet   LEVEL: Novice**
> **COORDINATES: 46.086614′N/-84.012111′W**

29. SPORT   (UPDATE -- *GLDG2* p. 304)

LOCATION: Three miles due east of Lexington, Michigan.

The historic, 1874 tug, *Sport,* the first built using composite construction (steel frame with wood overlays), sank in severe weather on December 13, 1920. Why was the tug out there so late in the season and in bad weather? It was going north from Port Huron to pick up an old barge the owner had just acquired! It was definitely not worth the effort.

Left: The Sport. (COURTESY OF ARTIST ROBERT McGREEVY) **Right and below:** *The* Sport's *wheel and whistle.* (PHOTOS BY JOYCE HAYWARD)

30. CHARLES A. STREET (UPDATE -- *GLDG2* p. 297)

> **DEPTH: 5 to 15 feet   LEVEL: Novice**
> **COORDINATES: 43° 35.6990′ N/082° 35.4449′ W**

This wooden steamer burned, stranded and broke up on July 20, 1908.

31. NEW YORK (UPDATE -- *GLDG2* p. 297)

> **DEPTH: 95 to 118 feet   LEVEL: Advanced**
> **COORDINATES: 43° 36.2468′ N/082° 28.2575′ W**

LOCATION: This wreck, the wooden steam-barge, *New York,* which foundered with the loss of one life on October 14, 1876, lies 12.3 miles north-northeast of Port Sanilac, Michigan.

This is the ship that collided with the small schooner named the *Dawn* on Lake Erie, sending that vessel to the bottom on Oct. 21, 1859. (see p. 69 of this book for that shipwreck).

Joan Forsberg follows the upright starboard bracing arch on the New York. (PHOTO BY CRIS KOHL)

32. COL. A. B. WILLIAMS (UPDATE -- *GLDG2* p. 296)

> **DEPTH: 73 to 84 feet   LEVEL: Advanced**
> **COORDINATES: 43° 36.7430′ N/082° 30.8087′ W**

This 110-foot-long schooner and her coal cargo foundered in an 1864 storm.

33. GLENORCHY (UPDATE -- *GLDG2* p. 322)

> **DEPTH: 100 to 120 feet   LEVEL: Advanced/Technical**
> **COORDINATES: 43° 48.580′N/082° 31.792′W**

This Canadian ship, lying about 10 miles east-southeast of Harbor Beach, Michigan, sank in a collision with another steel freighter, the *Leonard B. Miller,* on October 29, 1924, reportedly caused by smoke on the water, a result of forest fires, fortunately with no lives lost. This big wreck lies upside-down, with limited openings offering access. NOTE: Penetration diving requires specialized training and preparation.

Left: *When the propeller hovers this far above the bottom of the lake, then the shipwreck is probably upside-down.*

Right: *Shipwreck penetration requires specialized, technical training and intense preparations. The wreck of the* **Glenorchy** *offers a few entry and exit places for the specially trained.*

(PHOTOS BY VLADA DEKINA)

34. *ANNA DOBBINS* (UPDATE -- *GLDG2* p. 316)

> **DEPTH: To 90 feet   LEVEL: Advanced**
> **COORDINATES: 44° 08.111′N/082° 51.277′W**

The 102-foot-long, wooden tug, **Anna Dobbins,** *built at Buffalo, New York, in 1862, foundered on September 24, 1886. No lives were lost.*

(ARTWORK COURTESY OF ROBERT MCGREEVY)

35. *TROY* (UPDATE -- *GLDG2* p. 313-314)

> **DEPTH: To 97 feet   LEVEL: Advanced**
> **COORDINATES: 44° 08.655′N/083° 01.939′W**

Built in 1849 at Cleveland, the wooden steamer, *Troy* (163′ x 21′1″ x 10′2″), foundered in heavy seas on October 24, 1859, with 18 of 26 lost.

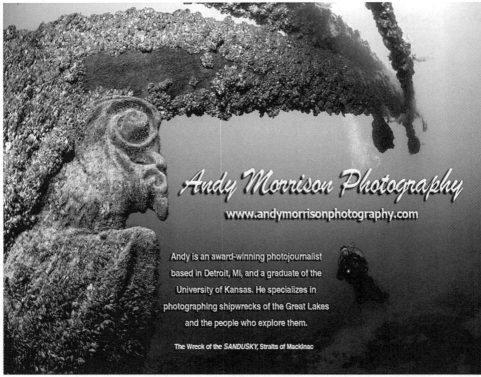

36. DETROIT   (UPDATE -- *GLDG2* p. 318)

> **DEPTH: To 180 feet   LEVEL: Technical**
> **COORDINATES: 44° 13.611′N/082° 45.436′W**

LOCATION: This 1846 sidewheel steamer, located 10 miles north of Grindstone City, Michigan, sank in a collision with a sailing ship on the foggy night of May 25, 1854.

Right: *One of the Detroit's zebra-mussel-encrusted paddlewheels occupies the foreground, while the walking beam of the steam engine is silhouetted in the background.* (PHOTO BY ANDY MORRISON)

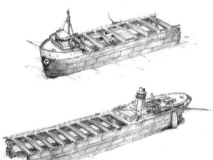

Left: *The wreck of the steamer,* **Detroit.**
(ARTWORK COURTESY OF ROBERT MCGREEVY)

37. DANIEL J. MORRELL   (UPDATE -- *GLDG2* p. 319)

> **DEPTH: To 218 feet   LEVEL: Technical**
> **COORDINATES: See *GLDG2*, p. 319, for both bow and stern #'s**

One of the last of the modern-era maritime tragedies on the lakes, this 60-year-old, 600-foot-long, steel ship broke in half in a storm on November 29, 1966, with the stern half steaming on for another five miles before sinking! Of the 29 crew, there was only one survivor, rescued from a raft after drifting on it for 36 hours (see more information about sole survivor Dennis Hale on page 208). The U.S. Coast Guard almost immediately located the stern half; the team of Larry Coplin, Dave Trotter, and others found the bow half in 1979.

Left: *The two halves of the wrecked* **Daniel J. Morrell.** (COURTESY OF THE ARTIST, ROBERT MCGREEVY)
Below row: *Divers examine the superstructure, an unused lifeboat, and inside the galley of the* **Daniel J. Morrell.** (PHOTOS BY JITKA HANAKOVA)

38. *ARGUS* (UPDATE -- *GLDG2* p. 318)

> **DEPTH: To 220 feet**   **LEVEL: Technical**
> **COORDINATES:**

Lost with all hands in the Great Storm of 1913, this 416-foot-long, steel freighter was found by shipwreck hunter Dick Race in 1972.

39. *MINNEDOSA* (UPDATE -- *GLDG2* p. 312)

> **DEPTH: To 210 feet**   **LEVEL: Technical**
> **COORDINATES:**

This four-masted-schooner-turned-into-towbarge, the largest sailing vessel ever built on the Canadian side of the Great Lakes, sank with all hands in a storm on Oct. 20, 1905.

Left: *The Minnedosa's bowsprit and figurehead were impressive.*   (KOHL-FORSBERG ARCHIVES)
Middle and right: *Divers study the Minnedosa's wheel and a lifeboat.*   (PHOTOS BY VLADA DEKINA)

40. *W. C. FRANZ* (UPDATE -- *GLDG2* p. 310)

> **DEPTH: 200 to 230 feet**   **LEVEL: Technical**
> **COORDINATES: 44° 38.862′N/082° 54.379′W**

NOAA Thunder Bay Sanctuary researchers located this shipwreck independently (after it had been found by Dave Trotter) and publicized its location. This 346-foot-long, steel freighter sank after a collision with another ship on Nov. 21, 1934, with four lives lost.

 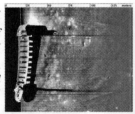

Left: *A Pesha photo of the W. C. Franz.* (KOHL-FORSBERG ARCHIVES)
Right: *Sidescan sonar image of the W. C. Franz.* (COURTESY OF NOAA THUNDER BAY SANCTUARY)
Below: *Divers examine the superstructure and the ship's wheel on the W. C. Franz.* (PHOTOS BY JITKA HANAKOVA)

42. SPORT DIVING WRECKS: ALPENA (UPDATES)

These updated shipwrecks are in the same order in which they appear in the book, *The Great Lakes Diving Guide,* 2d Edition (2008). The workers at the NOAA Thunder Bay Sanctuary have done a fantastic job of documenting and publicizing all of the shipwrecks -- whether shallow, sport diving range, or deep -- in the Alpena, Michigan, area, and providing location coordinates for most of them (excluding a few very deep, recent discoveries).

OSCAR T. FLINT (UPDATE -- *GLDG2* p. 324-325)

DEPTH: 28 to 36 feet	LEVEL: Novice
COORDINATES: 45° 01.568′N/083° 20.843′W	

This wooden steamer burned to a total loss near Alpena on November 25, 1909.

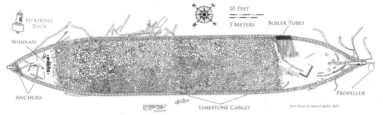

Left: Layout drawing of the wreck of the Oscar T. Flint. (COURTESY OF NOAA THUNDER BAY SANCTUARY)

BARGE NO. 1 (UPDATE -- *GLDG2* p. 325)

DEPTH: 35 to 45 feet	LEVEL: Intermediate
COORDINATES: 45° 00.919′N/083° 18.238′W	

This 310-foot-long wooden barge was storm-wrecked on November 8, 1918.

MONTANA   (UPDATE -- *GLDG2* p. 326)

**DEPTH: 33 to 74 feet   LEVEL: Intermediate-Advanced
COORDINATES: 44° 59.025′N/083° 16.013′W**

This 236-foot, wooden steamer burned, with no lives lost, on September 7, 1914.

GRECIAN   (UPDATE -- *GLDG2* p. 326-327)

**DEPTH: 70 to 105 feet   LEVEL: Advanced
COORDINATES: 44° 58.099′N/083° 11.991′W**

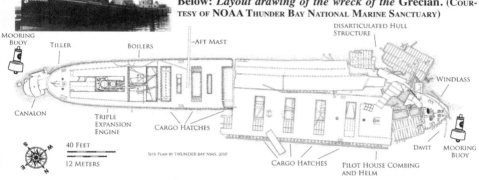

This 296-foot-long, steel freighter sank while under tow, heading towards repairs, on June 15, 1906. No lives were lost, but subsequent salvage efforts failed.

Left: *The steamer,* **Grecian.** (KOHL-FORSBERG ARCHIVES)
Below: *Layout drawing of the wreck of the* **Grecian.** (COURTESY of NOAA THUNDER BAY NATIONAL MARINE SANCTUARY)

E. B. ALLEN   (UPDATE -- *GLDG2* p. 334)

**DEPTH: 92 to 106 feet   LEVEL: Advanced
COORDINATES: 45° 00.976′N/083° 09.899′W**

This small schooner, sunk in a collision on Nov. 18, 1871, is popular among divers.

(PHOTOMOSAIC OF THE *E. B. ALLEN* COURTESY OF THE NOAA THUNDER BAY NATIONAL MARINE SANCTUARY)

JAMES DAVIDSON   (UPDATE -- *GLDG2* p. 327)

**DEPTH: 70 feet   LEVEL: Intermediate-Advanced
COORDINATES: 45° 01.944′N/083° 11.563′W**

This wooden steamer stranded and sank on Oct. 4, 1883, NE of Thunder Bay Island.

O. E. Parks   (UPDATE -- *GLDG2* p. 331)

> **DEPTH: 63 feet   LEVEL: Intermediate-Advanced**
> **COORDINATES: 45° 03.114′N/083° 10.527′W**

No lives were lost when this wooden steamer sank in a storm on May 3, 1929.

W. P. Thew   (UPDATE -- *GLDG2* p. 331, 334)

> **DEPTH: 76 to 86 feet   LEVEL: Advanced**
> **COORDINATES: 45° 02.705′N/083° 09.205′W**

This 25-year-old, wooden steamer sank in a collision on June 22, 1909.

Lucinda Van Valkenburg   (UPDATE -- *GLDG2* p. 331)

> **DEPTH: 62 to 70 feet   LEVEL: Advanced**
> **COORDINATES: 45° 03.380′N/083° 10.180′W**

This 25-year-old, three-masted schooner sank in a collision on June 1, 1887.

D. M. Wilson   (UPDATE -- *GLDG2* p. 331)

> **DEPTH: 46 feet   LEVEL: Intermediate**
> **COORDINATES: 45° 03.920′N/083° 10.928′W**

On October 27, 1894, this wooden steamer sprang a leak and sank; no lives were lost.

Nordmeer   (UPDATE -- *GLDG2* p. 332-333)

> **DEPTH: To 40 feet   LEVEL: Novice**
> **COORDINATES: 45° 08.161′N/083° 09.586′W**

This German freighter stranded on rocks 17 miles off Alpena on November 19, 1966, becoming a total loss. A salvage vessel, *Barge No. 12*, lies at coordinates **45° 08.193′N/083° 09.554′W** off the *Nordmeer's* port side.

Left: *The* **Nordmeer** *shortly after the sinking.* (Courtesy of the George Thomas Archer Marine Arts Collection)

42. *W. H. Gilbert*   (UPDATE -- *GLDG2* p. 334)

> **DEPTH: 255 feet   LEVEL: Technical**
> **COORDINATES: 44° 50.195′N/082° 58.722′W**

This 328-foot-long, steel freighter, built at West Bay City, MI, in 1892, was nearly cut in two and sank in a collision with a bigger, steel freighter, the six-year-old, 504-foot-long *Caldera*, on May 22, 1914, about 18 miles off Thunder Bay Island. No lives were lost.

The deep steamer, **W. H.Gilbert:** *stern, collision damage, and bow.* (Photos by Jitka Hanakova)

43. *PEWABIC* (UPDATE -- *GLDG2* p. 329)

> **DEPTH: 149 to 170 feet   LEVEL: Technical**
> **COORDINATES: 44° 57.890′N/083° 06.236′W**

This "death ship/treasure ship" sank in a collision, killing many, on August 9, 1865.

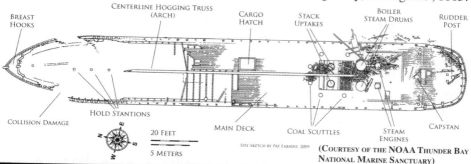

Site sketch by Pat Labadie, 2009
(COURTESY OF THE NOAA THUNDER BAY NATIONAL MARINE SANCTUARY)

(PHOTOMOSAIC OF THE *PEWABIC* COURTESY OF THE NOAA THUNDER BAY NATIONAL MARINE SANCTUARY)

44. VIATOR (UPDATE -- *GLDG2* p. 333)

> **DEPTH: 188 feet   LEVEL: Technical**
> **COORDINATES: 44° 59.480′N/083° 02.229′W**

Kent Bellrichard found this shipwreck in 1976 (not in 1975, as reported earlier). The

Viator was a "saltie," a 231-foot, steel freighter built in Norway in 1904, delivering sardines, pickled herring, and cod liver oil to the Great Lakes, when a collision with the 250-foot, steel freighter, *Ormidale,* on October 31, 1935, sank her. No lives were lost in this pre-St.-Lawrence-Seaway mishap (ships limited to "canal size," about 250 feet long and with relatively shallow draft, could make it into the Great Lakes then).

The **Viator.** (KOHL-FORSBERG ARCHIVES)   International miscommunication caused this noontime sinking in dense fog. When the *Viator* saw the downbound *Ormidale* closing in, she reversed her engines and gave three short blasts on her whistle. On the ocean, three short blasts mean, "I have reversed my engines and am going astern," but on the inland seas, they mean, "I am caught in a fog." Result: the *Ormidale* sliced her bow deep into the *Viator's* side, but kept her bow embedded in the gash until the 34 sailors jumped to safety onto the *Ormidale.* Coincidentally, when first launched in 1917 at Manitowoc, Wisconsin, as a war ship for World War One, the *Ormidale* was placed under Norwegian registry!

45. D. R. HANNA (UPDATE -- *GLDG2* p. 331)

> **DEPTH: 97 to 138 feet   LEVEL: Advanced-Technical**
> **COORDINATES: 45° 05.050′N/083° 05.193′W**

Another victim of a collision in this area's well-known, dense fog, the 532-foot-long *D. R. Hanna* rolled over and sank upside-down after being struck by the 504-foot-long *Quincy A. Shaw* on May 16, 1919. The *Hanna* is the largest shipwreck in the NOAA Thunder Bay National Marine Sanctuary.

Right: *A diver and the upside-down* **D. R. Hanna's** *stern.* (PHOTO BY JOE HOYT, COURTESY OF THE NOAA THUNDER BAY NATIONAL MARINE SANCTUARY)

46. DEFIANCE (UPDATE -- *GLDG2* p. 342)

> **DEPTH: 186 feet   LEVEL: Technical**
> **COORDINATES: 45° 14.058′N/083° 16.707′W**

This ship sank on Oct. 20, 1854, in a collision with another schooner, which also sank.

A profile photomosaic (left)*; divers do survey work* (right) *on the amazingly intact, deep wreck of the twin-masted* **Defiance.**   (COURTESY OF THE NOAA THUNDER BAY NATIONAL MARINE SANCTUARY)

47. *TYPO*   (UPDATE -- *GLDG2* p. 344)

DEPTH: 160 feet   **LEVEL: Technical**
COORDINATES: 45° 17.475′N/083° 18.951′W

The 1873 schooner, *Typo,* was located by Michigan shipwreck hunter Stan Stock in 1988, and he identified it when he found the ship's official number stamped into a main beam on the forward hatch. On October 14, 1899, four lives were lost when the wooden steamer, *W. P. Ketcham*, rammed into the coal-laden *Typo*. (The *Ketcham*, which moved off-lakes in 1907, foundered in the Atlantic Ocean in 1915.)

Left: *The* Typo *under construction.* (KOHL-FORSBERG ARCHIVES)
Below: *The impressive bow and complete bowsprit of the* Typo; *a diver shines a light on the ship's bell.* (PHOTOS BY JITKA HANAKOVA)

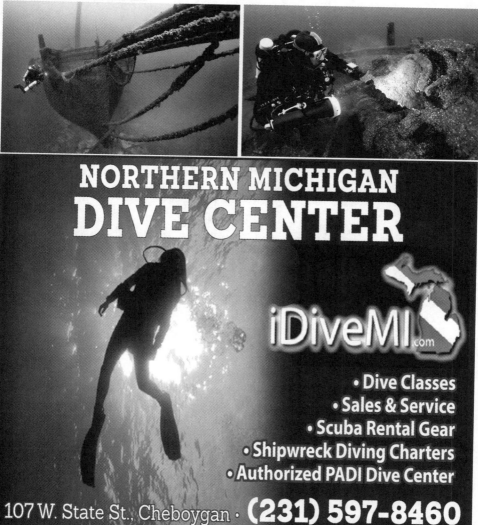

48. *FLORIDA* (UPDATE -- *GLDG2* p. 344)

> **DEPTH: 205 feet   LEVEL: Technical**
> **COORDINATES: 45° 17.781′N/083° 17.011′W**

Again in dense fog, this steamer sank after a collision on May 21, 1897.

Divers examine the collapsed stern of the Florida *and engine gauges.* (PHOTOS BY JITKA HANAKOVA)

49. *NORMAN* (UPDATE -- *GLDG2* p. 344)

> **DEPTH: 210 feet   LEVEL: Technical**
> **COORDINATES: 45° 18.694′N/083° 16.737′W**

The *Norman* (sunk in a collision on May 30, 1895) and the *Cornelia B. Windiate* were found on the same day by shipwreck hunters John Steele and Paul Ehorn in May 1986.

The steel freighter, Norman, *damaged in midship, lies tilted to port.* (PHOTOS BY JITKA HANAKOVA)

50. *CORNELIA B. WINDIATE* (UPDATE -- *GLDG2* p. 340-341)

> **DEPTH: 165 to 188 feet   LEVEL: Technical**
> **COORDINATES: 45° 19.526′N/083° 13.106′W**

This one-year-old, three-masted schooner, which disappeared in Lake Michigan with its entire crew in late November 1875, surprised Great Lakes historians and divers in May 1986, when John Steele and Paul Ehorn found this wreck in Lake Huron! Somehow it had made it through the Straits of Mackinac in severe, early-winter weather without being seen by anyone. This very intact shipwreck remains one of the most impressive in the entire Great Lakes

Left: *The breathtaking* **Cornelia B. Windiate.**
(COURTESY OF THE ARTIST, ROBERT MCGREEVY)

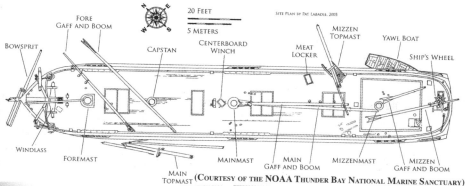

FORE GAFF AND BOOM | 20 FEET | SITE PLAN BY PAT LABADIE, 2005 | MIZZEN TOPMAST | YAWL BOAT | BOWSPRIT | 5 METERS | CAPSTAN | CENTERBOARD WINCH | MEAT LOCKER | SHIP'S WHEEL | WINDLASS | FOREMAST | MAINMAST | MAIN GAFF AND BOOM | MIZZENMAST | MIZZEN GAFF AND BOOM | MAIN TOPMAST

(COURTESY OF THE NOAA THUNDER BAY NATIONAL MARINE SANCTUARY)

Divers explore the bow and stern of the deep **Cornelia B. Windiate.** (PHOTOS BY JITKA HANAKOVA)

51. *KYLE SPANGLER* (UPDATE -- *GLDG2* p. 334)

DEPTH: 158 feet   LEVEL: Technical
COORDINATES: 45° 23.011'N/083° 26.115'W

Stan Stock located this impressive shipwreck in 2003. It sank in a collision on Nov. 7, 1860,

Left: *Both masts, with crowsnests, remain upright.* (PHOTO BY BECKY KAGAN SCHOTT)
Right: *A port bow view.* (PHOTO BY JOE HOYT, COURTESY OF THE NOAA THUNDER BAY NATIONAL MARINE SANCTUARY)

52. *NORTHWESTERN* (UPDATE -- *GLDG2* p. 342)

DEPTH: 129 to 135 feet
LEVEL: Advanced-Technical
COORDINATES: 45° 26.885'N/083° 41.817'W

Sunk in a collision with a wooden steamer on Sept. 30, 1850, with no lives lost, this early schooner off Presque Isle, MI, is a popular dive site.

Left: *View from the bow.* (PHOTO BY JOE HOYT, COURTESY OF THE NOAA THUNDER BAY NATIONAL MARINE SANCTUARY)

53. *CEDARVILLE* (UPDATE -- *GLDG2* p. 363)

> **DEPTH: 40 to 106 feet   LEVEL: Intermediate-Technical**
> **COORDINATES (bow): 45° 47.238′N/084° 40.249′W**

This immense, 38-year-old, steel freighter sank in the Straits of Mackinac after a collision with a Norwegian ship on May 7, 1965, with severe loss of life.

Left: *The* **Cedarville** *underway.* (KOHL-FORSBERG ARCHIVES)
Right: *A diver approaches the nearly overturned bow.*
Below, left: *The self-loading mechanism near midship.*
Below, right: *Inside the dangerous engine room.*
(PHOTOS BY JITKA HANAKOVA)

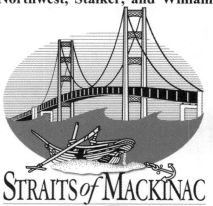

54. WILLIAM YOUNG (UPDATE -- *GLDG2* p. 360-361)

DEPTH: 100-118 feet   LEVEL: Advanced
COORDINATES: 45° 48.765'N/084° 41.941'W

On Oct. 5, 1891, this 139-foot-long schooner-barge waterlogged and sank in the Straits of Mackinac. The wreck lies one mile east of today's Mackinac Bridge.

SCHR. WILLIAM YOUNG
139 x 26 x 12

Built 1863, Bailey Shipbuilding, Madison Dock Ohio. A typical schooner of the Civil War era, she was lost in the Straits of Mackinac while towed by the stmr Nashua. The Young's entire crew were rescued. Discovered in August 2002, she was identified by her registration number inside the main hatch.

Illustrations by Marine Artist Robert McGreevy

The **William Young.** (COURTESY OF THE ARTIST, ROBERT McGREEVY)

Updates on the Wreck of the *GRIFFON*

"The *Griffon* -- isn't that the wreck somebody's finding every ten minutes?" -- Clive Cussler.
     Those words, spoken in the summer of 2014 when we told Clive that we were writing a book about the very first shipwreck in the upper Great Lakes, reflect the recent media attention.
     Steve Libert, who claimed in 2004 that he found the *Griffon's* bowsprit sticking out of the bottom of Green Bay in Lake Michigan, finally won permission from the State of Michigan to excavate it in 2013 -- but there was no *Griffon* shipwreck underneath it. His search continues.
     Two divers from the Muskegon, Michigan, area, in December, 2014, announced their *Griffon* claim of discovery, but it turned out to be a tugboat, ending their hopes for a TV reality show.
     Of the 22 claims of discovery made so far, all are either disproven or unproven, and all are described in our book, *The Wreck of the* GRIFFON, *The Greatest Mystery of the Great Lakes*. The strongest claim to date remains the Mississagi Strait wreck at Lake Huron's Manitoulin Island.

Left: *Four-year-old Richard Tappenden, Jr. gave this portion of the Mississagi Strait shipwreck some scale in this 1932 photo taken by his father.* (COURTESY OF RICHARD TAPPENDEN, JR.)
Below, l. to r.: *In August, 2015, Richard Tappenden, Jr. (pictured with Cris Kohl) hosted a visit by the authors to discuss this wreck* (PHOTO BY JOAN FORSBERG). *The trek to where the Mississagi Strait wreck lay (until washed away by a storm) is an adventure. A white "G" marks the spot.* (PHOTOS BY CRIS KOHL)

9. Lake Michigan

"NEW SHIPWRECKS" refers to those that are not in the book, *The Great Lakes Diving Guide,* second edition, 2008 (*GLDG2*), either because they had not yet been discovered, or because the authors had not yet learned about their locations.

NEW SHIPWRECKS

A. 'Shale Scow'
B. 'Yuba Wreck'
C. *Flora*
D. *Jessie Scarth*
E. *Westmoreland*
F. *Jane*
G. *C. E. Redfern*
H. *Comanche*
I. *L. C. Woodruff*
J. *John V. Moran*
K. *St. Peter*
L. *Aurora* and *L. L. Barth*
M. *Hamilton*

N. *Joseph P. Farnan*
O. *William Tell*
P. *Hattie Wells*
Q. *A. P. Dutton*
R. *Farmer*
S. *Horace A. Tuttle*
T. *Buccaneer*
U. *L. R. Doty*
V. *M. H. Stuart*
W. *Alice E. Wilds*
X. *Lottie Cooper*
Y. *I. A. Johnson*
Z. *Robert C. Pringle*

"UPDATED SHIPWRECKS" refers to ones that are in the book, *The Great Lakes Diving Guide* (shortened to *GLDG2* when referenced in this chapter). The UPDATED information about each of these shipwrecks could be new or corrected GPS coordinates, additional maritime history, and/or modern-day news about that particular wreck.

UPDATED SHIPWRECKS

1. *Eber Ward*
2. *Fred McBrier*
3. *Uganda*
4. *Carl D. Bradley*
5. *Keuka*
6. *Metropolis*
7. *Tramp*
8. 'Elmwood Wreck'
9. *Anna C. Minch*
10. *Daisy Day*
11. *Brightie*
12. *Interlacken*
13. *Salvor*
14. *Helen*
15. *Henry Cort*
16. *Ironsides*
17. *Louisville*

18. *David Dows*
19. *Barge No. 2*
20. *Luther Loomis*
21. *Tacoma*
22. *Silver Spray*
23. *Flora M. Hill*
24. *Thomas Hume*
25. *Rotarian*
26. Zion schooners
27. *Wisconsin*
28. *Lumberman*
29. *Dredge No. 6*
30. *Norlond*
31. *Edward E. Gillen*
32. *Prins Willem V*
33. *St. Albans*
34. *EMBA*

35. *Milwaukee*
36. *Tennie and Laura*
37. *Northerner*
38. *Byron*
39. *Selah Chamberlain*
40. *Rouse Simmons*
41. *Gallinipper*
42. *J. Evenson*
43. *Adriatic*
44. *Joseph L. Hurd*
45. *Frank O'Connor*
46. *F. J. King*
47. Pilot Island Wrecks
48. *Iris*
49. *Roen Barge and Tug*
50. *Erastus Corning*

This map is not to be used for navigation, as details, such as potential hazards, are not marked. Use the maps in this book only for general orientation.

Straits of Mackinac

Manistique

Escanaba

Beaver Island

Fox Islands

Death's Door

Menominee

Manitou Islands

Charlevoix

Sturgeon Bay

Green Bay

Kewaunee

Traverse City

Frankfort

Manitowoc

MICHIGAN

WISCONSIN

Ludington

Sheboygan

Pentwater

Port Washington

Muskegon

MILWAUKEE

Grand Haven

Racine

Holland

Kenosha

South Haven

Waukegan

Benton Harbor

ILLINOIS

St. Joseph

CHICAGO

Michigan City

Burns Harbor

INDIANA

Lake Michigan

Map by Joan Forsberg

A. 'SHALE SCOW' (NEW)

> **DEPTH: 12 feet   LEVEL: Novice**
> **COORDINATES: 44° 53.280′N/085° 25.680′W**

This 100-foot-long scow, which sank in 1903 while tied up at the Elk Rapids Cement Company dock, lies just south of the Elk Rapids harbor.

B. 'YUBA WRECK' (NEW)

> **DEPTH: 15 feet   LEVEL: Novice**
> **COORDINATES: 44° 49.615′N/085° 27.970′W**

This shore-dive shipwreck is that of a small schooner that sank in 1894, and could possibly be the *Ada* or the *Morning Star*, each one being 52 feet long.

C. *FLORA* (NEW)

> **DEPTH: 12 feet   LEVEL: Novice**
> **COORDINATES**
> **45° 127320′N/-86° 611777′W**

Located just off Bay Front Park Beach in Northport, Michigan, this tug boat (44′8″ x 12′ x 3′8″), built at Saugatuck, MI, in 1889, reportedly was swamped and sunk in a storm in either 1893 or early 1894, as the vessel's enrollment was surrendered on May 4, 1894, with the cause written as "t. l." (total loss.)

The small and simple, yet very photogenic shipwreck, Flora.
(PHOTO BY CHRIS DOYAL)

D. JESSIE SCARTH (NEW)

LOCATION: This wreck lies approximately 12 miles north of Manistee, Michigan.

This three-masted schooner (140′ x 26′3″ x 12′), built at Hamilton, Ontario, in 1871 for Toronto's Scarth brothers, foundered in a severe storm while at anchor on October 4, 1887, with its corn cargo, but no lives lost, her crew reaching shore with difficulty in their yawl boat. The ship, heading from Chicago to Midland, ON, reportedly sank in 132 feet of water. Capt. Roberts, who had lost another ship three years earlier on Georgian Bay, later became Chicago's harbormaster and removed many derelict ships from the river there.

This wreck was located on August 16, 2005, by Michigan diver Matthew Higgins. Its stern is relatively intact, while both anchors and chain run off the collapsed bow.

E. WESTMORELAND (NEW)

> **DEPTH: 180 feet   LEVEL: Technical**
> **COORDINATES (approx.): 44.777549N/-86.131120W**

LOCATION: About 2.5 miles off shore in NW Platte Bay, south of the Empire Bluffs.

Almost immediately after this steamship sank on December 7, 1854, with the loss of half of the 34 lives on board, a legend sprang up that it was a "treasure ship" hauling gold and whiskey. The "gold rush" by many wreck hunters to find this historic shipwreck spanned 150+ years, with no luck, until Michigan diver Ross Richardson did extensive research and located it on July 7, 2010. However, to date, he has found no gold or whiskey on board this intact (still with steam engine and boiler that were incorrectly claimed to have been recovered in 1874!) wreck. The *Westmoreland* (200′3″ x 28′3″ x 12′3″), built at Buffalo, NY, in 1853, was one of the "ghost-ship-treasure-wreck" legends of the Great Lakes.

Above: *The amazing wreck of the long lost* **Westmoreland.** (COURTESY OF THE ARTIST, CAL KOTHRADE)

Left: *The wreck of the* **Westmoreland** *rises about 30 feet off the lake bottom, an enormous profile of the wreck's bow.*

Right: *An impressive focal point of any shipwreck: the intact wheel!*
(PHOTOS BY CAL KOTHRADE)

F. JANE (NEW)

> **DEPTH: 100 feet**   **LEVEL: Advanced**
> **COORDINATES:**

The *Jane* was a small tugboat, approximately 60 feet long, that sank on May 30, 1927. Discovered by cable layers in the 1990's, the wreck was documented by members of Save Ontario Shipwrecks (S.O.S.).

G. C. E. REDFERN (NEW)

> **DEPTH: 275 feet**   **LEVEL: Technical**
> **COORDINATES:**

LOCATION: Approximately four miles off Point Betsie Light, Michigan.

This wooden ship (181' x 35' x 13'1"), built at West Bay City, MI, in 1890 and converted from a schooner to a motorship in 1926, foundered in a violent storm on September 19, 1937, with the 15 crew rescued by the USCG *Escanaba* and the *Ann Arbor No. 7*.

In the summer of 1997, legendary shipwreck hunter John Steele retired from that activity and sold his boat and sidescan equipment to Thaddeus Bedford, a well-known,

deep wreck diver from Michigan. The purchase included some of Steele's wreck coordinates, including the *Redfern's,* but he had never dived it due to the depth. Bedford explored and identified the wreck in the early 2000's, and the Michigan DNR located the wreck independently in 2008.

The motorship, **C. E. Redfern,** *with a cargo of lumber.* (KOHL-FORSBERG ARCHIVES)

H. COMANCHE (NEW)

> **DEPTH: 75 feet**   **LEVEL: Advanced**
> **COORDINATES: 43° 50.253'N/086° 29.023'W**

LOCATION: The wreck lies approximately five miles north of Pentwater, Michigan.

"Comanche" may be a nickname, as no records for a ship this type and size, with that name, exist. This 80-foot-long tug displays a three-bladed propeller and a steam engine.

I. L. C. WOODRUFF (NEW)

> **DEPTH: 6 feet**   **LEVEL: Snorkel**
> **COORDINATES: 43° 22.960'N/086° 25.685'W**

LOCATION: This wreck lies approximately 1000 feet north of Montague Channel, MI.

The three-masted barkentine, *L. C. Woodruff* (170'3" x 33' x 12'9"), launched on April 27, 1866, at Buffalo, NY, stranded and sank in 13 feet of water off Whitehall, Michigan, on November 1, 1878, during a violent storm that also sank several other vessels. The crew desperately clung to the ship's rigging about 400 feet from shore, awaiting the arrival of a rescue crew from the Grand Haven Life Saving Station. Numerous attempts at rescue initially failed. A whip line from shore reached the sailors on the ship and, in frantic desperation, four of

The **L. C. Woodruff** *resembled this ship, the* **Zack Chandler.** (KOHL-FORSBERG ARCHIVES)

them jumped into the water to try to follow this line to the safety of shore. When it broke off the doomed ship, men on shore pulled hard on that line to bring in the four sailors. Three were rescued and one died on shore from injuries received. Then the ship, with the six remaining sailors still on it, began to break up. Four reached shore safely on hatch covers, while two drowned. The ship and its corn cargo were a total loss.

This wreckage, long covered by sand, reappeared on shore in 1975.

J. JOHN V. MORAN (NEW)

> **DEPTH: 365 feet**   **LEVEL: Technical**
> **COORDINATES:**

LOCATION: Approximately 20 miles off Muskegon, Michigan.

Launched on August 16, 1888, at West Bay City, MI, this wooden steamer (214′ x 37′ x 22′2″) was cut and sunk by ice on February 7, 1899, showing that Lake Michigan shippers, alone in all the Great Lakes, stubbornly refused to recognize winter as a reason to stop operations. The crew was rescued by the passing freighter, *Naomi* (later renamed the *Wisconsin*, and today a popular shipwreck dive site off Kenosha, WI; see page 168.)

The deep, upright, intact wreck of the *John V. Moran* was found on June 5, 2015, by the Michigan Shipwreck Research Association (MSRA) team.

Left: *The* **John V. Moran.**
Right: *An account of the ship's demise* **(Detroit Free Press,** *Feb. 12, 1899).*
(KOHL-FORSBERG ARCHIVES)

K. ST. PETER (NEW)

> **DEPTH: 350 feet**   **LEVEL: Technical**
> **COORDINATES:**

LOCATION: Approximately 20 miles off Grand Haven, MI (although a Wisconsin state web site gives coordinates that place it about 17 miles southeast of Sheboygan, WI.)

The two-masted, 90-foot-long schooner, *St. Peter* (the patron saint of sailors), built at New Baltimore, Michigan, on Lake St. Clair in 1868, sprang a leak and sank on May 5, 1874, with a wheat cargo enroute from Chicago to Buffalo, the crew safely abandoning ship in a yawl boat. A shipwreck in deep water, believed to be the remains of the *St. Peter*, was located by Michigan Shipwreck Research Association (MSRA) in spring, 2012.

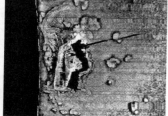

Above: *A sidescan sonar image of this wreck, possibly the* **St. Peter.** (NUMA/MSRA) **Right:** *The* **St. Peter (?)** *today.* (ART BY ROBERT DOORNBOS/MSRA)

WHEN
ICE
SANK SHIPS

The most famous shipwreck in the world, *Titanic*, went to the bottom after striking an iceberg in 1912. Lesser known are the many ships that sank due to ice in the "inland seas."

Great Lakes shipping cannot be done year-round due to thick ice formation in the winter that dramatically hinders the forward motion of ships, a serious climatic reality that usually "laid up" vessels in harbors between December and April. Some years, those in which winter came early or lingered long into spring, were worse than others.

The end of the year 1904 was long remembered for the early arrival of a bitterly frigid winter that struck all five of the Great Lakes, and several ships and lives were lost, directly or indirectly, due to the cold. The schooner, *Annie Falconer*, sank in Lake Ontario on November 12, 1904, and the only death was the mate, who perished from exposure -- but only after he and the rest of the crew reached shore safely! (see *GLDG2*, p. 108-109.) On November 20th, the wooden steamer, *Philip Minch*, caught on fire in western Lake Erie, with the crew "suffering severely from burns and the cold" (see *GLDG2*, p. 195-196). On November 28th, the steamer *B. W. Blanchard* and its towbarge, the *John T. Johnson*, were blown ashore near Alpena on Lake Huron "by the terrific gale which accompanied a snow storm" (see *GLDG2*, p. 327). By December 3rd, five inches of ice blocked many harbors, such as Ashland, Wisconsin, and most ships ceased operations. On that date, the 37-year-old schooner, *Thomas Dobbie* (launched as the *Comanche*), had her hull cut through by the ice a half mile out of Deseronto, Ontario. No lives were lost in this sinking, but the ship was not recovered.

The narrow bottleneck called the Straits of Mackinac was often the last place to be cleared of ice by the increasing warmth of spring weather, a situation reflected by a higher number of ships sunk by ice there than anywhere else in the Great Lakes:

The steamer, *William H. Barnum*, sank on April 3, 1894, after ice cut into her hull (see *GLDG2*, p. 362). The very next day, the steamer, *Minneapolis*, was sunk by ice nearby (see *GLDG2*, p. 359-360).

The wooden steamer, *Eber Ward*, sank five miles west of Mackinaw City on April 20, 1909, after ice holed her hull, with the loss of five lives (see *GLDG2*, p. 357-358).

The steamer, *Uganda*, was cut by ice and sunk on April 19, 1913 (see *GLDG2*, p. 354).

Dozens more Great Lakes ships were lost because of ice, including:

-- the paddlewheel steamer, *George Dunlap*, sunk by ice on November 20, 1880, in Lake Huron's Saginaw Bay, 14 miles out of Bay City, Michigan.

-- the wooden barge, *Morning Star*, on Lake Erie on April 19, 1873.

-- the steamer, *F. A. Meyer*, 20 miles east of Point Pelee in Lake Erie on December 18, 1909, the crew rescued by a passing steamer (see *GLDG2*, p. 174-175.)

-- the small schooner named the *Brothers*, caught in an ice field and crushed in the spring of 1869 off Goderich, Ontario, on Lake Huron.

-- the scow-schooner, *T. G. Lester*, cut by ice, sunk, and abandoned in the Detroit River on March 30, 1908.

-- the tug, *George Nelson*, sunk by ice in the St. Clair River on December 7, 1910.

-- the iron freighter, *Michigan*, crushed by ice and sunk about 17 miles off Holland, Michigan, on March 10, 1885 (see *GLDG2*, p. 383)

-- and, in this book, on page 143, the steamer, *John V. Moran*, on Lake Michigan.

So, for those of you who stretch your activities on the Great Lakes, heed those immortal words of wisdom uttered *ad infinitum* after *Titanic's* loss: "Beware of icebergs."

L. *L. L. BARTH* AND *AURORA* (NEW)

LOCATION: These abandoned wrecks lie in the harbor at Grand Haven, Michigan.

A challenge remaining for maritime historians is determining exactly what happened to ships described as "abandoned." This is much more difficult than listing shipwrecks that received newspaper coverage over their dramatic demises. Valerie van Heest and the Michigan Shipwreck Research Association are among the few doing such Great Lakes research. They identified the remains of the *L. L. Barth* (185' x 35' x 13'8"), launched as the *S. S. Wilhelm* in 1889 at West Bay City, Michigan, and abandoned in 1927, and the *Aurora* (290' x 41' x 22'4"), built at Cleveland in 1887, and burned and abandoned in 1932.

Above: *In their primes, the steamers,* **L. L. Barth** *and* **Aurora**, *both underway.*
(KOHL-FORSBERG ARCHIVES)

Left and right: *In their abandonments, the steamers,* **L. L. Barth** (PHOTO BY VALERIE VAN HEEST/MSRA) *and* Aurora. (PHOTO BY BILL MARTINEZ/MSRA)

M. *HAMILTON* (NEW)

DEPTH: Approximately 275 feet   LEVEL: Technical
CORDINATES: 42° 37.501'N/086° 31.635'W

LOCATION: This wreck lies approximately 15 miles off Saugatuck, Michigan.

Built in Oswego, New York, in 1847, the two-masted, 255-ton schooner, *Hamilton* (113' x 22' x 8'10"), foundered after springing a leak in heavy seas on October 15, 1873, while enroute to Chicago from Muskegon hauling 117,000 board feet of lumber. After 19 hours in their yawl boat, the 7 crew, hungry but safe, reached South Haven, Michigan.

This unidentified shipwreck was initially found by a local marine contractor, and independently located in 2007 by MSRA, whose technical dive team believe it to be the *Hamilton*.

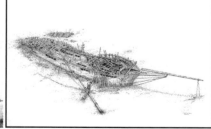

Left: *Archival artwork of the* **Hamilton** *underway.* (MSRA)
Right: *Modern artwork of the* **Hamilton** *today.* (ART BY ROBERT DOORNBOS/MSRA)

N. JOSEPH P. FARNAN (NEW)

DEPTH: 170 feet   LEVEL: Technical
COORDINATES: 42° 20.919′N/086° 34.339′W

LOCATION: This wreck lies about 14 miles WSW of South Haven, Michigan.

During Michigan Shipwreck Research Association's (MSRA) and NUMA's search for a missing aircraft off South Haven, MI, the team located a badly broken up, wooden hull, with sides fallen outwards and the superstructure absent, containing a steam engine and a boiler. They later identified this wreck as the *Joseph P. Farnan* (sometimes incorrectly seen as "Farnam"). The *Farnan* (151′4″ x 33′6″ x 9′6″), built in Cleveland Ohio, in 1887, was on her way up, light, on July 20, 1889, to load ore at Escanaba, after unloading coal at St. Joseph, Michigan, when fire broke out in the engine room. After the spreading flames de-

stroyed their lifeboat, the captain, his wife, and the nine crew hastily built a raft out of hatch covers and fenders, and stayed afloat long enough after their ship sank to be rescued by the South Haven Life Saving station. Conflicting newspaper accounts indicate the ship was either insured for $30,000, or carried no insurance at all.

Left: *The* **Farnan** *ablaze.* **Below, left:** *The* **Farnan** *wreck.* (BOTH BY R. DOORNBOS/MSRA) **Below, right:** *Approaching the* **Farnan's** *bow.* (PHOTO BY VALERIE VAN HEEST/MSRA)

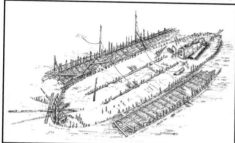

O. WILLIAM TELL (NEW)

DEPTH: 160 feet   LEVEL: Technical
COORDINATES: 42° 15.794′N/086° 40.111′W

LOCATION: This shipwreck lies about 12 miles northwest of Benton Harbor, MI.

The small, 44-ton, 60-foot-long, two-masted scow schooner, *William Tell,* launched in 1861 at New Baltimore, Michigan, was hauling a cargo of lime from Milwaukee to St. Joseph, Michigan, when the ship caught on fire on August 20, 1869. Having originated in the cargo, the flames had already eaten through the deck when the fire was discovered, but the crew escaped in their small yawl boat. Michigan Shipwreck Research Association, working with Clive Cussler's NUMA, found this shipwreck in 2009.

Left: *The wreck of the* **William Tell.** (ART BY ROBERT DOORNBOS/ MSRA)

Right: *Videotaping the wreck's bow.* (PHOTO BY VALERIE VAN HEEST)

P. *HATTIE WELLS* (NEW)

DEPTH: Approximately 210 feet   LEVEL: Technical
COORDINATES: 42° 19.9663′N/086° 43.5318′W

LOCATION: About 17 miles northwest of Benton Harbor, MI.
This old, three-masted schooner (135′1″ x 26′3″ x 11′2″), built at Port Huron, MI, in 1867, foundered in a storm on November 9, 1912, with no lives lost. This wreck was located by MSRA and NUMA.

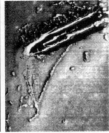

MARINE
WAVES OVERWHELM
ANCIENT VESSEL

Schooner Hattie Wells is Swamped in Heavy Sea Crossing Lake Michigan.

Swamped beneath the battering blows of mighty waves in the storm tossed sea, the little schooner Hattie Wells, which for 45 seasons had defied the power of storms, was overwhelmed and sank in Lake Michigan Wednesday night.
News of her loss was brought to St. Joseph, Mich. Thursday, by the tug James H. Martin, which had the schooner in tow and succeeded after great difficulty in rescuing the five members of her crew.
The Martin and her consort, the latter carrying a cargo of lumber, were bound from Waukegon, Ill., to Muskegon, Mich. Bravely the little schooner breasted the giant waves, fighting her way across the lake.
Worn by many other fierce battles in which she was victorious over the ever-treacherous attacks

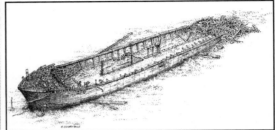

Left: *Reporting the loss;* **Detroit Free Press,** *Nov. 8, 1912.* **Middle:** *Sidescan sonar of the* **Wells.** (NUMA/MSRA) **Right:** *The wreck of the* **Hattie Wells** *today.* (ART BY ROBERT DOORNBOS/MSRA)

Q. *A. P. DUTTON* (NEW)

DEPTH: Approximately 160 feet   LEVEL: Technical
COORDINATES: 42° 20.378′N/086° 34.240′W

LOCATION: About 15 miles west of South Haven, Michigan.
This 43-ton, twin-masted schooner (65′ x 15′ x 6′), built at Racine, WI, in 1856, foundered with all hands on Dec. 8, 1868. The hull lies embedded, with little upper structure.

ART BY ROBERT DOORNBOS/MSRA

L. to r.: **Dutton** *sonar image; the wreck today; wreck photo by Valerie van Heest* (NUMA/MSRA)

R. *FARMER (?)* (NEW)

DEPTH: 72 feet   LEVEL: Advanced
COORDINATES:

The bow, samson post, and windlass of the Farmer. (COURTESY OF WOLF'S DIVERS SUPPLY/YOUTUBE)

This wreck may be the *Farmer.* This two-masted schooner (87′ x 18′ x 7′), built at Salem (later Conneaut), OH, in 1837, capsized off New Buffalo, MI, on April 3, 1863, during a storm, with the loss of everyone (2 passengers and 5 or 6 crew). Only ribs and a bow portion with an old windlass remain unburied. The site is nicknamed "Mac's Wreck" after Don McAlhany, who provided the coordinates to it.

The Indiana Department of Natural Resources has been researching and promoting Indiana's Lake Michigan shipwrecks, such as the *J. D. Marshall,* the *Material Service,* the *Car Ferry Barge No. 2,* and others. Check out their web site, with its amazing 3-D shipwreck imagery, at https://secure.in.gov/dnr/lakemich/8482.htm

S. HORACE A. TUTTLE (NEW)

> **DEPTH: 24 feet**   **LEVEL: Novice**
> **COORDINATES:**

LOCATION: Off the mouth of the harbor at Michigan City, Indiana.

This wooden steamer (250′ x 38′8″ x 20′), built at Cleveland in 1887, was wrecked in a very damaging storm on October 26, 1898, grain-laden from Chicago, with no lives lost.

Left and right: *The wooden steamer,* **Horace A. Tuttle,** *enjoyed only 12 years working on the Great Lakes before ending as a shipwreck blocking the mouth of the harbor at Michigan City, Indiana. The wreck was removed to deeper water a year later.* (KOHL-FORSBERG ARCHIVES)

T. BUCCANEER (NEW)

> **DEPTH: 72 feet**   **LEVEL: Advanced**
> **COORDINATES: 41° 51.288′N/087° 23.862′W**

LOCATION: Approximately eight miles east of the mouth of the Chicago River.

The 9th ship to be scuttled in the Great Lakes for the express purpose of creating a new scuba dive shipwreck site is named the *Buccaneer* -- and it is perhaps the most historic of them all!

Launched as the *Dexter* in 1925 at Bay City, MI, for the U.S. Coast Guard to combat rumrunning during Prohibition (1920-1933), this 100-foot-long, steel ship gained international notoriety when it sank a Canadian rumrunning schooner, the *I'm Alone*, in international waters in the Gulf of Mexico,

L. to r.: *The* **Dexter** *at launch, 1925* (COURTESY OF RALPH ROBERTS); *the Chicago party boat,* **Bucca-** **neer,** *in 2000* (PHOTO BY CRIS KOHL); *a UASC crew on the final clean-up day, 2009: Bob Rushman, Scott Reimer, Joan Forsberg, Cris Kohl, Dean Nolan, and Bob Mueller.* (PHOTO BY BILL MESSNER)

killing one, on March 20, 1929. Six years later, the USA apologized and paid reparations to the crew and Canada. The *Dexter* went on to serve as a U.S. Navy ship in World War Two, actually fighting U-boats in the Caribbean. After the war, the ship was sold to civilians in Boston, who turned it into a party boat named the *Trinidad* and later, at Chicago, the *Buccaneer*. The tired, old ship was about to be scrapped in 2008 when the Underwater Archaeological Society of Chicago, under President Joan Forsberg, arranged to clean the ship and sink it off Chicago -- a grueling, two-year, 1800-man-hour task requiring a multitude of formal permissions. The *Buccaneer,* with its colorful history, is the only shipwreck in the Great Lakes that engaged in actual enemy combat in World War Two!

L. to r.: *After a two-year clean-up, the* **Buccaneer** *was finally sunk off Chicago on June 18, 2010* (BOTH PHOTOS BY JOAN FORSBERG); *diving on the* **Buccaneer's** *bow in 2010.* (PHOTO BY SCOTT REIMER)

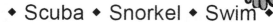

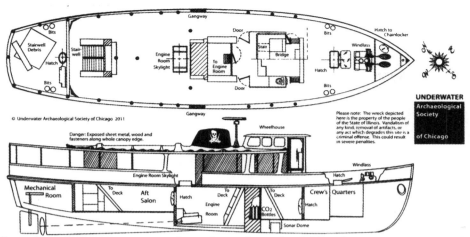

Above: *Some* **Buccaneer** *survey work was done prior to the sinking* (Courtesy of the Underwater Archaeological Society of Chicago); *more underwater views of the* **Buccaneer** *-- inside the pilot house, at the bow, and wall artwork below deck* (Photos by Scott Reimer). *Despite now being under water, this historic vessel remains with us instead of having been turned into razor blades.*

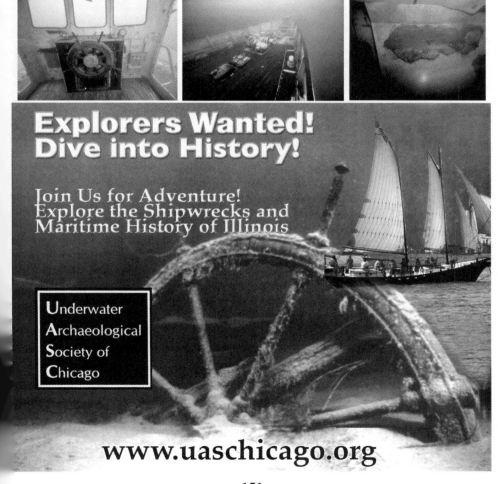

U. *L. R. DOTY* (NEW)

> **DEPTH: 300+ feet**   **LEVEL: Technical**
> **COORDINATES:**

LOCATION: Approximately 20 miles off Oak Creek (Milwaukee), Wisconsin.

In 1991, a commercial fish tug snagged its nets on a deep wreck near the middle of Lake Michigan, and on June 16, 2010, a boat operated by charter captain Jitka Hanakova relocated that site and, with the crew on board -- including Brendon Baillod, Peter Scotland, John Janzen, and John Scoles -- determined that the wreck was that of the *L. R. Doty*.

The *L. R. Doty* had left Chicago towing the schooner-barge *Olive Jeanette*, both laden with corn cargoes, on October 24, 1898, bound for Midland, Ontario, when the ships sailed

WENT DOWN
TO DEATH!

FEARED THAT THE STEAMER L. R. DOTY FOUNDERED.

SHE WAS OUT IN TUESDAY'S FRIGHTFUL STORM.

HAD NOT BEEN SIGHTED AT ANY LAKE MICHIGAN PORT.

WRECKAGE FROM THE BOAT DISCOVERED OFF KENOSHA.

Her Crew of Fifteen Contained Many Michigan Men.

Chicago, October 27.—The steamer L. R. Doty, with her crew of fifteen men, is believed by marine men to have been lost

age from a large steamer had been found off Kenosha was quick confirmation.

It was figured out by marine men that Capt. Smith, having ample confidence in his steamer, would have kept on after the storm came, with the idea that it would go to the northwest, and he could creep down along the lee of the west shore and reach the foot of the lake before crossing over to the straits. In consequence of his faith, he did not, like so many other captains, run for shelter, but kept on his way.

Something went wrong, doubtless, and it may never be known what it was, but the steamer probably became disabled and driven by a sixty-mile gale, both the Doty and Jeanette drifted to the southward. Whether the accident on board the Doty occurred before or after the Jeannette broke adrift will not be known until that schooner is brought into port and the story of the crew learned. The Doty must have drifted over a hundred miles before she went down. In the sheets of rain and the furious gale of Tuesday night her signals of distress could have been seen or heard but a short distance, and other boats, which might have been in the vicinity, had all they could do to keep afloat without rendering assistance even if the signals had been seen.

Above: *The steamer,* L. R. Doty, *in the Soo Locks.*
Right: *These dramatic headlines reporting the loss of the* L. R. Doty *appeared in the* **Detroit Free Press** *on October 28, 1898.*
(BOTH: KOHL-FORSBERG ARCHIVES)

John
Janzen

Underwater Videography & Photography

Technical Diving & Rebreather Training

Deep Water Projects and Recovery Diving

Engineering & Consultation

janzen_john@hotmail.com

right into a severe storm. The towline between the *Doty* and the *Olive Jeanette* broke, or was dropped or cut, at about 5 P.M. on October 25th, when both ships were in mid-lake just north of Milwaukee, with north winds blowing hard. The *Doty* and her 17 crewmembers disappeared, and two days later, the tug, *Prodigy,* found wreckage from the *Doty* 25 miles off Kenosha, WI. Meanwhile, the *Olive Jeanette* struggled to limp back to Chicago under her own sail, arriving there on Oct. 28th (but see p. 196 for this ship's fate).

The *Doty* (291' x 41' x 19'8"), which carried 1,900 tons of soft coal on its maiden voyage on June 16, 1893, was the last of six identical ships, all enormous, wooden bulk freighters, constructed by F. W. Wheeler at West Bay City, MI, in the early 1890's (the others were, in order of construction, the *Tampa*, the *Willliam F. Sauber*, the *Iosco*, the *Uganda* -- see p. 158 -- and the *C. F. Bielman*. All met violent ends, including the *Bielman*, which, despite ending up quietly placed as a breakwall at northern Lake Huron's Great Duck Island, did not go quietly into that good night, instead violently sinking the first tug that tried to tow her up there in 1934 to her final resting place, killing four sailors -- see "The Short, Unhappy Life of Duane Precious" in *Wreck Diving Magazine* #20).

The discovery of the *Doty* solved one of Lake Michigan's maritime mysteries.

 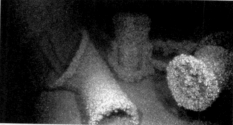

Left: *A diver explores walkways on the* L. R. Doty. **Right:** *Some on-deck debris.* (PHOTOS BY JOHN JANZEN)

V. *M. H. STUART* (NEW)

DEPTH: Deep   **LEVEL: Technical**
COORDINATES:

LOCATION: Approximately seven miles east of Milwaukee.

The wooden, "rabbit" steambarge, *M. H. Stuart* (131'3" x 24'8" x 9'1"), built at Sturgeon Bay, WI, in 1921, despite nearly becoming a permanent loss in 1937, lived on for several more years, finally being scuttled in LakeMichigan in 1948.

Left: *The steamer,* M. H. Stuart (KOHL-FORSBERG ARCHIVES). **Below:** *Jitka Hanakova shines a light on the upright wreck's stern; the* Stuart's *collapsed bow.*   (PHOTOS BY JOHN JANZEN)

 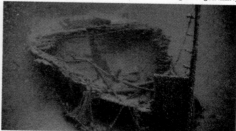

Lake Michigan shipwreck hunter Jerry Guyer located three shipwrecks in the autumn of 2015, but didn't have a chance to dive on them; that will have to wait until the summer of 2016. Stay tuned for more shipwreck information!

W. ALICE E. WILDS (NEW)

DEPTH: 200+ feet   LEVEL: Technical
COORDINATES:

LOCATION: This shipwreck lies in deep water off Milwaukee, Wisconsin.

The wooden steamer named the *Alice E. Wilds* (136' x 28'3" x 10'8") was launched at Detroit in 1883, but the ship lasted less than a decade. On May 28, 1892, the *Wilds,* traveling light from Chicago towards Escanaba, MI, collided with the similarly-sized, 120-foot-long passenger steamer, *Douglas,* which was bound from Milwaukee to Muskegon, and sank quickly, with the *Douglas* rescuing the *Wilds'* distressed crew. Fortunately, no lives were lost. Despite the heavy fog, both ships had been traveling at a high rate of speed, but it was the *Douglas* that was found to be at fault, ultimately paying for the loss of the *Wilds.* The *Douglas,* built at Saugatuck, MI, in 1882, was abandoned after a long career at Detroit in 1920.

The wreck of the *Alice E. Wilds* was found by Jitka Hanakova and her team in 2015.

Left to right: Divers explore the ghostly bow, as well as the open deck, of the **Alice E. Wilds** (BOTH PHOTOS BY BECKY KAGAN SCHOTT); *a diver gets close to the ship's wheel.* (PHOTO BY JITKA HANAKOVA)

X. LOTTIE COOPER (NEW)

LOCATION: These shipwreck remains are in a park near the marina in Sheboygan, WI.

With interest in building a marina at Sheboygan, WI, a mandatory survey of the harbor bottom for signs of historic shipwrecks revealed, on July 16, 1990, a wreck embedded about 100 feet from the existing city boat launch ramp. The wreck was removed in sections in September 1992; examination and research proved it to be the remains of the three-masted schooner, *Lotttie Cooper* (131'1" x 27'3" x 9'4"), built at Manitowoc, WI, in 1876 and wrecked in a violent storm on April 9, 1894. The ship had dropped anchor outside Sheboygan to ride out the storm, but the anchors dragged and the vessel, with its 230,000 board feet of elm lumber, capsized and sank, with the loss of one life, the other four being rescued by the life saving crew. Neither the $7,000 ship nor its $3,500 cargo was insured. Despite some local opposition, these shipwreck remains were placed on public exhibition.

Large sections of the wreck of the schooner, **Lottie Cooper,** *can be explored and closely examined in a public park during any season at Sheboygan, Wisconsin.*   (BOTH PHOTOS BY CRIS KOHL)

Y. *I. A. Johnson* (NEW)

> **DEPTH: 90 feet**   **LEVEL: Advanced**
> **COORDINATES:**

LOCATION: This shipwreck lies off Sheboygan, Wisconsin.

In 2014, longtime shipwreck hunter from Sheboygan, Steve Radovan, found this shipwreck, sunk in a collision with another sailing ship, about seven miles from where the collision occurred. Built in 1866 at Dover Bay, Ohio, the two-masted scow schooner, *I.A. Johnson* (83' x 22' x 6'), was doomed after a collision with the 115-foot-long schooner *Lincoln Dall*, on September 23, 1890. While being towed to shore, the *Johnson* sank. The sides of this small vessel have collapsed, and its profile is low on the lake bottom.

Z. *Robert C. Pringle* (NEW)

> **DEPTH: From 290 to 310 feet**   **LEVEL: Technical**
> **COORDINATES:**

LOCATION: This wreck lies about 12 miles off Sheboygan, Wisconsin.

On June 19, 1922, this wooden tug (101' x 22'4" x 9'6") sank in deep water after striking an obstruction. No lives were lost. This ship, launched as the excursion steamer, *Chequamegon*, at Manitowoc, WI, in 1903, was renamed *Pere Marquette No. 7* in 1911, and *Robert C. Pringle* in 1918.

Right: *The wooden steamer,* **Robert C. Pringle,** *enjoyed only 19 years on the Great Lakes.* (KOHL-FORSBERG ARCHIVES)

The intact nature of this small shipwreck has made it a photographer's delight!

The deep wreck of the **Robert C. Pringle** *features an intact pilothouse (complete with the ship's wheel!) and a bell and searchlight on the deck.* (BOTH PHOTOS BY JOHN JANZEN)

1. *EBER WARD* (UPDATE -- *GLDG2* p. 357-358)

DEPTH: 110 to 148 feet   LEVEL: Advanced-Technical
COORDINATES: 45° 48.7503′N/084° 49.1213′W

LOCATION: This wreck lies 4.6 miles west-northwest from Old Mackinac Point.

This wooden steamer, sunk by thick ice on April 20, 1909, with the loss of five lives, remains a popular dive destination. The wreck is intact and upright, offering many items of interest to examine. An overturned lifeboat lies on the bottom just off the starboard stern.

Left: *The intact bow of the wooden steamer,* **Eber Ward,** *in the Straits of Mackinac.* (PHOTO BY ANDY MORRISON)

2. *FRED MCBRIER* (UPDATE -- *GLDG2* p. 354-355)

DEPTH: 96 to 104 feet   LEVEL: Advanced
COORDINATES: 45° 48.339′N/084° 55.320′W

LOCATION: This wreck lies 9.3 miles west of Old Mackinac Point.

The wooden steamer, *Fred McBrier*, sank in a collision with another steamer on October 3, 1890. Michigan artist Robert McGreevy has drawn the wreck as she looks today:

The **Fred McBrier.** (COURTESY OF THE ARTIST, ROBERT MCGREEVY)

3. *UGANDA* (UPDATE -- *GLDG2* p. 354)

DEPTH: 185 to 207 feet   LEVEL: Technical
COORDINATES: 45° 50.30′N/085° 03.49′W

The large, wooden steamer, *Uganda,* was sunk by ice in deep water in April, 1913.

Left: *A diver approaches the damaged hull of the* **Uganda** *in the Straits of Mackinac.* **Right:** *The upright engine and gauges poke through the collapsed decking.*   (PHOTOS BY JITKA HANAKOVA)

4. *CARL D. BRADLEY* (UPDATE -- *GLDG2* p. 367)

The 623-foot-long *Carl D. Bradley*, the second-largest shipwreck in the Great Lakes (only the 729-foot-long *Edmund Fitzgerald* is larger), was lost in 1958 with only two survivors. It is also one of the last Great Lakes shipwrecks of the modern era. In 2007, technical divers John Janzen and John Scoles, in several dives to the wreck, removed the original ship's bell and replaced it with a memorial bell of similar dimensions, engraved with the names of the lost crew. Frank Mays, then the only remaining survivor, was present.

Above: *Suddenly, out of the darkness in 300 feet of water, appears a bell atop the* **Carl D. Bradley's** *pilothouse.* **Below:** *Inside the pilothouse; John Scoles in the engine room.* (PHOTOS BY JOHN JANZEN)

5. KEUKA (UPDATE -- *GLDG2* p. 368)

The large schooner-barge, *Keuka,* built in 1889, reportedly spent her last years afloat as an offshore speakeasy near Charlevoix, Michigan, in the early 1930's.

Left and right: *On the wreck of the* Keuka.

(PHOTOS BY CHRIS DOYAL)

6. METROPOLIS (UPDATE -- *GLDG2* p. 368)

DEPTH: 8 to 120 feet

LEVEL: Novice to Advanced
COORDINATES:
Shallow: 44° 58.225′N/085° 27.944′W
Deep: 44° 58.341′N/085° 27.829′W

The two-masted schooner, *Metropolis,* sank after getting lost in a blinding snowstorm in November 1886, and running aground off Old Mission Point, near Traverse City, MI, before breaking up.

Left: *The very photogenic keelson of the* Metropolis *lies in very shallow water.*   (PHOTO BY CHRIS DOYAL)

7. TRAMP (UPDATE -- *GLDG2* p. 368)

DEPTH: 45 feet   LEVEL: Intermediate
COORDINATES: 44° 51.022′N/085° 36.070′W

This 1926 fish tug sank some time in the 1970's off southeast Marion Island.

8. 'ELMWOOD WRECK'

(UPDATE -- *GLDG2* p. 368)

DEPTH: 20 to 40 feet
LEVEL: Novice-Intermediate
COORDINATES: 44°47.261′N/085° 38.115′W

This unidentified fish tug, purposely moved from a depth of 80 feet to this shallow location just off the accessible shoreline, remains a popular location as a 'warm-up' dive at the start of the season.

Right: *The popular shipwreck site called the 'Elmwood Wreck.'*   (PHOTO BY CHRIS DOYAL)

9. ANNA C. MINCH (UPDATE -- *GLDG2* p. 379)

> **DEPTH: 36 to 45 feet   LEVEL: Intermediate**
> **Bow COORDINATES: 43° 45.705′N/086° 27.849′W**
> **Stern COORDINATES: 43° 45.784′N/086° 27.776′W**

The *Anna C. Minch* was one of the ships lost in the 1940 Armistice Day Storm.

10. DAISY DAY (UPDATE -- *GLDG2* p. 378)

> **DEPTH: 5 feet   LEVEL: Snorkel**
> **COORDINATES: 43° 31.670′N/086° 29.282′W**

This 103-foot-long, wooden steam barge was wrecked on October 11, 1891.

11. BRIGHTIE (UPDATE -- *GLDG2* p. 378)

> **DEPTH: 70 feet   LEVEL: Advanced**
> **COORDINATES: 43° 29.898′N/086° 29.892′W**

This schooner-barge, wrecked in Oct. 1891, lies 8 miles north of Whitehall, MI.

12. INTERLACKEN (UPDATE -- *GLDG2* p. 380)

> **DEPTH: 15 feet   LEVEL: Novice**
> **COORDINATES: 43° 27.056′N/086° 27.497′W**

This barge wrecked in 1934 was found from the air by Jonathan Freye in Sept. 2003.

13. SALVOR (UPDATE -- *GLDG2* p. 380)

> **DEPTH: 25 to 30 feet   LEVEL: Novice**
> **COORDINATES: 43° 15.615′N/086° 22.119′W**

This barge, wrecked in 1930, lies three miles north of the Muskegon lighthouse.

14. HELEN (UPDATE -- *GLDG2* p. 380)

> **DEPTH: 10 feet   LEVEL: Novice**
> **COORDINATES: 43° 15.003′N/086° 21.152′W**

This scow-schooner, wrecked in 1886, lies one mile north of the Muskegon Channel.

15. HENRY CORT (UPDATE -- *GLDG2* p. 380)

> **DEPTH: 20 to 30 feet   LEVEL: Novice**
> **COORDINATES: 43° 13.540′N/086° 20.891′W**

This whaleback, wrecked in 1934, lies broken and twisted along the north breakwall.

16. IRONSIDES (UPDATE -- *GLDG2* p. 382)

> **DEPTH: 109 to 122 feet**
> **LEVEL: Advanced**
> **COORDINATES:**
> **43° 02.931′N/086° 19.155′W**

This wooden, twin-propeller steamer foundered in 1873 four miles west of the Grand Haven (MI) Channel.

Left: *Although broken up, the* **Ironsides** *remains an interesting shipwreck.* (PHOTO BY VALERIE VAN HEEST)

17. LOUISVILLE (UPDATE -- *GLDG2* p. 398)

> **DEPTH: To 60 feet   LEVEL: Intermediate-Advanced**
> **COORDINATES: 41° 46.393′N/087° 20.277′W**

This steamer burned to a total loss seven miles off Indiana's shore on Sept. 29, 1857, with one life lost. Highlights include the upright steam engine on spindly legs and the propeller.

Above, left: Heyl's drawing of the **Louisville** (KOHL-FORSBERG ARCHIVES). *Left: The* **Louisville** *propeller. Right: Joan Forsberg scoots among the 8 legs of the engine.* (BOTH PHOTOS BY CRIS KOHL)

18. DAVID DOWS (UPDATE -- *GLDG2* p. 400-401)

> **DEPTH: 40 to 45 feet   LEVEL: Intermediate**
> **COORDINATES: 41° 46.072′N/087° 23.503′W**

The largest sailing ship ever built on the Great Lakes, the five-masted *David Dows*, sank in a storm off Chicago in 1889. The broken, half-buried wreck does not do it justice.

Middle: *The impressive* **David Dows** (KOHL-FORSBERG ARCHIVES). **Left and right:** *The less-than-impressive* **David Dows** *shipwreck, videotaped by Joan Forsberg and photographed by Cris Kohl.*

19. BARGE NO. 2 (UPDATE -- *GLDG2* p. 394-395)

> **DEPTH: 42 feet   LEVEL: Intermediate**
> **COORDINATES: 41° 44.965′N/087° 26.939′W**

This 1906 wreck, 3 miles off the Calumet breakwall, is the subject of an excellent, archaeological survey report, carried out under team leader John Loftus, and published in 2016 by the Underwater Archaeological Society of Chicago and available for purchase.

Left and right: *The wooden railroad car* **Barge No. 2,** *covers a huge area under water, most of the wreckage lying flat. Joan Forsberg descends to the wreck. Such a splayed-open shipwreck offers many views of construction techniques.* (PHOTOS BY CRIS KOHL)

20. *LUTHER LOOMIS* (UPDATE -- *GLDG2* p. 398)

The small, 29-gross-ton, wooden tug, *Luther Loomis*, (54′9″ x 13′ x 6′) built at Chicago in 1889, caught on fire and burned to a complete loss on the Calumet River on May 4, 1913, with no lives lost. The wreck was towed into Lake Michigan and sunk.

21. *TACOMA* (UPDATE -- *GLDG2* p. 402)

When it sank off Chicago on November 4, 1929, the 73-foot-long, wooden tug, *Tacoma*, was the oldest of the 29 tugs owned in Chicago on that date, having been built in 1894 at Benton Harbor, Michigan (the next oldest was the 1901 *Helen H. Upham*). The *Tacoma* "sprang a yawning leak" during the lunch hour and sank within five minutes, the crew barely having time to board a scow and free the towing cable before the tug sank.

Joan Forsberg examines the **Tacoma's** *decking and propeller.* (PHOTOS BY CRIS KOHL)

A Great Lakes Sidebar

Remembering the *Eastland* Disaster

The worst maritime disaster in Great Lakes history occurred 100 years ago, when the excursion steamer, *Eastland,* loaded to its 2,500 capacity, capsized at its dock in the Chicago River, killing more than 800 people in 22 feet of water about 50 feet from shore. It is also, by far, Chicago's worst disaster of many, including the Great Fire of 1871 (in which about 300 people died). In late July, 2015, special events were held in Chicago to commemorate the *Eastland* tragedy.

The last known survivor of this disaster, who was only three years old when her father took her in his arms and jumped into the Chicago River as the ship capsized, was Marion Eichholz, who died on Nov. 24, 2014, at the age of 102.

For more details about this disaster, see *GLDG2*, p. 408-409, and chapter 14, "Great Lakes Death Ship: The *Eastland*," in the book, *TITANIC, The Great Lakes Connections.*

The **Eastland**, *sleek and fast, was popular with excursionists until the ship tragically capsized opposite the Reid-Murdoch Building while loading passengers in the Chicago River on July 24, 1915.* (KOHL-FORSBERG ARCHIVES). *Today, across from the same, distinctive building, a historic plaque marks the site of the Great Lakes' worst maritime disaster.* (PHOTO BY CRIS KOHL)

22. SILVER SPRAY (UPDATE -- GLDG2 p. 402)

The passenger steamer, *Silver Spray* (109'2" x 21'9" x 8'3"), ex-*Bloomer Girl*, stranded on Morgan Shoal on July 15, 1914,

but did not catch on fire as was previously thought (but some wreckage that later washed ashore was used for beach bonfires.) No lives were lost, and waves broke up the ship only three days after the stranding.

Left: *The* **Silver Spray** *was a well-known, popular excursion steamer in Chicago.* (KOHL-FORSBERG ARCHIVES)

Below: *The news of the* Silver Spray's *loss,* Chicago Tribune, *July 19, 1914.* (KOHL-FORSBERG ARCHIVES)

SILVER SPRAY BREAKS UP

Small Steamer, Caught on a Sandbar, Goes to Pieces.

DECK IS CARRIED AWAY.

Taking Off Coal Makes Boat Easy Prey of Waves.

The Silver Spray, a small double decked steamer, which stuck on a sandbar in the lake about 400 feet off the foot of East Fifty-first street last Thursday, was wrecked by a rough sea yesterday after-

23. FLORA M. HILL (UPDATE -- GLDG2 p. 410-411)

The wreck of the *Flora M. Hill* (formerly a government lighthouse tender named the *Dahlia*), broken up in 37 feet of water off Chicago after ice sank it on March 11, 1912, is currently being surveyed by the Underwater Archaeological Society of Chicago. The first photomosaic of a portion of the the wreck site has been completed.

Right: *The* **Flora M. Hill**, *still named the* **Dahlia**, *at St. Joseph, Michigan, served as a backdrop for a life saving crew photo.* (KOHL-FORSBERG ARCHIVES)

24. THOMAS HUME (UPDATE -- GLDG2 p. 427)

DEPTH: To 150 feet   LEVEL: Technical
COORDINATES: 41° 56.455'N/087° 10.699'W

This ship was lost with all six hands in a storm on May 21, 1891, while on the Chicago-to-New-Buffalo (MI) route, much farther south than the ship's originally presumed Chicago-to-Muskegon route. The 2010 survey of this shipwreck, done in partnership with the first divers and the Michigan Shipwreck Research Association, confirmed its identity.

Left: *The schooner,* **Thomas Hume**, *under way.* (KOHL-FORSBERG ARCHIVES)

Right and below: *The* **Thomas Hume**, *despite its tragic loss, sits amazingly elegant and graceful on the lake bottom.*
(PHOTOS BY ROBERT UNDERHILL/MSRA)

Right: *A diver examines the many interesting artifacts grouped together in the* **Hume's** *cargo hold.* (PHOTO BY CAL KOTHRADE)

Below: *In this detailed artwork, the relative positions of the three masts can be seen. The wreck of the schooner,* **Thomas Hume,** *is a delight to explore.*

(ART BY ROBERT DOORNBOS/MSRA)

25. *ROTARIAN* (UPDATE -- *GLDG2* p. 411-412)

The steamer, *Rotarian*, started life innocently transporting families to fun islands in Lake Erie, and ended her days as a speakeasy ship in the Chicago River during Prohibition before being scuttled in Lake Michigan. We are often asked if the beer bottles on this shipwreck might have touched the lips of Al Capone, who supplied the ship's alcohol. Answer: unlikely. Reasons: found in the *Rotarian* article in *Wreck Diving Magazine* #36 (2015).

The **Rotarian:** *a section of flattened hull and the rudder post and steering quadrant.* (PHOTOS BY CRIS KOHL)

26. ZION SCHOONERS (UPDATE -- *GLDG2* p. 426)

One of the two abandoned schooners in 20 feet of water just off the Zion, Illinois, Power Plant might actually have been a steamer; steam machinery evidence is mounting.

27. *WISCONSIN* (UPDATE -- *GLDG2* p. 432-433)

The 209-foot-long steamer, *Wisconsin*, sank in a storm with the loss of nine lives on October 29, 1929, exactly one week after a worse tragedy occurred just a bit farther north, namely the foundering of the *Milwaukee* with the loss of all hands (see page 177).

This ship changed names far too frequently to be lucky: *Wisconsin* (1881-1899), *Naomi* (1899-1910), *E. G. Crosby* (1910-1918), *General Robert M. O'Reilly* (1918-1919), *E.G. Crosby* (1919-1920), *Pilgrim* (1920-1924), and finally, again, *Wisconsin* (1924-1929).

Left: *The* Wisconsin *when she carried that name for the* **first** *time (1881-1899).*

Right: *In 1910, this ship was renamed* E. G. Crosby, *after her new owner, a Great Lakes captain who, in 1912, perished in the* Titanic *sinking.*

(BOTH: KOHL-FORSBERG ARCHIVES)

Left and below: *The steamer,* Wisconsin, *sitting upright and mostly intact at a depth of 90 to 130 feet, is one of the more popular shipwreck dive sites in Lake Michigan.*
(PHOTOS BY CAL KOTHRADE)

28. *LUMBERMAN* (UPDATE -- *GLDG2* p. 435-436)

Capsized and sunk during her first trip of the season on April 7, 1893, the three-masted, 31-year-old schooner named the *Lumberman* was sailing light (meaning with no cargo) when a strong squall pitched her over. A passing steamer rescued her five crew. The wreck, found in 1983, sits in 53 to 70 feet of water several miles to the southeast of Milwaukee.

An overhead photomosaic of the wreck of the **Lumberman**. (PHOTOMOSAIC BY CAL KOTHRADE)

29. DREDGE NO. 6 (UPDATE -- *GLDG2* p. 436, 438)

This 42-year-old, wooden-hulled dredge sank off Milwaukee while under tow during a storm on May 23, 1956, with the tragic loss of nine lives. The wreck lies in 50 to 75 feet.

The shovel and arm -- the business end of any dredge like the No. 6. (PHOTO BY CAL KOTHRADE)

30. *Norlond* (UPDATE -- *GLDG2* p. 438)

Launched at Manitowoc, WI, in 1890, as the *Eugene C. Hart*, with her name changed to *Norlond* in 1919, this 152-foot-long, wooden steamer foundered in heavy weather in 65 feet of water on November 13, 1922. The 19 crew members reached shore in two life boats. Shipwreck hunter John Steele located the wreck of the *Norlond* (often incorrectly called or spelled *Norland*) in 1959, one of his earliest wreck discoveries.

Wreck of the
Norlond

The **Norlond** *as seen in an overhead photomosaic.* (Photomosaic by Cal Kothrade)

31. *Edward E. Gillen* (UPDATE -- *GLDG2* p. 440-441)

None of the four people on board the 56-foot-long, steel-hulled, diesel tugboat, *Edward E. Gillen*, built in 1908 at Buffalo, NY, was injured when their boat sank in 74 feet of water on June 3, 1981 (that's in relatively modern times!) The tug was helping the Coast Guard ship, *Westwind*, test its towing winch when the wire parted suddenly, and the tug rolled over and sank. The Coast Guard immediately rescued the four men in the water.

A profile view of the tug, **Edward E. Gillen.** (Photo by Cal Kothrade)

32. *PRINS WILLEM V* (UPDATE -- *GLDG2* p. 441-442)

Before the St. Lawrence Seaway opened in 1959 to allow huge ships of the world into the Great Lakes, smaller vessels (those of "canal size," about 250 feet long, that the old Welland Canal could accommodate) traded with ports on the inland seas. The 250-foot-long, Dutch *Prins Willem V* was such a ship. But upon leaving Milwaukee on Oct. 14,

1954, a freak accident with a tug's tow and towline sank the foreign visitor in 90 feet of water. No lives were lost, but several salvage attempts over the next few years all ended in failure. The *Prins Willem V,* affectionately nicknamed the *"Willy"* by divers, is one of the most visited shipwrecks in Lake Michigan. Exploring a wreck's interior is called "penetration diving" and requires special training and preparation; the same applies to the *Willy*.

A magnificent photomosaic of the **Prins Willem V.** (PHOTOMOSAIC BY CAL KOTHRADE)

The Dutch **Prins Willem V** *on one of her visits to the Great Lakes.* (KOHL-FORSBERG ARCHIVES)

The wreck sits severely tilted -- angle-corrected in the photo on right. (PHOTOS BY CAL KOTHRADE)

33. *St. Albans* (UPDATE -- *GLDG2* p. 445-446)

Another vessel sunk by ice, the 13-year-old, wooden steamer, *St. Albans*, went to the bottom of Lake Michigan in 178 feet of water on January 30, 1881, with no lives lost.

The bow is recognizable as such; the stern is in better shape. (PHOTOS BY CAL KOTHRADE)

34. *EMBA* (UPDATE -- *GLDG2* p. 446-447)

The *EMBA* was a 128-foot-long schooner-barge scuttled in 170 feet of water in 1932 due to old age, a practice thankfully not yet applied to old divers.

The EMBA -- for "Excelsior Marine Benevolent Association." (PHOTOS BY CAL KOTHRADE)

35. *MILWAUKEE* (UPDATE -- *GLDG2* p. 448, 450)

This steel, railroad car ferry, 338 feet long, sank in a storm on Oct. 22, 1929, with the loss of all 52 people on board. The zebra mussel invasion has greatly increased visibility.

Above: *The* **Milwaukee.** (KOHL-FORSBERG ARCHIVES)
Right and below: *Divers can explore the tall bow and the four-bladed propeller on the* **Milwaukee** *in 90 to 125 feet of water.* (PHOTOS BY CAL KOTHRADE)

36. TENNIE AND LAURA   (UPDATE -- *GLDG2* p. 450)

This small, 73-foot-long, two-masted scow-schooner capsized and sank in 319 feet of water on August 8, 1903, about 12 miles northeast of Milwaukee, with one life lost.

The **Tennie and Laura:** *mast "crowsnest," and bowsprit and anchor*   (PHOTOS BY JOHN JANZEN)

37. NORTHERNER   (UPDATE -- *GLDG2* p. 452)

The *Northerner*, a twin-masted, 78-foot-long schooner built in 1859, sank in severe weather with its cargo of coal on November 29, 1868, southeast of Port Washington, WI. No lives were lost. The figureheaded wreck sits upright in 122 to 138 feet of water.

Above: *The wreck of the schooner,* **Northerner,** *as it appears today.* (ART BY CAL KOTHRADE)
Below: *This wooden wreck has been under water for about 150 years.* (PHOTOS BY CAL KOTHRADE)

38. BYRON (UPDATE -- *GLDG2* p. 454)

In 1975, commercial fisherman Danny Brunette snagged one of his fishing nets on this little schooner. In freeing his net, he lifted part of the wreck out of the sandy lake bottom in which most of it is embedded. As the net was pulled back on board, he noticed an anchor came up in it. Realizing he had snagged onto a shipwreck, he contacted local wreck hunters. John Steele, Bill Cohrs, and Steve Radovan were the first divers to explore this 40-foot-long wreck rising only three feet above the lake bottom in 135 feet of water.

39. SELAH CHAMBERLAIN (UPDATE -- *GLDG2* p. 456)

> **DEPTH: 75 to 88 feet   LEVEL: Advanced**
> **COORDINATES: 43° 46.02′N/087° 39.54′W**

Lying two miles north of Sheboygan Point, WI, the wooden steam barge, *Selah Chamberlain,* sank in a collision with another ship in dense fog on October 13, 1886, with the loss of five lives. This popular wreck sits upright on a sand bottom.

40. ROUSE SIMMONS (UPDATE -- *GLDG2* p. 462-464)

Gaining both fame and notoriety as "The Christmas Tree Ship" only in her final three years afloat, the 44-year-old schooner, *Rouse Simmons,* ended the years 1910, 1911, and 1912 by loading up evergreen trees from northern Lake Michigan to sell directly from the ship's deck for Christmas in the virtually-evergreen-treeless prairie port of Chicago. But the ship failed to reach port in 1912, having disappeared in a violent storm with all hands and its huge cargo of evergreen trees. The wreck was found in 1971 in 168 feet of water. For more details, read the book, *The Christmas Tree Ship,* by Cris Kohl and Joan Forsberg; it has 32 pages of color images, and includes the history of the Christmas tree tradition.

Above: *The schooner,* **Rouse Simmons,** *majestically underway.* (COURTESY OF THE DOOR COUNTY HISTORICAL MUSEUM)
Right and below: *The tragic, dramatic wreck of "The Christmas Tree Ship" in deep water off Two Rivers, WI.* (PHOTOS BY CAL KOTHRADE)

Wisconsin will soon have a Lake Michigan National Marine Sanctuary similar to the NOAA Thunder Bay National Marine Sanctuary at Alpena, Michigan, on Lake Huron. In October 2015, President Obama announced that NOAA (the National Oceanic and Atmospheric Administration) is moving forward with designating an area of 875 square miles (roughly an 80-mile-long section of Lake Michigan between Port Washington and Two Rivers, WI) as the 15th National Marine Sanctuary, and the first one designated since the year 2000. This area contains about 30 shipwrecks, the locations of which are known, including the famous *Rouse Simmons*, the "Christmas Tree Ship" (see p. 181). NOAA still has to draft an Environmental Impact Statement and management plan that will require public input.

41. GALLINIPPER (UPDATE -- GLDG2 p. 461)

The two-masted schooner named the *Gallinipper* (also seen as *Gallenipper*), built in 1846 in early Milwaukee, sank in a storm on July 7, 1851. In May 1994, commercial fisherman Ken Kolpa snagged one of his nets on a mast and marked it with a buoy. Divers Kent Bellrichard, Steve Radovan, and Jim Brotz were contacted for help, but could not free the badly entangled net. However, they explored the wreck and took fellow wreck hunter, John Steele, to it. Their collective explorations and research eventually identified it.

42. J. EVENSON (UPDATE -- link to F. J. King, GLDG2 p. 579)

A reward of $500 was offered several years ago by the Neptune Dive Club of Green Bay to anyone finding this tug (54'2" x 13'8" x 7'1"), built at Milwaukee in 1884 and sunk in a collision with the steamer, *I. Watson Stevenson*, on June 5, 1895, about five miles north of Ahnapee, Wisconsin. One life was lost. The $500 reward was recently cancelled, with this wreck still awaiting discovery.

43. *ADRIATIC* (UPDATE -- *GLDG2* p. 466)

An official survey of the 202-foot-long, three-masted schooner-barge, *Adriatic* (built at West Bay City, MI, in 1889 and abandoned in 2 to 15 feet of water near Sturgeon Bay, WI, in 1930), was undertaken by the Wisconsin Historical Society and East Carolina University in 2013.

In early 1914, the addition of conveyor belts for faster handling of bulk cargoes made the *Adriatic* the first self-unloading schooner-barge in the world.

The **Adriatic** *at Escanaba, MI.* (KOHL-FORSBERG ARCHIVES)

44. *JOSEPH L. HURD* (UPDATE -- *GLDG2* p. 468)

After a very long career laced with numerous strandings and collisions with other vessels and bridges, the wooden steamer, *Joseph L. Hurd* (1869-1913) was purposely sunk in 30 feet of water in Door County, Wisconsin, near Sturgeon Bay, following an on-board fire. The correct dimensions of this ship are 171' x 29'2" x 10'9". This vessel outlived the person after whom it was named, a successful grain shipper, by nearly 20 years.

45. *FRANK O'CONNOR* (UPDATE -- *GLDG2* p. 477-478)

This is one of the most popular scuba dive sites in Door County, WI. The 301-foot-long, wooden steamer, *Frank O'Connor,* built at West Bay City, MI, in 1892, burned off Cana Island on October 2, 1919, with no lives lost. The wreck lies in 70 feet of water.

The **Frank O'Connor's** *upright steam engine, propeller, and stern.* (PHOTOS BY CAL KOTHRADE)

46. *F. J. KING* (UPDATE -- *GLDG2* p. 579)

A reward of $1,000 was offered in 2007, announced with wild-west-type "Wanted" posters and creating quite a stir in the Great Lakes scuba diving community, by the Neptune Dive Club of Green Bay to anyone finding this 144-foot-long schooner, which sank several miles east of Cana Island with a heavy cargo of iron ore after springing a leak in a strong, southeast gale on September 15, 1886. The topmasts were reportedly seen above the water by the Cana Island lighthouse keeper for several weeks until they broke off. Despite that information, no one could locate the wreck. The dive club has some interesting stories to relate about shipwreck/bounty hunters who contacted them, but the wreck was not found and the offer of a reward was cancelled in 2015.

47. Pilot Island Wrecks (UPDATE -- *GLDG2* p. 481)

Pilot Island, the rocky sentinel marking the entrance to the Death's Door passage between Lake Michigan and Green Bay, has several shipwrecks in its history. Three of them lie together, broken and intermingled. These are the corrected dates of their losses:

The scow-schooner, *Forest,* stranded and wrecked here on October 28, 1891.

The schooner, *J. E. Gilmore,* stranded and wrecked here on October 16, 1892.

The schooner, *A. P. Nichols*, stranded and wrecked here on October 28, 1892.

Left: *Ruth Magnus and Bill Messner at the Pilot Island dock. Millions of zebra mussel shells lie several feet deep along the shore, covering rocks and, underwater, shipwrecks.*
Right: *The Pilot Island Lighthouse buildings are in dire need of restoration, but the island has been surrendered to cormorants.*
Below: *Pilot Island wreckage is explored by Joan Forsberg.* (ALL PHOTOS BY CRIS KOHL)

48. IRIS (UPDATE -- *GLDG2* p. 483)

> **DEPTH: To 4 feet   LEVEL: Snorkel**

A small, 74-foot-long schooner named the *Iris*, built in 1866 at Port Huron, MI, was abandoned at Jackson Harbor, Washington Island, WI, in 1913. The wreck lies off to one side of marina traffic.

Right: *The* Iris, *not long after being abandoned in 1913.* (COURTESY OF JIM BAYE) **Below:** *What remains of the* Iris *today lies in the shallows, with a portion above water.* (PHOTOS BY CRIS KOHL)

49. ROEN TUG AND BARGE (UPDATE -- *GLDG2* p. 484)

> **Tug: DEPTH: To 110 feet   LEVEL: Advanced**
> **COORDINATES: 45° 28.995′N/086° 41.070′W**
> **Barge: DEPTH: 75 to 110 feet   LEVEL: Advanced**
> **COORDINATES: 45° 28.956′N/086° 40.950′W**

A storm in October, 1969, sank the tug boat and steam barge owned by modern-day salvager John Roen. Nearly three miles south of the Poverty Island Lighthouse, the barge lies upside-down, and these two wrecks are far enough apart to make them separate dives.

50. ERASTUS CORNING (UPDATE -- *GLDG2* p. 486)

> **DEPTH: 12 to 65 feet   LEVEL: Intermediate-Advanced**
> **COORDINATES: 45° 31.425′N/086° 40.152′W**

The big wreck of this 204-foot-long schooner lies on a slope off the south side of Poverty Island, MI. Divers in the 1960s thought this was the tragic *Plymouth*, lost with all hands in 1913, but the iron ore cargo identifies it as the *Corning*, which was wrecked here on May 21, 1889.

Left: *A contemporary drawing of the* **Erastus Corning.** (KOHL-FORSBERG ARCHIVES) **Below:** *Joan Forsberg follows the length of the* **Corning** *into deeper water while videotaping.*   (PHOTOS BY CRIS KOHL)

Great Lakes Members of
the Women Divers Hall of Fame

Founded in 2000, the **Women Divers Hall of Fame** (WDHOF.org) is dedicated to honoring women divers whose achievements have had a significant impact on the exploration, understanding, safety, and enjoyment of the underwater world. WDHOF, with only 217 members world-wide as of 2016, has awarded over $300,000 in scholarships and training grants to more than 230 young people. The Great Lakes are well represented in WDHOF by the following extraordinary women, with the year of induction (all photos were submitted by the individuals, unless otherwise indicated):

Regina Bier (2011)

Regina, better known as Gina, is a dive instructor, having certified nearly 2000 divers, and runs the Wright State Scuba program in Dayton, Ohio, near Lake Erie. The legendary Joyce Hayward was Gina's mentor, and introduced her to Great Lakes shipwreck archaeology. Gina brought Joyce to Wright State where Joyce taught underwater archaeological survey techniques to local divers. Continuing the hands-on work, the university sponsored the underwater archaeological survey work that Gina did with Joyce on two Lake Erie shipwrecks off Kelley's Island, the *Adventure* and the *F.H. Prince*. In her twenty-year career as a police officer, she has used her underwater archaeology experience to lead underwater evidence recovery investigations, and was a female pioneer in the field of forensic diving.

Joan Forsberg (2010) See page 222

Lynn Funkhouser (2000)

Although famous for her extraordinary photography of the ocean's beautiful creatures, especially in the Philippines, it is not widely known that Lynn Funkhouser is a tireless activist for Lake Michigan clean water projects. Lynn was the first volunteer diver at the Shedd Aquarium in Chicago, doing every dive on weekends for two years, and now they have over 600 volunteers! She was the scholarship coordinator for Chicago's Our World – Underwater Scholarship Society from 1978-1982, and when she left the position, was replaced by five men! A popular speaker who has done presentations for every dive club in the Chicago area, she has also spoken at Columbia College, Shedd Aquarium, the Field Museum, and many other prestigious venues throughout the Midwest. Lynn has presented at Chicago's Our World – Underwater scuba show more often than any other woman and is closing in on the men who have retired. A passionate advocate for protection of our planet and its precious water, Lynn uses social media to help educate her more than 4000 friends about the problems of climate change, salt and fresh water issues, and marine life sustainability concerns.

Joyce Hayward (2001) See page 208

Sue Morra, Ph.D. (2000)

Sue is the ultimate dive instructor. Having grown up in Indiana, she began by diving in quarries, and eventually found her passion to be a dive instructor, becoming one of the first female PADI Course Directors. She has trained police department search and recovery teams, trained many Air Force divers, and helped develop the PADI Rescue Course. Having dove and taught all over the world, she assisted in the establishment of PADI Europe. Mid America Scuba, a dive shop she opened in Illinois, had 13 instructors on staff. With a B.S. in Biology, B.A. in Chemistry, M.A. in Plant Sciences, and a Ph.D. in Comparative Immunology, she studied the effects of acidic water conditions on the immune responses in fish, and also led to her interest in how these conditions affected scuba equipment.

Robin MacFadden Parish (2012)

In 1976, Robin Parish was the first female Rolex Scholar of Chicago's Our World – Underwater Scholarship Society, and has been national coordinator of the Rolex Scholarship of the OWUSS since 1994. As part of the Pew Environment Group's team, she lobbied the U.S. Senate to pass a shark conservation bill, representing divers across the Midwest, and showing the senators that protection of marine life is important to people living in the interior of the country, not just those living on the coasts. In her words: "I got a particular charge out of telling the senators how many Great Lakes scuba divers we have – they were shocked at the numbers!" The

bill did pass, and Robin was instrumental in getting a shark fin ban passed in the state of Illinois. "My main passion is encouraging young people to learn about the underwater world and getting people of all ages to take a look at what lies beneath...in both the sea and our lakes."

Becky Kagan Schott (2013)

Becky Schott is a multiple Emmy Award-winning underwater filmmaker, photographer, and accomplished technical diver whose work can be seen on major networks including National Geographic, Discovery, and Travel Channel. Co-owner of Liquid Productions, her projects have taken her all over the globe including exploring virgin wrecks in over 300 feet of Great Lakes water. She has participated in projects helping to document shipwrecks in 3D for the National Park Service in Isle Royale National Park in Lake Superior, and has searched for new wrecks in Lake Huron and Lake Michigan. In 2011 she worked with NOAA on a documentary called "Project Shiphunt" searching for shipwrecks with a group of high school students, which resulted in finding the schooner *M.F. Merrick* and the *Etruria* off Presque Isle, Michigan. In Becky's words: "I don't think a lot of people even to this day realize the incredible history and stories of tragedy and heroism that have gone on over the years. The lakes have been my favorite place to dive....I can't get enough of them...."

Pat Stayer on the Lake Huron wreck of the tug,
Mary Alice B. **(left),** *and cruising in the Straits*
of Mackinac **(right).** (PHOTOS BY CRIS KOHL)

Pat Stayer (2005)

For more than 40 years, Pat Stayer has been an extremely well-known and well-respected Great Lakes explorer. With her husband, Jim, Pat has written three books about Great Lakes shipwrecks and shipwreck survivors: *Shipwrecks of Sanilac*, *Sole Survivor: Dennis Hale's Own Story*, and *If We Make It 'til Daylight*. Pat and Jim, for over 20 years, ran a successful dive charter boat in Lake Huron, sharing their enthusiasm for the wrecks and maritime history of the inland seas. Often collaborating with Cris Kohl, they discovered, identified, and documented eight shipwrecks. Pat's stunning underwater videography and beautiful illustrations of the wrecks of the Great Lakes have been the hallmark of their popular lectures and more than 30 DVD documentaries, and her work has also been seen on television, notably on the History Channel. An ardent activist for Great Lakes shipwreck protection and conservation, she co-founded the Sanilac Shores Underwater Preserve and served as secretary of the Michigan Underwater Preserve Council. A skilled diver with thousands of dives under her weightbelt, she was one of the first female divers on the sheriff's dive team.

Tamara Thomsen (2014)

Tamara Thomsen is a maritime archaeologist with Wisconsin Historical Society's Maritime Preservation and Archaeology program. Her fieldwork has resulted in the listing of 41 Great Lakes shipwrecks and two submerged Historic Districts to the National Register of Historic Places. In 2014 as a result of this research, the governor of Wisconsin submitted a proposal to the National Oceanographic and Atmospheric Administration (NOAA) to establish a National Marine Sanctuary within the Lake Michigan waters of Wisconsin to protect these invaluable submerged cultural resources – that designation process is currently moving forward. Her work has been acknowledged with the Association for Great Lakes Maritime History's Joyce Hayward Award for Historic Interpretation and the Great Lakes Shipwreck Preservation Society's C.P. Labadie Special Recognition Award. An outstanding underwater photographer, Tamara is a popular

speaker on the stages throughout the Great Lakes. She founded and owns Diversions Scuba in Madison, Wisconsin, where she is an active technical instructor teaching the full range of mixed gas, rebreather, and cave diving courses.

Valerie Van Heest (2006)

Valerie began diving in 1978, while in high school growing up near the shore of Lake Michigan, and Great Lakes shipwrecks became her lifelong passion. She co-founded the Underwater Archaeological Society of Chicago, was instrumental in establishing Southwest Michigan's Underwater Preserve, and co-founded Michigan Shipwreck Research Association (MSRA). She uses her professional architectural, management and marketing talents to lead the fundraising, research, documentation, and interpretation of Great Lakes shipwrecks, producing drawings, articles, documentary films, and books, as well as museum exhibits. Since 2008, she has written six books about Great Lakes wrecks, including one for young readers. Her latest book recounts the tragic loss of Northwest Airlines Flight 2501 in Lake Michigan in 1950, and her work with author/explorer Clive Cussler to search for the wreck of the plane. She regularly lectures about shipwrecks and maritime history and has appeared on many television news features as well as on the History, Travel, and Discovery Channels. Preserving shipwrecks and contributing to the wealth of Great Lakes maritime knowledge is her hallmark.

Georgann Wachter (2013)

Georgann is a ranking expert on the shipwrecks of Lake Erie. A writer, researcher,

and illustrator, she has written five books, several multi-media programs and many magazine articles about Great Lakes wrecks with her husband, Mike. Having explored and documented more than 300 Great Lakes shipwrecks, this popular speaker is passionately devoted to spreading the word about the extraordinary underwater world of the Great Lakes. Often she has been the first person to investigate and identify a wreck, since the Wachters have discovered or re-discovered, (since shipwreck hunters are a secretive group) 35 shipwrecks. She and Mike will be investigating two more locations in the summer of 2016. Her work with the Maritime Archaeological Survey Team (MAST) based in Ohio has resulted in increased efforts for shipwreck conservation with the placement of mooring buoys at eleven sites for wreck protection and improved diver access and safety. Georgann is one of the organizers of the popular "Shipwrecks and Scuba" show in northern Ohio held each fall by the Bay Area Divers scuba club.

10. Lake Superior

"NEW SHIPWRECKS" refers to those that are not in the book, *The Great Lakes Diving Guide,* second edition, 2008 *(GLDG2),* either because they had not yet been discovered, or because the authors had not yet learned about their locations.

NEW SHIPWRECKS

A. *W. S. Crosthwaite*
B. *Yosemite*
C. *Jupiter*
D. *Phineas S. Marsh*
E. *Cleveland*
F. *Pacific*
G. *Starucca*
H. *Nelson*
I. *Henry B. Smith*
J. *Olive Jeanette*

K. *Ontario* (barge)
L. *Alice Craig*
M. *Scotiadoc*
N. **Thunder Bay (ON) Ships' Graveyard,** includes:

Mary H. Boyce	*Jed*
A. B. Conmee	*Mary Ann*
Corunna	*Niagara*
Jessie Hall	*W. H. Ritchie*
Henrietta	

"UPDATED SHIPWRECKS" refers to ones that are in the book, *The Great Lakes Diving Guide* (shortened to *GLDG2* when referenced in this chapter). The UPDATED information about each of these shipwrecks could be new or corrected GPS coordinates, additional maritime history, and/or modern-day news about that particular wreck.

UPDATED SHIPWRECKS

1. *Panther*
2. *Comet*
3. *Ora Endress*
4. *M. M. Drake*
5. *Saturn*
6. *Allegheny*
7. *Eureka*
8. *Indiana*
9. *A. A. Parker*
10. *Steven M. Selvick*
11. *Bermuda*
12. *Florida*
13. *T. H. Camp*
14. *Moonlight*
15. *Thomas Wilson*
16. *Harriet B.*

17. *Gray Oak*
18. *Robert L. Fryer*
19. *Green River*
20. *Puckasaw*
21. *Gordon Gauthier*
22. *Neebing*
23. *Mary E. McLachlan*
24. *Ontario* (steamer)
25. *Rappahannock*
26. *Gunilda*
27. *Judge Hart*
28. *Barge 115* (whaleback)
29. *Hiram R. Dixon*
30. *Columbus*
31. *Batchawana*
32. *Edmund Fitzgerald*

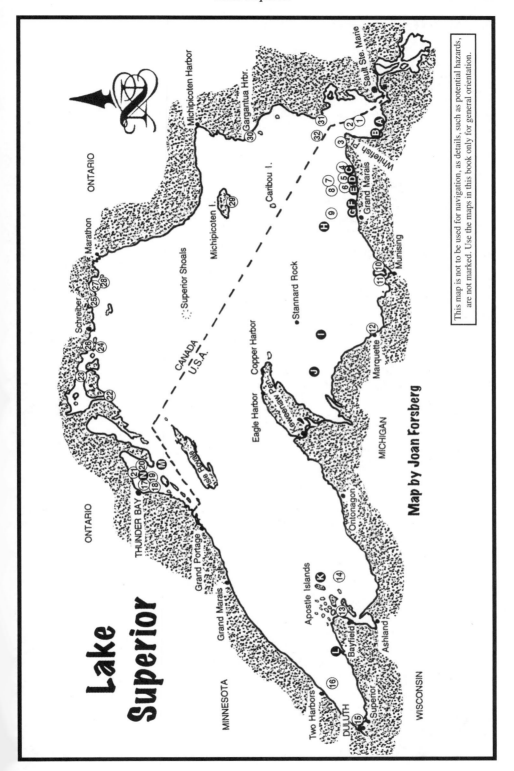

Lake Superior

This map is not to be used for navigation, as details, such as potential hazards, are not marked. Use the maps in this book only for general orientation.

Map by Joan Forsberg

A. W. S. CROSTHWAITE (NEW)

> **DEPTH: 15 feet   LEVEL: Novice**
> **COORDINATES: 46° 28.126'N/084° 52.346'W**

LOCATION: At the southern part of Whitefish Bay, Michigan.

While at anchor, this schooner-barge (197'8" x 34' x 13'3"), built at Saginaw, MI, in 1873, caught on fire from an on-deck stove heating laundry water on November 13, 1904, and burned to a total loss with no lives lost. This is one of the many area shipwrecks located from the air by diver Darryl Ertel.

The **W. S. Crosthwaite,** *lumber-laden.* (KOHL-FORSBERG ARCHIVES)

Right: *News of the loss,* **Duluth Evening Herald,** *Nov. 14, 1904.* (KOHL-FORSBERG ARCHIVES)

Marine News

SCHOONER BURNED.
William Crosthwaite a Total Loss at the Soo.

Sault Ste. Marie, Nov. 14.—(Special to The Herald.)—The schooner William Crosthwaite burned at her anchorage under Whitefish point last night and is a total loss. The crew of seven men had time only to escape from the burning boat, leaving money and clothing behind them.

The Crosthwaite was bound up Lake Superior without cargo in tow of the Saunders. On account of the northwest gale, the vessels remained under the

B. YOSEMITE (NEW)

> **DEPTH: 10 feet   LEVEL: Novice**
> **COORDINATES: 46° 31.274'N/085° 02.341'W**

LOCATION: Found by Darryl Ertel off Emerson, MI, in SW Whitefish Bay.

Launched on April 16, 1867, at Sandusky, OH, this steamer (152'3" x 28'8" x 9'6") burned while at anchor on April 30, 1892. No lives were lost.

Left: *The 146-foot-long* **Belle P. Cross** *closely resembled the* **Yosemite. Right:** *The burning was reported in the* **Duluth Daily News,** *May 2, 1892.* (KOHL-FORSBERG ARCHIVES)

TO THE WATERS EDGE.
The Steam Barge Yosemite, of Sandusky, Burned Off Emerson Last Night.

SAULT STE. MARIE, Special to the News, May 1.—The steam barge Yosemite, of Sandusky, owned by Walker and others, valued at about twenty thousand dollars, was burned to the waters edge while lying to an anchor off Emerson last night. The Yosemite is a small 203 ton vessel. She was built at Sandusky in 1867 and has had several partial rebuilds since then. She had an A-2½ rating for insurance purposes.

C. JUPITER (NEW)

> **DEPTH: 10 feet   LEVEL: Novice**
> **COORDINATES: 46° 43.898'N/085° 19.812'W**

LOCATION: Near Vermilion Point, west of Whitefish Point, MI. Lost with all hands in a storm on Nov. 27, 1872, this new, 400-ton schooner-barge was located by Darryl Ertel in 2007. The *Jupiter's* tow companion, *Saturn,* was also lost with all hands (see p. 201).

D. PHINEAS S. MARSH (NEW)

> **DEPTH: 15 feet   LEVEL: Novice**
> **COORDINATES: 46° 43.516'N/085° 20.746'W**

LOCATION: Five miles east of Two-Hearted River, MI, near Crisp Point. This three-masted schooner (177'2" x 31'1" x 12'9"), built at Black River, OH, in 1867, was stranded and wrecked on August 26, 1896, crew rescued by Lifesaving Service. This site was found aerially by diver/wreck hunter Darryl Ertel.

Left: *The 146-foot-long schooner,* **Phineas S. Marsh. Right:** *The loss as reported in the* **Duluth Evening Herald,** *August 27, 1896.* (KOHL-FORSBERG ARCHIVES)

MARINE MATTERS.

Schooner Marsh Did Not Founder. But is Ashore.

Chicago, Aug. 27.—A telegram from Capt. Somerville, of the schooner P. S. Marsh, lost on Lake Superior yesterday, says that the Marsh did not founder, but dragged ashore. He adds, however, that vessel has gone up the spout. The do not see it that way. Although Capt. Somerville telegraphs he is saving what he can. Wrecking Master Sinclair representing all the companies on the vessel will go to the wreck this afternoon and an effort will be made to get it afloat.

Deer Park, Mich., Aug. 27.—The schooner Phineas S. Marsh, laden with sandstone from Portage to Ashtabula, foundered at 8 o'clock yesterday morning in Lake Superior five miles east of Two Heart river. The crew of the Marsh were saved by the heroic efforts of the life-savers in charge of Capt. Small. The Marsh was owned by Joseph Davids, of Cleveland, and valued at $11,000. Insured for $9000, with $1200 insurance on the freight lost.

E. CLEVELAND (NEW)

> **DEPTH: 15 feet** **LEVEL: Novice**
> **COORDINATES: 46° 42.235'N/085° 24.326'W**

LOCATION: Off the mouth of the Two-Hearted River, Michigan.

This sidewheel steamer (196'7" x 27'8" x 11'), built at Newport (later Marine City), MI, in 1852, was storm-stranded and wrecked, with no lives lost, on October 28, 1864.

F. PACIFIC (NEW)

> **DEPTH: 15 feet** **LEVEL: Novice**
> **COORDINATES: 46° 40.770'N/085° 37.500'W**

LOCATION: Near Deer Park, Michigan, about 20 miles west of Whitefish Point.

Grounded on a shallow shoal with a cargo of lumber enroute from the dock at Deer Park, MI, to Michigan City, Indiana, on November 16, 1887, the steambarge, *Pacific* (191'4" x 29'4" x 11'2"), broke up in a gale three days later before the ship could be towed off the reef. The Lifesaving Service rescued the entire crew, plus the captain's dog. The ship was built as a freight-and-passenger steamer in 1864 at Cleveland, OH, but had just been reduced to a lumber carrier in April 1887. Darryl Ertel found this wreck in 2007.

Left: *The* **Pacific,** *pictured here, had this appearance for more than 20 years before being reduced to a cut-down lumber carrier.*

Right: *News of the ship's loss appeared in the* **Duluth Tribune,** *Nov. 18, 1887.*

(KOHL-FORSBERG ARCHIVES)

A PROPELLER STRANDED.

The Pacific Ashore Twenty Miles West of White Fish Point.

BUFFALO, Nov. 18 —A special dispatch states that the propeller Pacific stranded today twenty miles west of White Fish Point, Lake Superior. She was lumber laden and bound down. The Pacific was built in Cleveland in 1864, and valued at $22,000. She was owned by Cook & Wilson, of Michigan City, Ind.

G. STARUCCA (NEW)

> **DEPTH: 15 feet** **LEVEL: Novice**
> **COORDINATES: 46° 42.106'N/085° 48.510'W**

LOCATION: Off Deer Park, about ten miles west of Grand Marais, Michigan.

Launched on December 1, 1874, at Buffalo, NY, this wooden steamer (218'3" x 34'5" x 13'6") worked on the Great Lakes for 14 years before being stranded well off shore on a shallow, sandy bar in a blizzard on November 15, 1888. The crew jettisoned part of the cargo (general merchandise and heavy railroad wheels), but the vessel stayed stuck. Men from the Deer Park Lifesaving Station rescued the entire crew when the ship broke her spine and her arches collapsed. The vessel was enroute from Buffalo to Duluth at the time.

Left: *With her spine broken and her arches gone, the* **Starucca** *was doomed (pictured here on a better day).*

Right: *News of the loss,* **Marquette Daily Mining Journal,** *Nov. 19, 1888.*

(KOHL-FORSBERG ARCHIVES)

PROBABLY DOOMED.

Such is the Condition of the Steamer Starucca, Ashore at Grand Marais.

THE LAST FLEET OF ORE-CARRIERS FOR THE SEASON NOW IN PORT.

Who Wants to Run the Snow Plow?—Arrived Last Evening—Laid to Rest. Kind Regards.

The Doomed Starucca.

The steamer Starucca, of the Union Steamboat company, ashore ten miles east of Grand Marais, about half way between Whitefish Point and Grand Island, is probably doomed, owing to the fact that so far it has been impossible to get close enough to her with a tug to render her assistance. The large and powerful tug Andrew J. Smith, of the Sault, which was sent to her relief Saturday has returned and reported her in very bad shape. She

H. NELSON (NEW)

LOCATION: This wreck is situated well off Grand Marais, Michigan.

A severe, 55-mile-an-hour, northeast gale on May 13, 1899, snapped (or was it cut?) the towline connecting the ice-covered *Nelson* (163'5" x 32'2" x 12'1") to the steamer, *A. Folsom*, and the other tow, the *Mary B. Mitchell*. After finding herself alone in very heavy seas, the *Nelson* began to break up. The old ship's lifeboat was lowered with the captain's wife, their two-year-old son, and the five sailors in it, but when Captain Hagney tried to jump into it, he missed, landing in the icy lake. When he surfaced, the *Nelson* and the yawl had disappeared. Apparently a line connecting the yawl to the *Nelson* had not been cut, and the yawl was dragged to the lake bottom with the ship. Hagney clung to the floating pilot house, and drifted ashore about 12 hours later at 2 A.M. He wandered for hours, fol-

The **Nelson**.
(KOHL-FORSBERG ARCHIVES)

lowing a telephone line, before reaching a house. With seven lives lost and the ship valued at only $1,400 compared to the $12,000 value of her 1,300 tons of coal, the *Nelson* became the first disaster of the year 1899 on the lakes.

The wreck of the *Nelson* was found in just over 200 feet of water in August 2014, by the Great Lakes Shipwreck Historical Society. The ship's name painted on the stern is still legible, and her wheel, although damaged in the sinking, remains in place.

ALL BUT ONE LOST

Schooner Nelson Sinks Off Grand Marais, Mich. in Saturday's Northwest Gale.

NONE BUT CAPTAIN SURVIVE

Ancient Bay City Boat Goes Down in Strong Wind Saturday Afternoon.

The **Duluth News Tribune**,
May 15, 1899.
(KOHL-FORSBERG ARCHIVES)

I. HENRY B. SMITH (NEW)

LOCATION: Thirty miles north of Marquette, Michigan.

This ill-fated freighter was one of 12 ships lost with their entire crews during the worst cataclysm of nature to hit the Great Lakes in recorded history -- the Great Storm of 1913, which killed 250+ mariners. Built at Lorain, OH, in 1906, the immense *Henry B. Smith* (525' x 55' x 31') loaded her iron ore cargo at Marquette, MI, on Nov. 9, 1913, and headed out into the storm -- while men scrambled to lock down hatches -- the ship never to be seen again above water.

Left: *This archival postcard shows the* **Henry B. Smith** *at Ashtabula, Ohio, in the early 1900s.*

Right: *News of the* Smith's *loss,* **Duluth Herald**, *Nov. 15, 1913.*
(KOHL-FORSBERG ARCHIVES)

PROBABLY ALL OVER.

Steamer H. B. Smith Has Evidently Foundered in Superior.

Marquette, Mich. Nov. 15.—Four oars and a pike pole marked "Henry B. Smith" were picked up on the shore east of Marquette here yesterday by Ban Johnston, a land looker. The steamer Henry B. Smith cleared Marquette in the height of the storm on Sunday night, and finding of the oars and other small wreckage, tends to confirm the fears of the last two days that she has foundered.

It is thought that the boat gave up the attempt to make the Soo and sought to battle her way to shelter east of Keweenaw point.

Three highly experienced Lake Superior shipwreck hunters, Jerry Eliason, Ken Merryman, and Kraig Smith (plus one computer-analysis-savvy wife, Karen Eliason), found this wreck sitting amidst her iron ore cargo in 535 feet of cold, fresh water on May 24, 2013, after a 20-minute search. The intact bow and the heavily damaged stern (the wreck appears to be broken in two), resting on iron ore, suggest the ship broke in half on the surface and spilled her cargo before sinking on top of it.

L.to r.: *Wreck hunters on their boat: Ken Merryman, Jerry Eliason, and Kraig Smith* (PHOTO COURTESY OF JERRY ELIASON). *The* Smith's *wheel house and stern name.* (ROV IMAGES COURTESY OF KEN, JERRY, & KRAIG)

Annual Show in March

Located in Minneapolis Minnesota

Join us for a full day of entertainment, learning, excitement, and fun for the whole family. See what's happening in the dive community, what's new, and where to dive, Travel and Adventure.

Featuring: Excellent Speakers, Shipwrecks, Maritime History, Dive sites, Travel, Exhibitors, New Diving technology, Raffle, Discover SCUBA, Friday Night at the Movies, and more.
Go to www.umsatshow.org for more info

Sponsored by the

Great Lakes Shipwreck Preservation Society

Dedicated to Saving our Shipwrecks from Prevention to Preservation since 1996

First non-profit organization to: Stabilize a shipwreck in a National Park; Implement a Put-it-Back Program; Nominate a shipwreck and have it placed on the National Register of Historic Places, five so far.

GLSPS programs are: Shipwreck preservation and monitoring, Diver access, Placing mooring buoys on Shipwrecks, Put it Back, Annual Upper Midwest SCUBA and Adventure Travel show, National Register of Historic Places nominations, SS Meteor Restoration Project, Shipwreck Documentation, Education, Preserving Maritime History, and more.

For more information and to join GLSPS go to www.glsps.org

J. OLIVE JEANETTE (NEW)

LOCATION: Four miles north of the Huron Island lighthouse, NW of Marquette, MI.

The schooner-barge, *Olive Jeanette,* was a victim of the first of three major storms to strike the Great Lakes, with most of the destruction being done on Lake Superior, in, respectively, September, October, and November, 1905.

Launched at West Bay City, MI, on May 24, 1890, the huge, four-masted *Olive Jeanette* (242' x 39' x 16') toiled on the freshwater seas as a bulk freight schooner-barge being towed by a steamer. Such was the case when the vessel, heavily loaded with iron ore from Superior, WI, for Sandusky, OH, and being towed by the similarly-cargoed steamer, *Iosco,* encountered a violent storm on September 2, 1905. Both the schooner barge, with seven lives, and the steamer, carrying 19 crewmembers, foundered with all hands lost.

While the wreck of the *Olive Jeanette* was located recently by Jerry Eliason and his team, the steamer, *Iosco,* last seen off Stannard Rock lighthouse, remains missing.

Left: *The tragic* **Olive Jeanette.** **Middle:** *The* **Duluth Evening Herald** *reported the loss of the* **Olive Jeanette,** *amidst the tales of many other losses, on Sept. 5, 1905* (BOTH KOHL-FORSBERG ARCHIVES). **Right:** *The* **Olive Jeanette** *in deep water.* (ROV IMAGE COURTESY OF JERRY ELIASON)

K. ONTARIO (BARGE) (NEW)

LOCATION: This wreck lies off Outer Island, Apostle Islands, WI.

Built as a steel, railroad car ferry at Owen Sound, ON, in 1890 for the Canadian Pacific Railway Company, the *Ontario* (297' x 41'3" x 14'9") spent her first 26 years working on the river between Detroit, MI, and Windsor, ON. Later, in 1924, a Lake Superior company in Port Arthur, ON, bought her and reduced the ship to a pulpwood barge. This ship foundered on Oct. 13, 1927, the five-man crew being "rescued with great difficulty." Possibly operating as a Prohibition rumrunner between Canada and the USA in the 1920s, the wreck today lies in 450 feet of water, heavily embedded in, and partly covered with, mud. The *Ontario* was found by Jerry Eliason and his team in 2013.

Left: *The* **Ontario** *worked as a railroad car ferry on the Detroit River between 1890 and 1916.* (KOHL-FORSBERG ARCHIVES). **Right:** *Part of the* **Ontario's** *deep wreckage, and the mud around it.* (ROV IMAGE COURTESY OF JERRY ELIASON)

L. ALICE CRAIG (NEW)

LOCATION: This wreck reportedly lies off Bark Point, near the Apostle Islands, WI.

The small, two-masted schooner, *Alice Craig* (57'6" x 17'6" x 5'10"), launched in 1858 as the *John B. Floyd,* USRC (United States Revenue Cutter), at Milan, OH, and renamed when sold civilian in 1864, was driven ashore in a blinding snowstorm on November 18, 1887, while running between Bayfield, WI, and Siskiwit Bay, WI, "with camp supplies." The crew, while suffering terribly from the bitter cold, survived, and the wreck was later stripped of her rigging and abandoned. A Wisconsin diver stated, in March 2016, that this wreck was recently found; stay tuned.

Right: *The* **Alice Craig's** *"unfortunate sailors" had their story told in the* **Duluth Tribune** *on November 25, 1887.* (KOHL-FORSBERG ARCHIVES)

UNFORTUNATE SAILORS.

The Schooner Alice Craig Driven Ashore Near Ashland, Wis.

The Entire Crew Wander About for Hours—The Captain Frozen.

Other Vessls Meet With Similar Disasters in Various Places.

Narrow Escape.

ASHLAND, Nov. 24.—Monday night the schooner Alice Craig, laden with camp supplies, was driven ashore near Bayfield and went to pieces. The crew escaped in yawls and landed in a dense forest. A

M. *Scotiadoc* (NEW)

LOCATION: This wreck lies in deep water off Trowbridge Island, Ontario.

Sunk in a collision with the steamer, *Burlington*, on June 20, 1953, with the loss of one life, the *Scotiadoc* (424' x 48'1" x 23'9"), launched on May 14, 1904, at Cleveland as the *Martin Mullen*, is the deepest shipwreck found to date in the Great Lakes, a fact not known until 2013 when Jerry Eliason and his team located this wreck in 870 feet of water.

Left: *The* Scotiadoc *underway.*
Right: *The* Scotiadoc *loss, as reported in the* **Toronto Evening Telegram** *on June 22, 1953.* (BOTH KOHL-FORSBERG ARCHIVES)
Below: Scotiadoc *machinery and the ship's name on the hull.* (ROV IMAGES COURTESY OF JERRY ELIASON)

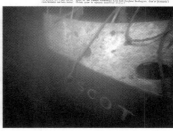

N. THUNDER BAY (ON) SHIPS' GRAVEYARD (NEW)

INTRODUCTION:

Several locations around the Great Lakes stand out as having "Ships' Graveyards" just off their shores. Ships that grew too old and/or too damaged to be of any further use were patched up just enough to tow them out into the lake and purposely sink them. In those environmentally worry-free days, out of sight meant out of mind. Places such as Kingston (ON), Toledo (OH), Detroit (MI), Sarnia (ON), Bay City (MI), Grand Haven (MI), Milwaukee (WI), Sturgeon Bay (WI), and others, have many deliberately discarded vessels lying in their waters or embedded in their shorelines. However, as far as numbers are concerned, the top prizes would go to Chicago (IL) and Thunder Bay (ON).

Research on Chicago's ships' graveyard is still a big work in progress, but in Ontario's Thunder Bay on Lake Superior, a group of divers/researchers, under the leadership of Ryan LeBlanc, has, since July 2001, been doing amazing work in locating, researching, and identifying the ships that were just taken out of the harbor and sunk with little or no fanfare, and with no official and media notice or record. As any scuba diver will tell you, these non-catastrophic ships are, indeed, interesting wrecks of ships worthy of exploration and research, despite lacking dramatic tales behind their demises. In terms of Great Lakes maritime history, the catastrophic, highly-publicized ship losses have been the "easy" ones for historians to document. The easy-to-reach apples have all been plucked from the tree. Difficult work must now be done to document ships that were purposely abandoned. (Another challenging area just barely begun is researching pre-1860's ships that existed prior to mandatory documentation, ships that left little or no paper trail relating to their existence and histories... but that's another story.)

THUNDER BAY SHIPS' GRAVYARD:

More than three dozen hulls of abandoned and scuttled ships have, in recent years, been located off Thunder Bay, Ontario, in water ranging from 190 to 250 feet in depth. The histories of three of them (the *Corunna*, the *Niagara*, and the *Mary Ann*, with archival photographs of each), appeared in *GLDG2* on page 557, so they will not be repeated here, with the exception of the *Mary Ann* for a reason that will be given. Here are some of the other abandoned ships that have been identified to date:

The **Mary Boyce.**

The wooden steambarge, *Mary H. Boyce* (181'4" x 34'2" x 14'), built at Grand Haven, Michigan, by Duncan Robertson in 1888, was the ship that carried the steel plates, frames, boilers, and engine from Cleveland, OH, to Port Arthur, ON, in 1914 for the new vessel named the *Noronic* that was being built there. Ownership of the *Boyce* was transferred in 1917 from Chicago's Robert McCormick to the Ontario Transportation Company. After burning at Fort William, ON, in 1928 and lying abandoned in the boneyard there for years, the *Boyce* was finally scuttled in 1933 off the Welcome Islands.

The **Jessie Hall.**

Launched on May 11, 1881, as the wooden tug, *Superior* (92' x 18'3" x 10'), at Owen Sound, ON, and renamed the *A. B. Conmee* in 1917, this vessel was dismantled and scuttled in deep water in May 1937.

The 56-gross-ton tugboat, *Jessie Hall* (84' x 17' x 9'), built in 1867 at Buffalo, NY, and transferred to Canadian ownership in 1874, had its registry closed in 1909, after which the boat lay idle in the harbor for years. In 1936, her boiler was removed, but was lost in the harbor while enroute to the dock. A navigational hazard, this boiler damaged several ships and led to the clean-up of the harbor, with this old tug being moved to the graveyard's deep waters.

The **Mary Ann.**

The *Henrietta* (126'2" x 28' x 6'7"), a sternwheel steamer (perhaps the only one ever to appear on Lake Superior) built at Oshkosh, WI, in 1879, was sold to Canadian interests in 1904, ending up in the deep graveyard of ships.

Launched as the huge steamer, *Cherokee*, at Marine City, MI, in 1889, renamed *Maplegrove* in 1918 when it was sold Canadian, and again renamed, this time **Jed** (208'7" x 35'7" x 14'5") in 1921, this wooden ship was abandoned and scuttled in deep water in 1935.

The **Jed.**

The very first vessel registered in 1867 in the new country called the Dominion of Canada was the tug, *Mary Ann* (78' x 15' x 8'). Built at Stromness, ON, this little boat rescued the crew of the steamer, *A. Neff,* when it was wrecked on October 20, 1886. But in 1901, the 34-year-old vessel was condemned and abandoned, and much later scuttled in 1933. Initially thought to be one of the wrecks in deep water, the *Mary Ann* was accidentally found in 2013 in 70 feet of water, and eventually identfied, by two divers, David Shepherd and Rob Valley, who were heading out to a different wreck. The *Mary Ann's* coordinates are

The **W. H. Ritchie.**

48° 21' 15.66"N/089° 7' 10.56"W.

The *W. H. Ritchie* (161'2" x 30'4" x 10'7"), originally named the *Stephen C. Hall* when launched at Grand Haven, MI, in 1880, was given her new name in 1921, just in time for the ship to be burned to a total loss at the Port Arthur, ON, dock on Sept. 27, 1921. What remained of the hull was later scuttled in the deep waters of the ships' graveyard.

Stay tuned for more identifications of the many wrecks in this cemetery of ships.

1. PANTHER (UPDATE -- *GLDG2* p. 494)

This 247-foot-long, wooden steamer sank in 110 feet of water in a collision with another ship on June 26, 1916, with no lives lost.

The sinking of the **Panther** *was publicized in the* **Duluth Herald** *on June 27, 1916. Features of the* **Panther** *shipwreck include its engine and steering post.* (VIDEO FREEZE-FRAMES BY CRIS KOHL)

2. COMET (UPDATE -- *GLDG2* p. 494-495)

Lying in 230 feet of water southeast of Whitefish Point, MI, this 1857, wooden steamer sank in a collision with another steamer on August 26, 1875, with the tragic loss of 10 lives. The engine, now exposed, has the ship's name painted on it (see photo below.)

Many small items that are of great interest to divers litter the Comet *site, such as dishes* (left) *and a safe* (right).
Larger items also appear, such as the Comet's *engine, rudder, and propeller* (below).
(PHOTOS BY JITKA HANAKOVA)

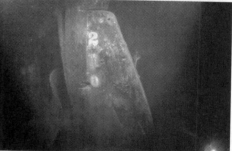

3. ORA ENDRESS (UPDATE -- *GLDG2* p. 498)

> **DEPTH: To 10 feet   LEVEL: Novice, or snorkle**
> **COORDINATES: 46° 46.395′N/084° 58.657′W**

This little tugboat, built in 1910 and lost in 1914 when it capsized off Whitefish Point, MI (no lives were lost), lies mostly embedded in the sandy bottom of Lake Superior.

The **Ora Endress** (KOHL-FORSBERG ARCHIVES)*--and under water.* (VIDEO FREEZE-FRAMES BY CRIS KOHL)

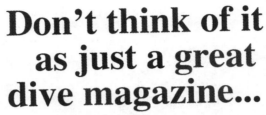
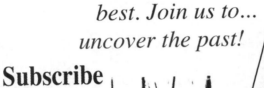

4. *M. M. Drake* (UPDATE -- *GLDG2* p. 500-501)

> **DEPTH: 42 to 50 feet   LEVEL: Intermediate**
> **COORDINATES: 46° 46.588′N/085° 05.933′W**

This wooden steamer sank in late 1901 after colliding with a sinking barge whose crew the *Drake* was trying to rescue. One life from the barge was lost.

Left: The M. M. Drake's propulsion mechanism remains nearly intact.
Right: The Drake's enormous boiler is a highlight of this interesting shipwreck site.
(VIDEO FREEZE-FRAMES BY JOAN FORSBERG)

5. *Saturn* (UPDATE -- *GLDG2* p. 501-502)

> **DEPTH: 20 feet   LEVEL: Novice**
> **COORDINATES: 46° 45.952′N/085° 01.547′W**

The *Saturn* and the *Jupiter* (see p. 192) were both lost with all hands while being towed by a steamer in late 1872. Shifting sands alternately cover/uncover this shipwreck.

Left: *The bow draught markings.*   **Middle:** *The* **Saturn** *resembled the* **Bay City.** (KOHL-FORSBERG ARCHIVES). **Right:** *The* **Saturn's** *hull and iron ore cargo.* (VIDEO FREEZE-FRAMES BY JOAN FORSBERG)

6. *Allegheny* (UPDATE -- *GLDG2* p. 502-503)

> **DEPTH: 30 feet   LEVEL: Novice-Intermediate**
> **COORDINATES: 46° 46.016′N/085° 10.601′W**

Stranded and wrecked in a spring-of-1913 storm, this site is subject to shifting sands.

7. *Eureka* (UPDATE -- *GLDG2* p. 506)

> **DEPTH: 48 to 54 feet   LEVEL: Intermediate**
> **COORDINATES: 46° 50.029′N/085° 10.808′W**

Lying on one of the shallow rises in Lake Superior's bottom far off shore, the *Eureka*, foundered in a late 1886 storm with the loss of all six hands and an iron ore cargo.

MARINE NEWS.

The Barge Eureka Lost and all Hands Supposed to Have Perished.

SAULT STE. MARIE, October 22—The barge Eureka, reported yesterday as having broken loose from her tow, foundered in Lake Superior on the 20th inst. ten miles above Whitefish Point and five miles from shore in seven fathoms of water, and is abreast of life-saving station No. 8. From present information all hands are lost. Had any of the crew been rescued information would without doubt have been received at this place. Several steamers have passed the wreck and would have brought the survivors down either from the wreck or Whitefish Point had there been any. The vessel's foremast and mainmast are above water. She was ore laden from Marquette and in tow of the steam barge Prentice.

Left: *The Eureka resembled the* **Minerva.**   **Middle:** *The* **Detroit Free Press,** *Oct. 23, 1886.*
(KOHL-FORSBERG ARCHIVES). **Right: Eureka's** *bow in the sand.* (VIDEO FREEZE-FRAME BY CRIS KOHL)

8. *INDIANA* (UPDATE -- *GLDG2* p. 506)

DEPTH: 103 to 118 feet   LEVEL: Advanced
COORDINATES: 46° 48.574′N/085° 17.184′W

Despite the Smithsonian recovering the engine and its components, this historic wreck, lost in 1858, remains very interesting, with decking that defies both weight and gravity.

Left: *The* **Indiana's** *bow features some unique, extended, structural arms.* **Right:** *The iron ore cargo remains on the wreck, along with an 1850's hand cart.* (VIDEO FREEZE-FRAMES BY CRIS KOHL)

9. *A. A. PARKER* (UPDATE -- *GLDG2* p. 506)

This was the last shipwreck for which famous wreck hunter John Steele (unsuccessfully) searched in July, 1997, before retiring from the lakes. The wooden *Parker*, located in deep water in 2001, foundered after springing a leak in September, 1903.

Left: *The* **A. A. Parker** *remains considerably intact.*
Right: *The* **Parker's** *name is still visible on the stern.*
Below: *An amazing sight, exposed after the collapse of some decking, is the steam engine with its gauges.*
(ALL PHOTOS BY JITKA HANAKOVA)

Left: *The historic, remote Crisp Point (Michigan) lighthouse has been restored. Many ships sank off this shoreline.* **Right:** *Shipwreck hunter Darryl Ertel recovers part of the washed up, thick, polypropylene line that he had tied to the wreck of the* **Jupiter** *near Crisp Point, but which Lake Superior's shifting sands had covered again at this point in time.* (PHOTOS BY CRIS KOHL)

10. STEVEN M. SELVICK (UPDATE -- *GLDG2* p. 510-511)

This 1915 tug, a popular wreck site, lies in 65 feet of water off Munising, Michigan.

The tug, Steven M. Selvick, *was purposely sunk in 1996.* (PHOTOS BY CAL KOTHRADE)

11. BERMUDA (UPDATE -- *GLDG2* p. 514)

This upright, beautiful schooner, resting here since October 1883, sits in shallow water (about 30 feet) in a protected bay (hence its hull still being intact) off Munising, Michigan. Boaters, divers, and tourists enjoying the shipwreck views from glassbottom boats are frequently seen at this popular site.

Left: *The schooner,* **Bermuda,** *is the most visited shipwreck in Lake Superior.* (PHOTO BY CAL KOTHRADE)

12. FLORIDA (UPDATE -- *GLDG2* p. 517)

The correct depth of this novice level shipwreck dive at Marquette, MI, is 10 to 15 feet.

13. T. H. CAMP (UPDATE -- *GLDG2* p. 528-529)

This tug sank off Madeline Island, WI, on November 16, 1900, with no lives lost.

14. MOONLIGHT (UPDATE -- *GLDG2* p. 530)

This wrecked schooner-barge foundered off Michigan Island, WI, on Sept. 13, 1903.

15. THOMAS WILSON (UPDATE -- *GLDG2* p. 532)

This whaleback steamer, sunk in a collision with another ship on June 7, 1902, lies about one mile outside Duluth, MN, harbor in about 70 feet of water.

Above: *Divers Cris Kohl and Elmer Engman (Elmer wrote a book about this wreck in the 1970's) explore and photograph the* **Thomas Wilson** *in 2008.* (VIDEO FREEZE-FRAMES BY JOAN FORSBERG)

Left: *A winch, part of the* **Wilson's** *below-deck machinery.* (PHOTO BY CRIS KOHL)

Below: *Joan Forsberg sneaks up on a drowsy burbot, nestled between the fairleads on the* **Wilson's** *bow and initially dazed by the unexpected lights before it slowly glides off into the darkness.* (PHOTOS BY CRIS KOHL)

16. HARRIET B. (UPDATE -- *GLDG2* p. 540)

This huge barge, lost in a 1922 collision, lies in about 650 feet off Two Harbors, MN.

Above: *Paint remains discernible in these scenes featuring bitts and a wheelbarrow.* **Below:** *A ladder and thick lines on bitts make the wreck come alive.* (ROV IMAGES COURTESY OF JERRY ELIASON)

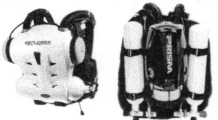

17. GRAY OAK   (UPDATE -- *GLDG2* p. 555)

> **DEPTH: 108 feet   LEVEL: Advanced**
> **COORDINATES: 48° 20′ 50.2582″N/089° 7′ 17.1731″W**

This 133-foot-long scow-schooner was scuttled in 108 feet of water in about 1911.

18. ROBERT L. FRYER   (UPDATE -- *GLDG2* p. 556)

> **DEPTH: To 35 feet   LEVEL: Novice-Intermediate**
> **COORDINATES: 48° 21′ 50.8249″N/089° 8′ 30.5591″W**

Burned as a public spectacle in 1930, the appropriately-named *Fryer* lies in 35 feet.

19. GREEN RIVER   (UPDATE -- *GLDG2* p. 556)

> **DEPTH: 50 to 80 feet   LEVEL: Advanced**
> **COORDINATES: 48° 21′ 55.943″N/089° 8′ 34.511″W**

Only 450 feet from the *Fryer*, this wooden steamer was scuttled in 80 feet in 1932.

20. PUCKASAW   (UPDATE -- *GLDG2* p. 556)

> **DEPTH: 55 to 80 feet   LEVEL: Advanced**
> **COORDINATES: 48° 22′ 0.3″N/089° 8′ 32.7011″W**

This 96-foot-long tug, scuttled in 1934, lies in 80 feet of water near the *Green River*.

21. GORDON GAUTHIER   (UPDATE -- *GLDG2* p. 557)

> **DEPTH: 15 feet   LEVEL: Novice**
> **COORDINATES: 48° 30′ 16.6645″N/088° 59′ 4.7975″W**

Dive shop owner Wally Peterson recently returned the propeller to this wreck site.

22. NEEBING   (UPDATE -- *GLDG2* p. 558)

> **DEPTH: 60 to 100 feet   LEVEL: Advanced**
> **COORDINATES: 48° 39′ 47.9989″N/088° 7′ 48″W**

This gravel carrier, in 100 feet of water, took five lives with it in 1937.

23. MARY E. McLACHLAN   (UPDATE -- *GLDG2* p. 558)

> **DEPTH: 16 to 33 feet   LEVEL: Novice-Intermediate**
> **COORDINATES: 48° 54′ 39.6″N/087° 48′ 3.6″W**

This 251-foot-long, 1893 schooner foundered in 33 feet of water in 1921.

24. ONTARIO (STEAMER)   (UPDATE -- *GLDG2* p. 562)

> **DEPTH: 10 to 40 feet   LEVEL: Novice-Intermediate**
> **COORDINATES: 48° 45′ 11.9988″N/087° 31′ 59.4012″W**

A boiler on shore marks the general location of this steamer wrecked in 1899.

25. RAPPAHANNOCK   (UPDATE -- *GLDG2* p. 562-563)

> **DEPTH: 35 to 85 feet   LEVEL: Advanced**
> **COORDINATES: 48° 48′ 57.996″N/086° 57′ 31.23″W**

This 308-foot-long steamer, sunk in 1911, lies on a slope in Jackfish Bay, Ontario.

26. GUNILDA (UPDATE -- *GLDG2* p. 560-561)

> **DEPTH: 257 feet   LEVEL: Technical**
> **COORDINATES: 48° 47' 3.0012"N/087° 25' 19.9992"W**

Proclaimed by the 1980 Cousteau expedition as being "the most beautiful shipwreck in the world," the *Gunilda* is infrequently visited due to its extreme depth.

L. to r.: *The luxury yacht,* Gunilda, *sank in deep water in 1911 due to a rash accident* (Kohl-Forsberg Archives); *Fred Broennle, who, for the last half of his life, claimed ownership of the* Gunilda, *recovered a grate and other items* (Photo courtesy of Wally Peterson); *Cris Kohl gets a grip on that brass* Gunilda *grate at Thunder Country Diving, Wally's dive shop in Ontario* (Photo by Wally Peterson). Gunilda *binoculars that Wally also purchased from Fred Broennle.* (Photo by Cris Kohl)

27. JUDGE HART (UPDATE -- *GLDG2* p. 563-564)

> **DEPTH: 180 to 210 feet   LEVEL: Technical**
> **COORDINATES: 48° 47' 20.4"N/086° 38' 13/8012"W**

This steel freighter, lost with a grain cargo in 1942, lies near Neys Provincial Park.

28. BARGE 115 (WHALEBACK) (UPDATE -- *GLDG2* p. 564)

> **DEPTH: 40 to 80 feet   LEVEL: Intermediate-Advanced**
> **COORDINATES: 48.698190N/086.654579W**

This is the most dramatic, Christmas-time, survival story in the Great Lakes.

29. HIRAM R. DIXON (UPDATE -- *GLDG2* p. 566)

> **DEPTH: 10 to 15 feet   LEVEL: Novice**
> **COORDINATES: 47.714465N/085.7709906W**

This wooden steamer burned in 1903 in the harbor of remote Michipicoten Island.

30. COLUMBUS (UPDATE -- *GLDG2* p. 567)

> **DEPTH: To 27 feet   LEVEL: Novice**
> **COORDINATES: 47.566842'N/084.969400W**

This tug, burned in 1909, could be the most difficult Great Lakes shore dive to reach.

31. BATCHAWANA (UPDATE -- *GLDG2* p. 570)

> **DEPTH: 4 to 35 feet   LEVEL: Novice-Intermediate**
> **COORDINATES: 46.990208N/084.790388W**

Lying alongside Rousseau Island, this steamer burned in 1907.

32. EDMUND FITZGERALD (UPDATE -- *GLDG2* p. 568-569)

The most famous (plus the largest and the most recent) commercial shipwreck in the Great Lakes, the *Fitzgerald* sank in 529 feet of water with the loss of all 29 hands on Nov. 10, 1975. At the request of the victims' families, the Ontario government (the wreck lies 900 feet inside Canada) has made this wreck legally off-limits to any and all explorations.

Great Lakes -- *In Memoriam*

We would like to pay tribute to some of the many people who are no longer with us, but who contributed to the promotion of the Great Lakes and their shipwrecks/maritime history. All photos were taken by Cris Kohl or Joan Forsberg:

Joyce Hayward (d. August, 2009) -- the Lady of the Lakes

Great Lakes shipwrecks were Joyce Hayward's passion. An accomplished underwater photographer, she loved presenting multi-media programs to educate the public about the importance of

preservation and protection of these non-renewable cultural resources. Her work in shipwreck and marine biology education resulted in her being featured in a PBS special, "The Great Lakes in Depth." A member of all, and officer of many, U.S. and Canadian Great Lakes wreck conservation organizations, she was appointed by the governor to be Ohio's shipwreck management advisor. She founded the "Shipwrecks and Scuba" show in Ohio, one of the premier dive shows in the Midwest that is still going strong today. Volunteer divers from all over the Great Lakes were eager to work with Joyce as she spearheaded the underwater archaeological survey of the deep wreck of the *Cornelia B. Windiate*, which resulted in the expansion of the boundaries of the NOAA Thunder Bay National Marine Sanctuary to include this wreck. A mentor and role model for generations of other women divers, she was inducted into the Women Divers Hall of Fame in 2001. With her passing from cancer in 2009, the Great Lakes lost the best friend they ever had.

Dennis Hale (d. September, 2015) -- Sole Shipwreck Survivor

The gales of November had claimed the 60-year-old *Daniel J. Morrell* and her entire crew except for Dennis Hale, who survived a freezing, 38-hour ordeal on a life raft, clad only in his underwear and a peacoat. Although the ship had sunk in 1966, it was 15 years before he could talk about

it, so great was the effect of having been the sole survivor on him. The subject of two books, *Sole Survivor* by Jim and Pat Stayer and Tim Juhl, and the autobiographical *Shipwrecked – Reflections of a Sole Survivor*, Dennis became a sought-after speaker and inspired all who heard his dramatic, deeply-felt, moving story. Cris Kohl recalls the night in late November 1996, when he and Dennis nervously peeked out from behind the curtains to a full house of 1,100 people in the audience at Port Huron's McMorran Place Auditorium. "Have you ever presented to this many people?" "No, have you?" "No!" They both ended up doing fine at this 30th anniversary of the loss of the *Morrell* show. Although he was a big man, Dennis had an impish quality and a twinkle in his eye, and a boatload of hilarious, bawdy tales.

John Steele (d. January, 2016) -- King of the Shipwreck Hunters

A banker by profession, but an aquatic adventurer with a love of maritime history in his real life, John found his first Great Lakes shipwreck in 1959, using primitive World War Two submarine detection equipment. John persisted in this exciting pastime, gaining proficiency with the early equipment available to him, right up until the time he hung up his fins in 1997. He gave away all of the artifacts he recovered to museums and libraries, and he openly shared the locations of the shipwrecks he found. In his 38 years of wreck hunting, he located, or helped locate, more than 60 of the most popular and historic shipwreck sites in the inland seas.

James P. Barry (d. July, 2011) -- Great Lakes Maritime Historian

With book titles ranging from *Wrecks and Rescues of the Great Lakes:A Photographic History* to *Ships of the Great Lakes, 300 Years of Navigation* to two books about the maritime history of Georgian Bay, and numerous others, including books for young people, Ohioan James Barry packed and publicized a lot of fascinating nautical facts into his 93 years.

Ralph Roberts (d. June, 2014) -- Maritime Photographs Archivist

Ralph, as a consultant for the Institute for Great Lakes Research at Bowling Green State University, Ohio, spent summer vacations in the 1960's and 1970's visiting museums and libraries in the Great Lakes with Dr. Richard Wright, the institute's founder, shooting thousands of pictures of archival maritime photographs, making prints for the institute and for his personal collection. Ralph openly shared his maritime knowledge and photographs with everyone, and nearly every book about the Great Lakes includes his archival photos.

Mark Kistner (d. April, 2009) -- Hardy Great Lakes Promoter

A Michigan lawyer and volunteer firefighter in one life, and an outdoorsman who loved skiing, ice climbing, kayaking, and particularly shipwreck diving in another, Mark also worked as a scuba instructor, passionately promoting the shipwrecks of the Great Lakes and the Michigan Underwater Preserves. His endurance in cold water was legendary. Helping rescue a diver trapped inside the engine room of the *Cedarville* in the Straits of Mackinac in 2000, with the diver's head hanging out of a porthole, Mark shared air with him for half an hour in 70 feet of cold water before the diver was rescued -- with Mark wearing only a bathing suit for insulation!

Bill Patterson (d. Dec., 2012) -- St. Clair River Diving Pioneer

Bill took up scuba diving in the early 1950's and focused on what was in the water close to his home along the St. Clair River. He and his buddy, Fred Dufty, are credited with finding many of the shipwrecks in that river during those early years. Bill was instrumental in setting up the Lake Huron Lore Marine Museum and he donated many shipwreck artifacts to numerous museums for display.

Michael Schoger (d. 2013) -- Commercial Hardhat Diver

While working as a commercial hardhat diver for a gas company in the 1950's, 1960's and 1970's in southwestern Ontario, Mike located several historic shipwrecks in the waters of western Lake Erie. His collection of hardhat diving equipment, including a full outfit and pump from the 1850's that he painstakingly restored to perfection, impressed all who saw it. In the 1980's and 1990's, Mike was a popular speaker at a variety of shows and meetings.

Fred Broennle (d. April, 2013) -- Owner of the *Gunilda* Shipwreck

Fred is best remembered as the man who bought the salvage rights to the famous Lake Superior wreck of the luxury yacht, *Gunilda*, and for then trying to raise the wreck from its grave in 257 feet of water. He did succeed in raising a number of artifacts from it, but he is best remembered for raising the public's awareness of how exciting Great Lakes maritime history can be.

Nancy Boucha (d. January, 2016) -- Active Great Lakes Promoter

Becoming a diver in 1976 opened a wonderful new world for Nancy, and becoming an underwater photographer ignited her passion. Her photography won awards and one of her beautiful images graced the front cover of the book, *Our World – Underwater, the First 40 Years,* the scuba show at which she was a stalwart speaker and exhibitor. She was named Diver of the Year by the 20 Fathom Dive Club and was one of the founders of the Skyline Dive Club. Her 6,000 logged dives earned her the SSI Platinum Pro Award. Nancy became a dive instructor in 1980, was an Emergency First Responder Instructor Trainer and, over the course of her 35-year career, taught more than 1,500 divers how to be safe and enjoy the sport she loved so much.

Bernie Bloom (d. Nov., 2011) -- Divemaster of the *Alvin Clark*

Active in many shipwreck organizations like the Neptune Dive Club of Green Bay (the oldest dive club in Wisconsin) and the Underwater Archaeological Society of Chicago, with more than 50 years of shipwreck diving experience, Bernie's biggest job was divemastering the 1969 raising of the schooner, *Alvin Clark*, lost in 1864, from 110 feet of Green Bay water (see *GLDG2,* p. 474, and the chapter, "Return from the Dead: Two Raised Shipwrecks" in the book, *Shipwreck Tales of the Great Lakes*.)

From the Debris Field...

Some miscellaneous Great Lakes photos and notes...

Joan, Rennie LaPointe, and Cris on Manitoulin Island in 2015. Rennie was captain of a dive boat at Tobermory in 1997 when Cris took Joan there for her first time, and, as captain, Rennie performed a marriage ceremony for them on board. He was relieved to find that they REALLY got married not long after that!

Fellow Great Lakes historian Frederick Stonehouse with Joan recently at Fred's home turf of Marquette, MI, on Lake Superior. (PHOTO BY CRIS KOHL)

Cris and Joan in 2008, dressed up,...and dressed down for cleaning up the Buccaneer *(see p. 149-151).*

Several musically-inclined underwater photographers (including the Great Lakes' Cris Kohl) formed a rock band, the Wetsuits, that went on a 2010 "World Tour," including lively performances at Chicago's Our World--Underwater Show and NYC's Beneath the Sea Show -- backed up by the Wet-ettes (which included the Great Lakes' Joan Forsberg and several other musically-inclined members of the Women Divers Hall of Fame.)

Patrick Folkes (left) and Art Amos (right) joined Cris and Joan on Manitoulin Island in 2015. Joan took this photo of the authors of the first two Ontario dive guides (by Patrick and Art in 1979, and Cris in 1985).

Cris, Richie Kohler, and John Chatterton take a break from their day jobs at the firm of Kohl, Kohler, and Kohlest. (PHOTO BY JOAN FORSBERG)

Bibliography

This bibliography covers mainly books and periodicals that were published or produced between late 2007 and late 2015, with few exceptions. For bibliographic information that appeared prior to late 2007, please see the bibliography found in *The Great Lakes Diving Guide* on pages 591-598.

A. Books

A Centennial Tribute to the Great Lakes Storm: 1913. Goderich, ON: Great Lakes Storm of 1913 Remembrance Committee, 2013.

Abrahamson, Robert M. *Luck of the Draw, The Mataafa Story*. Superior, WI: Robert M. Abrahamson, 2014.

Baillod, Brendon. *Fathoms Deep But Not Forgotten, Wisconsin's Lost Ships*. Madison, WI: Wisconsin Underwater Archaeology Association, 2010.

Brown, Curt. *So Terrible a Storm: A Tale of Fury on Lake Superior*. Minneapolis, MN: Voyageur Press, 2008.

Carroll, Paul. *The Wexford: Elusive Shipwreck of the Great Storm, 1913*. Toronto, ON: Natural Heritage Books, 2010.

Chicago Maritime Society, eds. *A Treasury of Chicago Maritime History*. Chicago, IL: Lake Claremont Press, 2008.

Daniel, Stephen B. *Shipwrecks along Lake Superior's North Shore, A Diver's Guide*. St. Paul, MN: Minnesota Historical Society Press, 2008.

Dear Ella,...I hope this is not like this in the fall, June 1913. A Tribute to Lost Mariners & Ships in the Great Lakes Storm of 1913 as Told by Their Descendants. Goderich, ON: Great Lakes Storm of 1913 Remembrance Committee, 2013.

Echo Soundings, Marine News from the Amherstburg Echo, 1936 and 1937, Volume XIII. Amherstburg, ON: Marsh Historical Collection, 2013.

Filey, Mike. *I Remember Sunnyside, The Rise & Fall of a Magical Era*. Toronto, ON: The Dundurn Group, 1996.

Hale, Dennis. *Shipwrecked! Reflections of the Sole Survivor*. Rock Creek, OH: Dennis Hale, 2010.

Halsey, John R., and Wayne R. Lusardi. *Beneath the Inland Seas, Michigan's Underwater Archaeological Heritage, 2nd edition*. Lansing, MI: Michigan Department of History, Arts and Libraries, 2008.

Keenan, Hudson. *Arrived on This Ship, Great Lakes Postcards from the Early Twentieth Century*. Holt, MI: Thunder Bay Press, 2012.

Kohl, Cris. *The Great Lakes Diving Guide*, 2nd edition. West Chicago, IL: Seawolf Communications, Inc., 2008.

Kohl, Cris, and Joan Forsberg. *The Christmas Tree Ship*. West Chicago, IL: Seawolf Communications, Inc., 2013.

.............*The Wreck of the GRIFFON, The Greatest Mystery of the Great Lakes*. West Chicago, Illinois: Seawolf Communications, Inc., 2014.

Leaves from the War Log of the Nancy, Eighteen Hundred and Thirteen. Huronia Historical Development Council and Ontario Department of Tourism and Information. n.d.

Longhurst, G. I. "Buck." *Steamers of the Turkey Trail*. Gore Bay, ON: Gore Bay & Western Manitoulin Museum, 2011.

Marcolin, Lorenzo. *A Great Lakes Treasury of Old Postcards, Canadian Harbour Scenes 1894-1960*. Midland, ON: Huronia Museum, 2007.

McGreevy, Robert. *Lost Legends of the Lakes, An Illustrated History*. Harbor Beach, MI: Robert McGreevy, 2011.

Ouderkirk, Capt. Gerry. *Shipwrecked on the Bruce Coast*. Published ca. 1995; 31 numbered pages; no other publishing information given.

Powers, Tom. *In the Grip of the Whirlwind, The Armistice Day Storm of 1940*. Holt, MI: Thunder Bay Press, 2009.

Richardson, Ross. *The Search for the Westmoreland, Lake Michigan's Treasure Shipwreck*. Traverse City, MI: Arbutus Press, 2012.

Smith, Arthur Britton. *Legend of the Lake, The 22-Gun Brig-Sloop Ontario, 1780, New Discovery Edition*. Kingston, ON: Quarry Heritage Books, 2009.

Stein, C. E. *The Wreck of the Erie Belle*. Wheatley, ON: Ship 'N Shore Publishing Company, 1970.

Stonehouse, Frederick. *The Last Laker, Finding a Wreck Lost in the Great Lakes' Worst Storm*. Duluth, MN: Lake Superior Port Cities, Inc., 2015.

Van Heest, Valerie. *Lost & Found, Legendary Lake Michigan Shipwrecks*. Holland, MI: In-Depth Editions, 2012.
..............*Lost on the Lady Elgin*. Holland, MI: In-Depth Editions, 2010.

Wrigley, Ronald. *Shipwrecked, Vessels Meet Doom on the North Shore* (of Lake Superior). Thunder Bay, ON: RW Publishing, 2013.

B. Periodical Literature

Birke, Scott. "Under The Bay." Interview with Cris Kohl and others. *On The Bay Magazine* (Georgian Bay). Vol. 8, No. 3 (Summer, 2011), 62-69.

Blake, Erica, photographs by Andy Morrison. "The Great Storm of 1913." *Wreck Diving Magazine*. Issue 14 (2007), 46-54.
..............photographs by Andy Morrison. "The *Nordmeer* is a Great Lakes shipwreck more than 40 years in the making." *Wreck Diving Magazine*. Issue 21 (2010), 28-33.

Daniel, Jared, and David and Mickey Trotter. "Desperate Voyage, The Loss of the Sidewheel Steamer *Keystone State*." *Wreck Diving Magazine*. Issue 32 (2014), 12-17.

Janzen, John. Underwater photography by Alan Williams. "Deep Inspirations, *Carl D. Bradley* Memorial." *Wreck Diving Magazine*. Issue 17 (2009), 46-55.

Kohl, Cris. "The 12-Fathom Lady of Lake Erie (the *Willis*)." *Wreck Diving Magazine*. Issue 26 (2012), 56-61.
..............*"America,* The Beautiful, Part 1 and Part 2." *Wreck Diving Magazine*. Issue 23 (2011), 44-53, and Issue 24 (2011), 50-55.
.............."The Brig *Sandusky* and the Figurehead Controversy." *Wreck Diving Magazine*.

Issue 22 (2010), 50-57.

.............."Collision on Lake Huron (the *F. T. Barney*)." *Wreck Diving Magazine*. Issue 21 (2010), 34-39.

.............."Deep in Lake Superior: Steamship *Samuel Mather*." *Wreck Diving Magazine*. Issue 17 (2009), 56-61.

.............."Ghost Fleet of the St. Clair River." *Wreck Diving Magazine*. Issue 37 (2015), 48-55.

.............."Great Lakes Treasure: Paddlewheeler *Comet*." *Wreck Diving Magazine*. Issue 18 (2009), 36-41.

.............."The Great Storm of 1913." *Wreck Diving Magazine*. Issue 31 (2013), 28-35.

.............."Hard Labor in a Large Graveyard (the *Cayuga*)." *Wreck Diving Magazine*. Issue 29 (2013), 58-65.

.............."Lake Erie's Surprising Mystery Shipwreck (the *Louis O'Neil*)." *Wreck Diving Magazine*. Issue 19 (2009), 48-55.

.............."The *Material Service*." *Wreck Diving Magazine*. Issue 16 (2008), 54-62.

.............."The Mystery of the Shipwrecked Barges (*Atlasco* and *Condor*)." *Wreck Diving Magazine*. Issue 25 (2011), 32-39.

.............."An Oddly Named Shipwreck, The *Joyland*." *Wreck Diving Magazine*. Issue 15 (2008), 12-21.

.............."One *Rotarian's* Loss of Innocence" *Wreck Diving Magazine*. Issue 36 (2015), 60-69.

.............."The *Sagamore,* A Whaleback of the Freshwater Seas." *Wreck Diving Magazine*. Issue 14 (2007), 64-71.

.............."The Short, Unhappy Life of Duane Precious (the tug, *Monarch*)." *Wreck Diving Magazine*. Issue 20 (2010), 28-37.

.............."A Small Workhorse Among Giants (the *Munson*)." *Wreck Diving Magazine*. Issue 32 (2014), 60-65.

.............."A *Sport* Diver's Delight." *Wreck Diving Magazine*. Issue 33 (2014), 28-37.

.............."Terror on the *Clarion!*" *Wreck Diving Magazine*. Issue 35 (2015), 36-45.

.............."Triumphs and Tragedies of the *Arabia*, Part 1 and Part 2." *Wreck Diving Magazine*. Issue 27 (2012), 42-49, and Issue 28 (2012), 54-61.

.............."The *Vienna's* Last Waltz." *Wreck Diving Magazine*. Issue 30 (2013), 26-35.

.............."When Haste Made Waste -- The *George M. Cox*." *Wreck Diving Magazine*. Issue 34 (2014), 38-47.

.............."Workhorse in the Wilderness" (the tug, *Columbus*.) *Wreck Diving Magazine*. Issue 38 (2016), 36-45.

Kovacs, Evan. Photographs by Becky Kagan Schott. "Project Shiphunt in Thunder Bay." *Wreck Diving Magazine*. Issue 26 (2012), 62-69.

Marsh, Betsa. Several photos by Cris Kohl. "Deep Secrets." *The Saturday Evening Post*. Vol. 283, No. 2 (March/April, 2011), 36-40.

Morrison, Andy. "Ice Diving Jana's Wreck." *Wreck Diving Magazine*. Issue 34 (2014), 30-37.

Schott, Becky Kagan. "Presque Isle Shipwreck Photography." *Wreck Diving Magazine*, Issue 38 (2016), 16-25.

Steinburger, Heather. Photos by Cris Kohl. "Get Wrecked" (a profile of Cris Kohl and Joan Forsberg). *Lakeland Boating*. Vol. LXIV, No. 8 (September, 2010), 34-38.

.............."Mystery Solved" (*L. R. Doty*). *Lakeland Boating*, Vol. LXIV, No. 8 (September, 2010), 8-9.

Trotter, Dave. "The Sole Survivor of the 1966 *Daniel J, Morrell* Dies." *Wreck Diving Magazine*. Issue 37 (2015), 8-9.

.............and Mickey Trotter, with Jared Daniel. "Ghost Ship of the White Hurricane (The Great Storm of 1913). *Wreck Diving Magazine*. Issue #38, 54-65.

Van Heest, Valerie. "Caught in the Vortex: The Armistice Day Blizzard of 1940." *Wreck Diving Magazine*. Issue 37 (2015), 42-47.

.............Underwater photographs by Robert Underhill. "A Hard Death -- The Sinking of the Steamer *Hennepin*." *Wreck Diving Magazine*. Issue 14 (2007), 56-63.

............."Lake Michigan's Most Visible and Visited Shipwreck (The *Francisco Morazan*)." *Wreck Diving Magazine*. Issue 34 (2014), 48-55.

.............Underwater photographs by Robert Underhill. "Message in a Bottle: Mysteries of the Schooner *Thomas Hume*." *Wreck Diving Magazine*. Issue 27 (2012), 62-67.

.............Underwater video captures by Dan Scoville and Jim Kennard, "Seek and Ye Shall Find, 228-year-old British warship found intact in Lake Ontario (the *Ontario*)." *Wreck Diving Magazine*. Issue 16 (2008), 68-73.

.............Photographs by Joe Oliver. "The Sidewheel Steamer That Took The Lives Of Over 300 People (the *Lady Elgin*)." *Wreck Diving Magazine*. Issue 26 (2012), 22-31.

.............Photographs by Robert Underhill. "Trapped in the Ice! The Ordeal of the S. S. *Michigan*." *Wreck Diving Magazine*. Issue 21 (2010), 18-27.

............."A Well-Kept Secret... Until Now -- First Dives on the *Carl D. Bradley*." *Wreck Diving Magazine*. Issue 18 (2009), 42-48.

C. Newspapers

Various issues of the following newspapers were utilized:

Bay City (Michigan) *Times*
Chicago Daily News
Chicago Daily Tribune
Chicago Herald
Chicago Herald-Examiner
Chicago Inter Ocean
Cleveland (Ohio) *Herald*
Cleveland (Ohio) *Plain Dealer*
Detroit Free Press
Detroit Journal
Detroit News
Door County (Wisconsin) *Advocate*
Duluth (Minnesota) *Herald*
Duluth (Minnesota) *News Tribune*
Escanaba (Michigan) *Daily Press*
Fond du Lac (Wisconsin) *Daily Reporter*
Grand Rapids (Michigan) *Press*
Kingston (Ontario) *Whig*
London (Ontario) *Free Press*
Manitoulin (Ontario) *Expositor*

Manitoulin (Ontario) *Recorder*
Marquette (Michigan) *Daily Mining Journal*
Milwaukee (Wisconsin) *Sentinel*
Owen Sound (Ontario) *Daily Sun*
Port Huron (Michigan) *Daily Times*
Port Huron (Michigan) *Times Herald*
Royal Oak (Michigan) *Daily Tribune*
Sandusky (Ohio) *Register-Star-News*
(Sault Ste. Marie, Michigan) *Evening News*
Sault (Ste. Marie, Ontario) *Daily Star*
Sarnia (Ontario) *Daily Observer*
Sheboygan (Wisconsin) *Press*
Toledo (Ohio) *Blade*
(Toronto) *Globe*
(Toronto) *Globe & Mail*
Toronto Daily Star
Toronto Evening Telegram
(Traverse City, Michigan) *Record-Eagle*
Windsor (Ontario) *Star*

Index

Words in *italics* denote a publication or a ship's name.
A number in **bold** denotes a photograph or a drawing on that page.

Advertisers' Index

About the Kohl-Forsberg Archives

It started as a hobby in the 1970's: collecting items about Great Lakes maritime history. After Cris Kohl's first book about Great Lakes shipwrecks was published in 1985, the collecting became serious. Several decades and many dollars later, the accumulation of maritime ephemera has grown so much that it exceeds any designation as a "collection" and has become "archives" -- 3,200+ books, 6,500+ archival photos of ships, 6,000+ archival maritime postcards, 6,200+ individual file folders (each one containing information about one Great Lakes shipwreck) in 22 filing cabinet drawers, 138 3-inch binders of photocopied newspaper articles (60,000+ pages), many maritime brochures, hours of audiotaped interviews, plus 21,000+ underwater shipwreck photos/slides taken by Cris Kohl, and many hours of underwater video shot by both Cris Kohl and Joan Forsberg. We are currently searching for a responsible, accessible, permanent repository for the Kohl-Forsberg Archives.

About the Authors

Cris Kohl and Joan Forsberg, well-known maritime historians, divers, photographers, videographers, authors, and speakers, are a husband-and-wife team who love to explore shipwrecks, particularly those in the Great Lakes. Starting with a double major in French and Russian for a diplomatic career, Joan switched to completing a degree in History. Cris has degrees in English and Education, and a Master of Arts degree in History. Both have underwater archaeology certifications from Great Britain's Nautical Archaeology Society (NAS). Their maritime history archives are one of the largest privately-held collections in the Great Lakes.

Joan, from Chicago, has been the Chairman of the Shipwrecks and Underwater Archaeology Room at Chicago's annual "Our World -- Underwater" Show since 1996. She is the author of the scuba celebrity cook-and-tell book, *Diver's Guide to the Kitchen*, and articles in magazines such as *Immersed, Great Lakes Boating*, and *Wreck Diving Magazine*, for which she became the Copy Editor in 2006. Joan appears behind the camera shooting underwater video, and in front of the camera as Cris' underwater model. In her three terms as President of the Underwater Archaeological Society of Chicago (2008, 2009, 2010), she spearheaded several significant maritime history projects and is the recipient of the 2011 UASC Award "for many years of leadership and dedication." Joan is a member of the international Women Divers Hall of Fame, has served as a Trustee of WDHOF for several years, and was elected WDHOF's Chairman of the Board in 2014 and 2015.

Cris, described in 2002 by California's *Skin Diver Magazine* as being "widely recognized as the world's preeminent Great Lakes wreck guru," is a prize-winning underwater photographer from Windsor, Ontario. He started writing about Great Lakes shipwrecks in 1982, with thirteen books and 300+ magazine and newsletter articles published since then. Several dozen of his articles have been published in Canada's *DIVER Magazine*, and his work has appeared in every issue of the international *Wreck Diving Magazine* since it began operations in 2003. He has helped locate and identify several Great Lakes shipwrecks. He served on the Executive Board of the Ontario Underwater Council from 1988 to 1997, is a Past President of the Underwater Archaeological Society of Chicago (2004), is the 2008 recipient of the annual "Our World -- Underwater" Outstanding Achievement Award, and in 2013, he received the Save Ontario Shipwrecks Marine Heritage Award "for his extensive body of work contributing to widespread appreciation of Ontario's maritime heritage." His expanded edition of *The Great Lakes Diving Guide* is the most comprehensive book ever published about Great Lakes shipwrecks.

Both Cris and Joan have appeared on numerous television programs, including on the History Channel, Discovery Channel, CBS, and Chicago's WTTW, and their underwater video has been broadcast on PBS and Canada's CTV network. They wrote the book detailing the first 40 years of Chicago's annual "Our World -- Underwater" Scuba Show. Co-authors of the recent books, *The Wreck of the* GRIFFON, *The Greatest Mystery of the Great Lakes, The Christmas Tree Ship*, and *Shipwrecks at Death's Door*, and producers of a variety of Great Lakes shipwreck maps, shipwreck postcards, and many maritime history documentaries, Cris and Joan are looking forward to their next big adventure.

The following articles provide more information about Cris Kohl and Joan Forsberg:

Hildebrand, Dick. "Shipwrecks of the Great Lakes, A World Class Dive Destination." (Biographical information about Cris Kohl and Joan Forsberg). *Windsor Life Magazine*. Vol. 22, Issue 5 (Summer, 2015), 20-24.

Steinburger, Heather. "Dynamic Duo." *Lakeland Boating*. Vol. LXIV, No. 8 (September, 2010), 30-33.

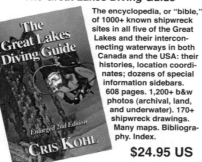

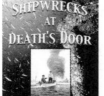

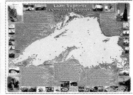